Increasing the Imj
of Your Research

MW00824620

This important resource helps researchers in all disciplines share their findings, knowledge, and ideas effectively and beyond their own field. By pursuing the practical recommendations in this book, researchers can increase the exposure of their ideas, connect with wider audiences in powerful ways, and ensure their work has a true impact.

The book covers the most effective ways to share research, such as:

- Social media—leveraging time-saving tools and maximizing exposure and branding.
- Media—landing interviews and contributing to public dialogue.
- Writing—landing book deals and succeeding in key writing opportunities.
- Speaking—giving TED Talks, delivering conference keynote presentations, and appearing on broadcasts like NPR.
- Connecting—networking, influencing policy, and joining advisory boards.
- Honors—winning awards and recognition to expand your platform.

Rich in tips, strategies, and guidelines, this book also includes clever "fast tracks" and downloadable eResources that provide links, leads, and templates to help secure radio broadcasts, podcasts, publications, conferences, awards, and other opportunities.

Jenny Grant Rankin is a Fulbright Specialist with two doctorates who lectures at universities and other institutions, such as the University of Cambridge, TED, and national research associations. Dr. Rankin is a prolific speaker and writer and has been honored by the U.S. White House for her work. See more at www.JennyRankin.com.

Increasing the Impact of Your Research

A Practical Guide to Sharing Your Findings and Widening Your Reach

Jenny Grant Rankin

Routledge
Taylor & Francis Group

NEW YORK AND LONDON

First published 2020
by Routledge
52 Vanderbilt Avenue, New York, NY 10017

and by Routledge
2 Park Square, Milton Park, Abingdon, Oxon, OX14 4RN

Routledge is an imprint of the Taylor & Francis Group, an informa business

Library of Congress Cataloging-in-Publication Data
Names: Rankin, Jenny Grant, author.
Title: Increasing the impact of your research : a practical guide to sharing
    your findings and widening your reach / Jenny Grant Rankin.
Identifiers: LCCN 2019058825 (print) | LCCN 2019058826 (ebook) |
    ISBN 9780367362355 (hardback) | ISBN 9780367363000
    (paperback) | ISBN 9780429345166 (ebook)
Subjects: LCSH: Communication in science. | Communication in
    learning and scholarship. | Science journalism. | Research.
Classification: LCC Q223 .R367 2020 (print) | LCC Q223 (ebook) |
    DDC 001.401/4—dc23
LC record available at https://lccn.loc.gov/2019058825
LC ebook record available at https://lccn.loc.gov/2019058826

ISBN: 978-0-367-36235-5 (hbk)
ISBN: 978-0-367-36300-0 (pbk)
ISBN: 978-0-429-34516-6 (ebk)

Typeset in Perpetua
by Apex CoVantage, LLC

Visit the eResources: www.routledge.com/9780367363000

This book is dedicated to Marek Ostoja-Zawadzki.

Thank you for being the best friend and big brother imaginable.

Contents

CONTENTS

 viii

Preface

This is a book full of secrets and shortcuts. It contains all the tips I gathered on my journey to share my research with the world. These strategies and sources allowed me to share my work widely (internationally and with large audiences) and in more compelling ways to help those impacted within my field. The most important reason for reading this book is to benefit more lives with your research findings.

The more time you have to devote to what you do best—like making new discoveries—the better for this world. So, this book is meant to save you time and introduce you to opportunities that can catapult your work's influence quickly and effectively.

Whether you are a researcher, graduate student, professor, or other faculty member, you likely have a vast store of expertise. Although your research benefits a field of knowledge, your findings need to be shared widely and effectively if they are to benefit our rapidly changing world. Sharing your findings outside the walls of your organization serves the field and provides you with validation beyond your immediate work environment. By sharing beyond common research communication silos (for example, researchers sharing mainly with other researchers), your work can reach varied audiences to improve decision-making, policies, studies, and practices on an expanded scale.

This book will guide you in winning opportunities such as book deals, radio and media interviews, conference presentations and keynotes, awards, consulting roles, panels, government involvement, magazine articles, journal papers, TED Talks, research, and more. This book will not just give you generalities; it will give you the specific web addresses, submission deadlines, contact information, and guidance to make it easy to share your voice in a variety of venues and formats.

Chapters will also highlight sharing opportunities that require very little time on your part (such as registering for databases used by journalists to reach out to you, rather than you spending time reaching out to journalists). The book will help you strike a balance of sharing that does not detract from your time spent researching.

Enjoy the contributions, connections, triumphs, and influence that come with these endeavors. Most of all, enjoy knowing your research will help as many lives as you work to reach.

AUDIENCE

This book is for those conducting studies, literature reviews, or other forms of research within any field. This book is written primarily for three groups:

- Researchers and those who promote research (through labs, universities, nonprofits, think tanks, policy shapers, knowledge brokers, etc.).
- University professionals (higher education professors, etc.).
- Graduate and postgraduate students who are conducting any form of research, from delving into literature review to conducting their own studies.

Professionals conducting less-formal research within their fields can also benefit from reading this book, as can professionals seeking to make the complicated findings of others (like scientific research they curate) accessible to varied audiences.

BOOK STRUCTURE AND CONTENT

The book's introduction provides a foundation that will help you with the other chapters' endeavors. Subsequent chapters focus on different means for sharing your research (media interviews, conference presentations, etc.). Most chapters provide:

- **Descriptions** of opportunities (avenues through which you can share your work, such as the media, broadcasting, publication, events, panels, etc.).
- **Lists of specific opportunities**—for example, being interviewed on National Public Radio (NPR)—via online eResources, including other details (web addresses, submission deadlines, etc.) you will need in order to apply for each specific opportunity.
- **Tips** to land the opportunities.
- **Strategies** to perform these endeavors well (deliver a riveting keynote, write a compelling article, etc.) so what you share has maximum impact.
- **Exercises** to help you apply key strategies shared in the chapter.

This book covers ways to increase the impact of research after it has been conducted. In other words, this book does not cover aspects like collecting pre-study data to craft a study more likely to have impact in needed areas or getting a well-known person or institution to partner on a study so its findings are more warmly welcomed. Instead, this book will help you take any valuable body of knowledge and spread that information successfully so it can have major impact.

ACCESSIBILITY

This book is written for all researchers: from novice to veteran, from armchair researcher to prolific scientist, and from any field one can study. Just as this book coaches readers to write in ways accessible to an entire audience, I use language meant to make the book's content accessible to all readers. You thus will find minimal academic jargon and will find examples any reader can understand. Do not mistake the absence of elitism as an indication that the book is not for those used to conferring in drier discourse. Rather, use this approach as an example for how you can make your own content understood by a wider and more diverse audience.

TERMINOLOGY

To avoid long phrasing within sentences, I will alternate the use of male (in odd-numbered chapters) and female (in even-numbered chapters) pronouns when not writing of specific individuals. No favoring of either gender is intended in any of these uses. For the sake of concision, I will also use "Google" as a verb, as it is shorter than "use a search engine to search for something on the internet."

Some who read this book will be interested in sharing their knowledge concerning *practice* (e.g., what they have learned from working in the field) with a wider audience, whereas others want to share their *research* findings or facets with a wider audience. Some readers will choose to share their research-informed opinions with the world, whereas others will abstain from taking a public stand on issues related to their areas of study. This book's concepts can be applied to any of these circumstances.

I will interchangeably use terms like research, science, findings, discovery, concept, expertise, knowledge, topic, and wisdom to describe what you are sharing with the world, but the book's concepts will apply to any of these. Note that these terms can encompass findings you make from studies you personally conduct, but they can also encompass knowledge you amass through practice or by studying others' research.

BENEFITS

Applying this book's strategies will allow you to efficiently and effectively share your research with a wider audience in a variety of venues and formats. This will typically enhance your resume and career and likely will enhance your sense of professionalism and accomplishment.

However, the main benefit of this book is that sharing your findings allows you to inform more people, and people in a wider spectrum of roles, in order to assist more lives. Helping the world is a worthwhile goal and renders an impact that few other professionals can enjoy.

eResources

AVAILABLE eRESOURCES

You have access to the following eResources:

- CV Template
- Sample Bios
- Guide to Creating a Website
- List of Writing Opportunities (specific weblinks and submission details to publish articles, papers, op-eds, whitepapers, reports, chapters, and other short-form written work; room to add and track more writing opportunities specific to your field)
- List of Book Publishers (specific weblinks to author or edit research-related books; room to add and track more publishers specific to your field)
- Guide to Slide Design
- Sample Handout
- Bad Slide vs. Good Slide
- Countdown Timer Slides

- List of Conferences (specific weblinks and submission details to present at conferences and other events where researchers speak; room to add and track more events specific to your field)
- List of Broadcasting Opportunities (specific weblinks and details to appear on radio, television, podcast, video, webcast, and more; room to add and track more broadcasting opportunities specific to your field)
- Guide to a Different Mentor
- List of Organizations (specific weblinks and details for organizations to join or subscribe; room to add and track more organizations specific to your field)
- List of Serving Opportunities (specific weblinks and submission details for fellowships, programs, internships, panels, boards, calls for input or participation, and opportunities to be a judge or reviewer; room to add and track more serving opportunities specific to your field)
- List of Awards (specific weblinks and submission details for awards, grants, and other honors; room to add and track more awards specific to your field)
- Guide to Hunting and Harvesting (to find and generate more opportunities to share your findings)

HOW TO ACCESS eRESOURCES

You can access these downloads by visiting the book product page at www. routledge.com/9780367363000. Once there, click on the tab that reads "eResources" and then select the file(s) you need, which will download directly to your computer.

HOW TO USE eRESOURCES

Most of the eResources are lists of specific opportunities you can pursue to share your research with the world. Many are specific to the education field, which intersects with other fields. Add any opportunities specific to your own field to your own copies of these lists after you store the files on your own computer. These Microsoft Excel files (indicated with "xlsx" after the file name) make it easy to:

- Find opportunities (sort a list of events by type, location, when the conference takes place, or when submissions to speak are due; sort a list of publishing prospects by publication title or type; sort a list of award and involvement opportunities by category or application deadline; etc.).
- Pursue opportunities (visit the provided website with a simple click, adhere to the given deadlines, etc.).
- Track opportunities for which you apply (use manipulation-friendly fields).

After downloading any eResource with "xlsx" after the file name (as explained in the previous "How to Access eResources" section):

1. Save your downloaded copy of the eResource to your computer. Close the file and reopen it on your computer to ensure any modifications you make will be saved for your future use.
2. Use your own saved copy of the eResource to add details on your own submissions (for example, when you submitted an op-ed to *The New Yorker* and what that submission's status is).
3. If you discover opportunities not already featured on a list, you can add them to your own copy of this spreadsheet by giving each new opportunity its own row.

Because application webpages vary from year to year, home page addresses are usually included on the eResource list. After visiting an opportunity's website, look for links based on what you seek to do (like "Call for Speakers" or "Apply to Present" if you seek to apply to speak at a symposium, or "Author Submission Details" or "Write for Us" if you seek to write for a publication).

Every time I apply for an opportunity, I store "P" (for Pending) in the spreadsheet's "Status" column for that opportunity's row, and I store my apply date in the "Applied for" column. I then change the status to "A" (for Accepted) or "R" (for Rejected) when I hear back from the folks in charge (e.g., editors, organizers, or organization members). These cells will automatically change color based on the letter you use, which makes each status easier to spot.

When I sort the file by its "Status" column, I can then more easily spot all of the

- Rejected opportunities, from which I can copy entry information (such as abstracts, papers, or session descriptions) to electronically paste into new prospects for which I apply;
- Pending opportunities, to which I can follow up (based on my noted submission date) to be sure my entry was received; and
- Accepted opportunities, which I can add to my CV, promotion efforts, and more.

Any technical learning curve you encounter while using these eResources will be worth pushing through to enjoy the enhanced organization and efficiency they provide. As you share your research with the world, you will come to enjoy this easy way to manage all the exciting venues that await you.

Acknowledgments

The inspiration for this book came from my own growth as a researcher and educator passionate about sharing my findings with the world. I owe many thanks to those who opened doors for me along the way. One of these doors was opened by my wonderful editor, Heather Jarrow. I will forever be grateful for her role in this book and those books that came before it. I also thank those who generously offered early feedback on the book.

I am thankful for those who have taken my classes, invited me to train their faculty, and applied this book's strategies. As always, I owe much gratitude to the tireless cheerleaders in my life: my family, Dr. Colette Boston, Nancy Grant, Dr. Margie Johnson, Marek Ostoja-Zawadzki, Piper Rankin, Steve Rees, Dr. Gail Thompson, Rufus Thompson, and my other dear friends. I feel blessed beyond words for everyone's support.

Meet the Author

Dr. Jenny Grant Rankin is a Fulbright specialist for the U.S. Department of State. She has taught how to best share research findings at University of Cambridge, as a lecturer for the PostDoc Masterclass, the American Educational Research Association (AERA) annual meeting, and other venues. She has two doctorates, a PhD and L.H.D., and has delivered approximately 200 keynotes and lectures (for Elsevier events and national research associations) and has served on many panels (for the National Science Foundation, non-research events like International Comic-Con, and others). Among her presentations is a TED Talk, which began as a TEDxTalk at TEDxTUM before spending a few years on the TED website.

Dr. Rankin's 11 books relate to sharing research, gifted education, sharing data, using data, and burnout. Her 145 papers and articles have appeared in 40 different publications, including *Psychology Today* (for which she writes an ongoing column), *Los Angeles Times*, and other magazines and journals.

Dr. Rankin's many media appearances include NBC News, *O: The Oprah Magazine*, NPR, *Newsweek*, *Good Housekeeping*, *HuffPost* (formerly *Huffington Post*), *The Washington Post*, *Reader's Digest*, *U.S. News & World Report*, Nonfiction Authors Association (NFAA), *The San Diego Union Tribune*, *The Orange County Register*, *The Seattle Times*, *Sunday Star-Times*, as well as frequent commendations in the media and congressional testimonies to inform legislation. She is an active member of Mensa (volunteering as Coordinator of the Mensa Gifted Youth Program in Orange County) and many research organizations, and she serves on multiple advisory boards.

Dr. Rankin has won Teacher of the Year and has been honored multiple times by the U.S. White House. For example, the American flag once was flown over the Capitol Building (the White House) in honor of Dr. Rankin and her professional contributions.

Dr. Rankin is regularly contracted by universities, school districts, nonprofits, government entities, and others to train faculty and staff on how best to share research, data, knowledge, and ideas with others. Dr. Rankin's complete CV is available at www.jennyrankin.com/bio and her press page (including social media links) is at www.jennyrankin.com/press.

Part I
Preparing

Chapter 1

Evolution of the Researcher for Modern Times

Climate change is threatening wildlife. Bigotry plagues society. Guns are killing children on school campuses. Cancer refuses to go away.

Whatever topic you study, there is a problem your findings could help solve. Even if you study inchworms and your focus feels inconsequential to the world's ills, your findings can advance understanding, spark ideas, and inspire future endeavors.

But no matter your discovery, it cannot help on a widespread scale if you are the only one who knows about it. And sharing your research can be harder than you think.

In fact, sharing your knowledge *effectively* can be downright counterintuitive. Consider that first example—climate change.

You are aware of climate change, whether you believe it is a problem or not, so we can conclude that scientists have talked extensively about it. But making you aware is not enough. Most researchers' goal in talking about climate change has been to *stop* what they have characterized as an unnatural crisis, which requires people to act in specific ways. That is where the communication of findings hit a snag, because people still are not doing enough to stop environmental temperatures from changing.

Researchers have shared all the frightening data: polar bears dying, natural disasters raging, sea levels rising. This is one of the largest science communication failures in history, because catastrophic scenarios are too overwhelming for people to handle (Stoknes, 2015). Grim statistics and forecasts cause people to detach from the issue—a mental state in which they are unlikely to change behavior. Though it is important to share data to provide proof, data shifts people into an analytical frame of mind that works against caring about or acting on the matter at hand.

An attractive story full of meaning, a positive image of a greener future, and fun ways for people to reduce carbon footprints are more effective at prompting people to conserve resources and curtail global warming (Brunhuber, 2016), a major aspect of climate change. For example, Jon Christensen reworked an environmental report that 50 University of California (UC) scientists shared with the United Nations so that it empowered people with easy ways to contribute, such as fun incentives to conserve water. The result was a straightforward, solutions-oriented report that has already changed behavior across 10 UC campuses and beyond.

Sharing findings can be especially hard when people are resistant to a message. Yet understanding our audiences allows us to approach them in ways they will accept. For example, a survey of 10,000 Americans indicated that evangelicals were particularly uninterested in environmental causes; however, 300 interviews revealed that evangelicals merely care more about people. Thus, decrying climate change's impact on wildlife will leave evangelicals indifferent, but focusing on the human impact (like what happens to children raised amid polluted air and water) holds great potential to move these groups (Ecklund & Scheitle, 2017).

Knowledge of overcoming political stances can also help. When Americans were asked what makes a fact likely to be true, 40% of Republicans versus 72% of Democrats respected the verification of scientists, and 30% of Republicans versus 57% of Democrats respected the verification of academics (AP-NORC Center for Public Affairs Research & USAFacts Institute, 2019). This indicates a disparity in the weight people of different political persuasions give to researcher input. Returning to our climate-change example, as Democrats and Republicans get better at comprehending science, they actually become more polarized over whether global warming is a valid concern (Kahan et al., 2012). Yet a Yale study revealed that priming people's scientific curiosity is such a powerful approach to increasing their acceptance of climate findings that it overcomes even political predispositions against such findings (Kahan, Landrum, Carpenter, Helft, & Jamieson, 2017).

The world needs researchers like you to share findings in ways that generate interest and change. Knowing the best ways to do that will maximize your impact. That is where this book comes in.

The strategies within these pages will help you reach a larger audience in compelling ways, so people care about, understand, remember, act on, and tell others about your discovery (see Figure 1.0). Pursuing the opportunities in this book can enhance your resume, CV, and career, and likely will increase your professional and personal satisfaction. However, the book's primary function is to help you increase your discoveries' benefit to the world, whether that means saving wildlife, advancing society, inspiring a cure for Parkinson's disease, or helping achieve something else entirely.

Whatever topic you study, you have knowledge that is more valuable when it is shared widely and effectively. Keep reading to enlighten decision-makers, inform communities, improve practices, further research, and widen your impact.

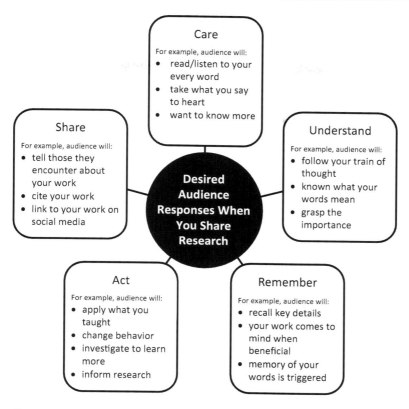

Figure 1.1 Desired Audience Responses When You Share Research

"Science and academia in general are not only a source of knowledge but also a guide to how reason can build a better society. Although most researchers do not intend to claim an ethics for humanity, they should nevertheless set an example of behavior for the rest of the population since they symbolize the wisdom of our epoch"

(Corredoira & Villarroel, 2019, p. 1).

WHY AND HOW RESEARCH NEEDS TO BE SHARED

People hold firm opinions on topics without being able to demonstrate knowledge on those topics, and many hold beliefs that do not match academic consensuses. For example, only 37% of U.S. consumers believe genetically modified (GM)

food is safe to consume, whereas 88% of *scientists* believe GM food is safe to consume, and consumers hold these beliefs regardless of whether they have knowledge on the subject (McFadden & Lusk, 2016). There are a number of reasons people outside (and even within) our fields are missing information or are misinformed. Research on behavioral economics reveals that shortcuts (such as biases and heuristics) inherent in people's decision-making processes lead to faster yet also frequently flawed conclusions (Kahneman, 2011).

Collective opinions, even when misguided, impact how the public thinks and talks about different issues, how the media frames the issues, how politicians make decisions related to the issues, how organizations do or do not fund research on the issues, how academics work on the issues, and more. Yet researchers' effective and comprehensive communication can enlighten audiences and overturn misconceptions. Going back to the example of GM food, informing consumers resulted in increased acceptance of GM foods, yet only when shared in specific ways, since mere statements from scientists are insubstantial and can even lead to backlash (Lusk, Roosen, & Bieberstein, 2014). Researchers can increase their impact when they share their research well and widen their reach.

This book is based on the premise that researchers should do what is best for the world (humanity, the environment, wildlife—whatever entity one's research has a chance to help). To further that objective:

- Researchers should share their research extensively.
- Researchers should share their research effectively.

This book helps with these endeavors, but the research community does not always encourage them. That needs to change.

Researchers Should Share Their Research Extensively

When Paul Revere learned British soldiers would march on the towns of Lexington and Concord, he went on a famous midnight ride warning communities. Local militia would have lost the next day's skirmishes, and possibly the entire American Revolutionary War, if Revere had instead kept his findings to himself. Even if Revere had left his silversmith shop to discuss his findings with those around him, it would not have been enough to save those who Revere had had the potential to help.

Important information needs to be shared with all those who can benefit. Only then can a discovery fulfill its potential for good.

Yet researchers often communicate in silos. This means that they commune with people in the same role (like researcher to researcher), field (like economist to economist), or at the same site (for example, the same university) when sharing knowledge, seeking knowledge, making decisions, and collaborating.

Consider the impact of transcending traditional communication silos. McGrath and Brandon (2016) shared how family-integrated care (FiCare) researchers increased family engagement in Canadian neonatal intensive care units (NICUs). The authors published findings in scholarly journals, but they also enlisted mainstream media, blogs, social networks, a researcher website, project videos, and a variety of conferences and venues. This caused most neonatal care providers to be familiar with the intervention strategy and several more trials were conducted in Canada, the U.S., and abroad.

Sometimes sharing does not even occur regularly and fluidly *within* silos, and the problem can be long established. Consider knowledge management, which is the process of exchanging and using information to maximize its value. Kidwell, Vander Linde, and Johnson (2000) found that while some examples of sharing knowledge within higher education existed, they were "the exception rather than the rule" (p. 28). When Veer Ramjeawon and Rowley (2017) examined this same issue years later, they found participants knew about knowledge management but more barriers than enablers to knowledge management were identified, and none of the universities had a knowledge management strategy. These same-silo and restricted-sharing paradigms limit awareness of knowledge available.

To meet this challenge, academics need to expand their reach when sharing knowledge. Researchers cannot share their discoveries only with readers of an academic journal, or practitioners too busy to read those journals will make decisions that do not benefit from those discoveries. Fields cannot keep findings to themselves, or cross-field innovations will never benefit society. Professors cannot share their discoveries only with their professor colleagues, or policymakers will make decisions that do not benefit from those discoveries. Additional examples can pair different stakeholders to the same effect.

Transcending the boundaries of traditional silos can occur if scholars make efforts to share their expertise with audiences of all natures, within their own traditional silos and outside their silos. As you share with varied constituents, you can also learn from them, so your research best serves society. As Leigh Hall of University of Wyoming and Teaching Academia (www.teachingacademia.com) said, "People will . . . ask you questions, and . . . their questions can actually push you in ways that other academics are not . . . because they are going to bring a different perspective, so that's another benefit to [interacting with the public]" (Hall, 2018a, 10:28).

Researchers Should Share Their Research Effectively

Research reporters Belluz, Plumer, and Resnick (2016) surveyed scientists of varied disciplines around the world and found that one of the biggest challenges facing science today is that "science is poorly communicated" (p. 1).

This book will teach you how to share your research effectively, but a common problem must first be addressed: researchers sometimes *choose* to present poorly.

To examine this point, compare research doctors to medical doctors for a moment. Physicians are notorious for wretched handwriting. If you have ever tried to decipher messily scrawled prescriptions, you know many physicians fit this stereotype. Yet poor penmanship is not a quality that physicians should emulate in an effort to appear "more physician-like." In fact, illegible writing is responsible for thousands of deaths each year (Chaturvedi, 2018).

Thus, it would be ridiculous for a doctor to say, "I know that indecipherable penmanship is less likely to help people, but it might make me look more like my colleagues, so I will write illegibly." It would be unethical for the physician to say, "My fear over not looking like all the other physicians will take precedence over others' well-being." Yet researchers—who also have life-saving information to communicate—often choose looking like a typical academic over presenting their findings in ways likely to have impact.

Standing behind a lectern "like researchers do" is comfortable. Reading study details from slide bullet points "like researchers do" is comfortable. There is no risk that attendees will perceive you as not being the credible researcher you are. However, there are much greater risks in the conventional path. Communicating "like researchers (typically) do" risks not moving your audience to care, understand, remember, share, and act in relation to what you disseminate.

There are other ways to establish credibility than communicating in the same ways that researchers have traditionally shared their findings. Thinking you have to present in a boring way to be perceived as a credible researcher is like thinking that wearing a stethoscope will make others view you as a credible doctor. Either is just a facade you can choose to wear. If your ideas have merit, they—along with your credentials—will convey your credibility.

When I train researchers how to present their findings so people will understand, remember, and care about those findings, I am told (usually by one student per class, though others lean in eagerly for the answer), "The ways you teach us to present are far better than the ways researchers currently present their findings. But I'm scared to present in this improved way, because so few researchers do it. I'm afraid I'll look silly."

Their fear is not unfounded. People fear change, particularly when they do not understand it or feel threatened by it. The first man to use an umbrella in England was ridiculed and shouted at by people who did not understand why he carried something they deemed feminine, and he was pelted with trash and abuse by coach drivers who feared the umbrella threatened their good business on rainy days (one driver even tried to run over the umbrella-carrying man with his hansom cab) (Waters, 2016). But this did not mean the umbrella was a bad idea. On the contrary, umbrellas protect people from inclement weather. Those who did not understand the umbrella's use merely needed to learn its value. The cab drivers feared the umbrella because they feared it was better than them: the umbrella enabled people to walk rainy streets without the recurring charge of a drive or inconvenience of finding a driver. The same is true when it comes to best practices for presenting and writing about research:

- Academics who come to understand the nature and value of better communication skills become advocates for these improvements . . . even when they are scared to apply them.
- Academics who witness presentations that are better than theirs (or read better writing than theirs) are fearful when they feel they cannot communicate their own research as well . . . but they can learn.

Even when our colleagues fear ways that are new or unfamiliar, we should not shun the chance to share our findings in ways that make people more likely to understand, care about, remember, tell others about, and act upon those findings. Just as we should not shun our umbrellas. Just as physicians should not try to write illegibly. Rather, the solution is for academia to evolve to embrace and practice improved ways to disseminate discoveries.

PRESSURE TO REMAIN CONFINED TO TRADITION

The examples presented earlier support the need to break from tradition. Yet academics often are not rewarded within academia for sharing research with non-traditional audiences. For example, although TED Talks are an immensely successful way to disseminate research and are in need of more academic presenters, giving a TED Talk has been found to have no impact on the number of citations a scholar receives in its wake and does not appear to promote researchers' work within academic communities (even though it popularizes the research *outside* academia) (Sugimoto et al., 2013).

The reality of our world is that the way people get their information has changed in substantial ways. The internet, in particular, has opened countless new channels to reach and help others with your findings. For example, "every day scholarly articles receive 12,000 new mentions across social media, news, and blogs. That's 1 mention every 7 seconds" (Elsevier, 2018, p. 1). Ignoring this reality is like the professor who says, "I shouldn't have to entertain my students to teach!" and continues to lecture his bored students in monotone while scoffing at the professor next door who engages his students in exciting educational activities more likely to result in learning.

9

"Your job . . . isn't to . . . crank out obscure academic publications by the dozens and amass a long list of peer citations. As scientists, your real job should be to make great discoveries and share them with the world" (Foley, 2016, p. 2).

—Jonathan Foley, Executive Director of the California Academy of Sciences

With all the opportunities for information exchange at our fingertips, it is commendable and encouraged that you use these avenues to share your wisdom with the world. Engaging with the public and experts in varied roles and in varied locales will multiply your impact. If you know something that is dramatically helping people in an area where your research is applied, why stop there? Why not let it dramatically help people who read an article you wrote, hear you on NPR, or watch your TED Talk—and let it dramatically help the people whom *those* people's new understanding reaches? If you imagine the enhanced impact that these (merely three) new avenues for sharing can have, then you can imagine the enormousness of the difference you can make by seizing many of the two thousand sharing opportunities waiting for you in this book.

If you are higher education faculty, your organization might be one that frowns upon "nonacademic" contributions, or it might be one that actively encourages the exchange between researchers and others. Either way, you can be part of the movement to modernize what it means to be a scholar. Interacting with the broader public can lead to more funding sources, new data sources, fresh perspectives and ideas, broader networks, and better research (Badgett, 2016; Ngumbi, 2018).

Knowledge sharing leads to grants, innovation, sustainability, and other perks in academia, yet it can also lead to increased competitiveness, and the academic community is often distrustful or unwilling to navigate sharing (Annansingh, Howell, Liu, & Nunes, 2018). Even though academia should embrace better communication strategies and better communication reach, researchers face pressure in the field to stick to

- Traditional dissemination strategies (such as dull, text-heavy slides in their presentations, and wordy, jargon-heavy writing) and
- Traditional dissemination venues (such as speaking only at research conferences and publishing only in academic journals).

For example, universities commonly discourage researchers from sharing outside of academia. Senior department members instruct scientists to not write for the general public, speak with journalists, talk at public events, or use social media because these do not lead to tenure or promotions, yet society suffers when researchers follow that advice (Scientific American Editors, 2018).

If you want to maximize the impact of your research, you must transcend these pressures. Share in ways likely to make a difference, even if some criticize you for doing so. If you encounter pressure in the field to "do what has always been done" or "do what everyone else is doing" when it comes to dissemination, you can be wary yet still find opportunities for more effective and extensive sharing.

For example, one of my students asked if she should use the PowerPoint template she had been encouraged to use by her Chair for her upcoming doctoral defense. As you can guess, it was a typical, uninspired template encouraging lots of text and bullet points . . . and I told her to use it. Offending or startling your dissertation committee is not the time to rock the research world with your unconventional—albeit highly effective—presentation skills. Better this graduate student achieve her PhD now, after which she can send the committee links to her groundbreaking presentations, rather than risk delaying her PhD and all the opportunities it will open for her.

Established academics can also push for progress. When professors learn better dissemination strategies but fear colleagues will scoff, they can arrange for a training workshop on this book's topic to take place at their institutions, or they can advocate for the department to read this book. This way, peers do not dismiss improved communication due to fear; rather, they are trained in how to be an engaging speaker, how to easily design improved slides, and other skills. Suddenly, the whole department or institution has an improved approach to dissemination and can support one another in making their research more impactful.

You might find times to temporarily hold back, but the times to let your new dissemination skills fully shine are far more numerous. Academia and the topics it touches are compromised when we share poorly, and academia will not evolve unless we change our own practices and reshape what a "normal" dissemination of findings looks like.

Plus, an audience's awe from a phenomenal presentation overshadows the audience's judgement you are not acting "researcher-like." I have never regretted an appearance or written piece in which I applied all I know about how to make my findings understandable, memorable, care-provoking, and actionable, no matter how unconventional the approach.

Consider Mike Morrison, a doctoral student at Michigan State University. He posted a video (www.youtube.com/watch?v=1RwJbhkCA58), to challenge the way research posters have always looked: text-heavy regurgitations of entire papers that cannot be easily consumed by the conference-goers walking past them. Morrison's design displays the study's main research finding in the middle of the poster in large letters above a QR code that conference-goers can scan with their smartphones for study details. This format allows visitors to learn something from each poster and quickly assess which posters appeal to their interests so they can approach those for more information.

The video quickly went viral; as I write this, Morrison posted it two and a half months ago and it already has 381,775 views. Scholars are starting to use this easy-to-skim poster format, sharing their redesigned posters on Twitter, greeting Morrison "like a rock star" at conferences, and even requiring all posters at a Harvard University Poster Day to adhere to Morrison's design (Greenfieldboyce, 2019, 3:27). In other words, breaking from traditional-yet-ineffective confines can receive a warm reception when it is done effectively.

EXAMPLES OF EFFORTS TO CONNECT RESEARCHERS WITH OTHERS

American Geophysical Union (AGU) Thriving Earth Exchange
Ecological Society of America (ESA) Public Affairs Program
Harvard Graduate School of Education's Usable Knowledge
Media Centre for Education Research Australia
Stanford University's Leopold Leadership Program
Three universities' Center for Research Use in Education
UMass Amherst's Public Engagement Project
University of Pennsylvania Graduate School of Education's CPRE
    Knowledge Hub

Your work is just as important as mine. People need to know about it. So get onto that stage, put your words into diverse readers' hands, shape professional and public dialogue, influence policy, and pursue any other avenues you choose to have a massive impact on the world.

DOMINO EFFECT

A single domino can knock down multiple dominos, or even a domino 50% larger than itself. This is an example of geometric progression: if you started with a regular-sized domino, the 18th domino to be knocked down could be as tall as the Leaning Tower of Pisa, and the 57th domino could reach from here to the moon (Keller & Papasan, 2013). As Malcolm Gladwell (2000) says of geometric progression, "Sometimes big changes follow small events, and . . . sometimes these changes can happen very quickly" (p. 11).

Brace yourself for the domino effect to knock open opportunities for you to share your research. When one door of opportunity falls open to you and you walk through it, this leads to more open doors of increasing stature. Walk through any of those, and yet more doors of ever-greater venues await you.

Even opportunities that seem minor can have unexpectedly huge pay-off. For example, maybe you speak at a fledgling conference but happen to influence a government official who will take your idea regionwide, or you sit next to someone who connects you with a BBC reporter, through whom your discovery reaches thousands.

Every time you "step out" of your routine and share in some way, you increase the likelihood of more great things happening. In this case, it is more chances to share your research and impact more lives.

BALANCE AND FINDING TIME

That said, be cognizant of how you allocate your time. As you follow this book's strategies you likely will get excited as you land more keynotes or book deals or whatever avenues you pursue to share discoveries with the world. However, amid increasing pressures of research agendas, you do not want to sacrifice the quality of your work in your pursuit of widening the audience that benefits from it. Thus:

- Be conscientious about striking balance between time spent sharing versus time spent on your actual research.
- Determine who can follow some opportunities on your behalf. If you work at a university, it likely has a Press Office, public relations (PR) staff, or communications team willing to reach out to journalists, write press releases, and more for you. Meet with such an individual to discuss this book. Give him a copy in which you have circled opportunities and strategies you especially want to pursue and discuss how you and this person can work together. University interdisciplinary centers and resource information managers (RIMs) are helpful as well.
- If you have written a book, your publishing house likely has a marketing team or PR contact who can reach out to the media on your behalf, boost your social media engagements, provide handouts for your appearances, and more.
- Read this book with a colleague and tackle your sharing efforts as a team. This could mean presenting together (such as during a conference session where you both get time to speak), co-writing articles, sharing

opportunities (for example, every time you get on the radio, you encourage the producer to feature your partner in another episode), or other ways to cut the dissemination workload.

- You can also collaborate on existing work duties to make it easier to carve out time to share your research. See the text box for a practical example of this. Successful collaboration holds great power to offset the increasing pressures of research agendas.

Remember, you do not have to do everything recommended in these pages. This book is written for researchers of all types and topics, so some opportunities might not feel like the right fit for what you, specifically, are trying to do. If a particular engagement or strategy does not fit your goals, then I am not suggesting you do it. Only pursue what is right for you.

TIME-SAVING TIP

See Hall (2018b) for a quick video explaining one highly practical way in which you can collaborate with a colleague to save your time while increasing your dissemination output. Sign up for more videos like this at www.teachingacademia.com.

REPRESENTATION AND INEQUITY

This book celebrates the need for all researchers to share what they know so the world can benefit from their wisdom. Yet women, people of color, LGBT+ individuals, and others face discrimination in their efforts to share findings within our professional arena. For example, in an Massachusetts Institute of Technology (MIT) Grand Challenges Summit report on information science and scholarly communications, Altman and Bourg (2018) detailed how participation in the development and evaluation of scientific knowledge is heavily skewed by gender, language, race, and class and that scientific benefits are unevenly distributed in our society. It is important to be aware of unfair obstacles and how they manifest themselves, so we can find ways to ensure that fields benefit from diverse voices.

See Rankin (2019) for a two-part series in *Psychology Today* that shares statistics and suggestions related to this topic. The series provides a glimpse at the added hurdles traditionally marginalized groups face in higher education institutions, in other research communities, and when seeking to publish their work.

Speak up for yourself, knowing you have a value too great to be quieted, and speak up for others so their voices can be heard too. If you come from a place of privilege or power, think deeply on how you can promote underrepresented voices. Recognize when obstacles or microaggressions have nothing to do with you, and do what you can to circumvent obstacles. As Congresswoman Shirley Chisholm said, "If they don't give you a seat at the table, bring a folding chair" (Vaidyanathan, 2016, p. 5). I had the honor of teaching Chisholm's mentee in one of my workshops on this book's topic, and she described Chisholm's encouragement of her—a researcher—to increase her impact and widen her reach.

Areas of inequity will never improve without courageous dialogue and conscientious actions. As researchers we are in prime position to further this charge.

PRIORITIZE EFFORTS AND BE SCRAPPY

Your workplace, specialties, preferences, and personality are all aspects that make your journey very individual. Thus, the way you use this book should be very individual. Not a fan of writing? Then spend less time tackling this book's writing recommendations than you do on speaking and other endeavors. Not able to live away from home for a White House fellowship? Then do not apply for one. Just want to try a few new things without setting up a webpage or brand? Then start small.

Use this book for your individual circumstances. However, note that stepping outside your comfort zone and pursuing a variety of opportunities is most beneficial. For example, public speaking increases writing opportunities and exposure, and writing increases public speaking opportunities and exposure. Social media presence and speaking engagements are something you put on your book proposal to get a book deal. All opportunities covered in this book are likely to increase other types of prospects, which will benefit the reach of your work. In addition, mere exposure effect dictates that the more people encounter something, the more they like it (Grant, 2016), so increasing your findings' exposure could increase its acceptance by stakeholders.

Sharing your research in a variety of ways results in a more well-rounded resume or CV, more well-rounded experience, and a much wider net to catch additional opportunities to tell the world your important information. This benefits more lives. So, use this book as you see fit, but be sure to push yourself as you do. Be brave, and do not be afraid to be scrappy.

SCRAPPY TIPS AND FAST TRACKS

Being *scrappy* means being determined and thinking outside the box to find numerous, creative ways to share what you know. It also means aiming high (while simultaneously seizing more accessible opportunities) for maximum impact.

Some call this moonshot thinking: shoot for the moon—10 times as high as might feel comfortable or typical—and see where it lands you. That approach worked for the first human to step on the moon: Neil Armstrong acquired his pilot's license *before* his driver's license.

This book offers many "scrappy tips" that offer clever, surprising ways to achieve a goal related to various sections in the book. This book also offers "Scrappy Fast Track" text boxes that offer action plans to get you from point A to point B as fast as possible. This will help you hit your mark when you aim high. For example:

- Publish a book even though your starting point includes no published writing.
- Give a TED Talk or keynote even though your starting point includes no notable speaking experience.
- Appear on NPR even though your starting point includes no radio interviews.
- Be honored by the White House even though your starting point includes no previous awards.
- Gain lots of exposure even though your starting point includes limited branding and social media presence.

You will have to scale up your skillsets quickly to achieve lofty goals (something this book helps you do), but these scrappy routes will help open those big doors for you. Be scrappy, walk through such doors, and see what happens.

HONESTY AND INTEGRITY

As you follow your path to maximum impact, commit to maintaining honesty and integrity. This means never lying on your CV, never taking credit for someone else's work, never undermining a colleague, and so on. Even if an underhanded move appears to have a positive result in the short term, it will likely damage you in the long term, such as by hurting your reputation.

You will feel your best if you operate with honesty and integrity, and people will respond better to you and your findings. For example, "when scientists are transparent about any conflicts of interest, sources of funding, or important affiliations related to their work, public views of their integrity can be enhanced" (National Academies of Sciences, Engineering, and Medicine, 2017, p. 25). You can still be scrappy (as covered in the previous section) but do so honorably.

RESOURCE TIP

The Committee of Publication Ethics (COPE) (www. publicationethics.org) can help you navigate topics (like authorship and publishing) with integrity.

HUMILITY

I reject the common notion that researchers are superior to "the general public," as if we have somehow removed ourselves from the latter group, and I find this humility keeps me open to new perspectives and better able to serve. Though this book focuses on ways to share research, it does so on the premise that one should listen to the needs of stakeholders with equal fervor. Doing so will improve your research and communication.

REFERENCES

Altman, M., & Bourg, C. (2018). A grand challenges-based research agenda for scholarly communication and information science. *MIT Grand Challenge PubPub Participation Platform*. https://doi.org/10.21428/62b3421f

Annansingh, F., Howell, K. E., Liu, S., & Nunes, M. B. (2018). Academics' perception of knowledge sharing in higher education. *International Journal of Educational Management, 32*(6), 1001–1015.

AP-NORC Center for Public Affairs Research & USAFacts Institute. (2019). *State of the facts*. Retrieved from www.apnorc.org/projects/Pages/State-of-the-Facts.aspx

Badgett, M. V. L. (2016). *The public professor: How to use your research to change the world*. New York, NY: NYU Press.

Belluz, J., Plumer, B., & Resnick, B. (2016, September 7). The 7 biggest problems facing science, according to 270 scientists. *Vox*. Retrieved from www.vox.com/2016/7/14/12016710/science-challeges-research-funding-peer-review-process

Brunhuber, K. (2016, January 4). Climate change is 'largest science communication failure in history'. *CBC News*. Retrieved from www.cbc.ca/news/technology/climate-change-science-communication-failure-1.3345524

Chaturvedi, S. K. (2018). What's wrong with doctors' handwriting? *The National Medical Journal of India, 31*(1), 47–48.

Corredoira, M. L., & Villarroel, B. (2019). How to make science and academia less hypocritical and more ecological. *RealClear Science*. Retrieved from www.realclearscience.com/articles/2019/05/13/how_to_make_academia_less_hypocritical_and_more_ecological.html

Ecklund, E. H., & Scheitle, C. P. (2017). *Religion vs. science: What religious people really think*. New York, NY: Oxford University Press.

Elsevier. (2018). *Get noticed: Increase the impact of your research*. Retrieved from www.elsevier.com/__data/assets/pdf_file/0014/201326/GetNoticed_A4_factsheet_2017.pdf

Foley, J. (2016, August 5). *Science communication as a moral imperative*. Retrieved from https://globalecoguy.org/science-communication-as-a-moral-imperative-14188eb7d797

Gladwell, M. (2000). *The tipping point: How little things can make a big difference*. London, United Kingdom: Abacus.

Grant, A. (2016). *Originals: How non-conformists move the world*. New York, NY: Penguin Books.

Greenfieldboyce, N. (2019, June 11). To save the science poster, researchers want to kill it and start over. *All Things Considered*. Podcast Retrieved from www.npr.org/sections/health-shots/2019/06/11/729314248

Hall, L. A. [Teaching Academia]. (2018a, October 5). *How to make your research accessible* [Video file]. Retrieved from www.youtube.com/watch?time_continue=2&v=qO5Pcj_H1WE

Hall, L. A. [Teaching Academia]. (2018b, November 26). *One simple trick for publishing more & getting tenure* [Video file]. Retrieved from www.youtube.com/watch?v=tNcpX18r7Zw

Kahan, D. M., Landrum, A., Carpenter, K., Helft, L., & Jamieson, K. H. (2017, August 1). Science curiosity and political information processing. *Advances in Political Psychology, 38*(51), 179–199. doi:10.1111/pops.12396

Kahan, D. M., Peters, E., Wittlin, M., Slovic, P., Ouellette, L. L., Braman, D., & Mandel, G. (2012, May 22). The polarizing impact of science literacy and numeracy on perceived climate change risks. *Nature, 2*(2012), 732–735.

Kahneman, D. (2011). *Thinking, fast and slow*. New York, NY: Farrar, Straus and Giroux.

Keller, G., & Papasan, (2013). *The ONE thing: The surprisingly simple truth behind extraordinary results*. Austin, TX: Bard Press.

Kidwell, J. J., Vander Linde, K., & Johnson, S. L. (2000). Applying corporate knowledge management practices in higher education. *Educause Quarterly, 23*(4), 28–33.

Lusk, J. L., Roosen, J., & Bieberstein, A. (2014). Consumer acceptance of new food technologies: Causes and roots of controversies. *Annual Review of Resource Economics, 6*(1), 381–405. doi:10.1146/annurev-resource-100913-012735

McFadden, B. R., & Lusk, J. L. (2016). What consumers don't know about genetically modified food, and how that affects beliefs. *The FASEB Journal, 30*(9), 3091–3096.

McGrath, J. M., & Brandon, D. (2016, August). Scholarly publication and social media: Do they have something in common? *Advances in Neonatal Care, 16*(4), 245–248. doi:10.1097/ANC.0000000000000319

National Academies of Sciences, Engineering, and Medicine. (2017). *Communicating science effectively: A research agenda*. Washington, DC: The National Academies Press. doi:10.17226/23674.

Ngumbi, E. (2018, July 3). We should reward scientists for communicating to the public. *Scientific American*. Retrieved from https://blogs.scientificamerican.com/observations/we-should-reward-scientists-for-communicating-to-the-public

Rankin, J. (2019, February 6). Researchers battle discrimination. *Psychology Today*. Retrieved from www.psychologytoday.com/blog/much-more-common-core/201902/researchers-battle-discrimination-part-1-higher-education

Scientific American Editors. (2018, February 1). Universities should encourage scientists to speak out about public issues. *Scientific American*. Retrieved from www.scientificamerican.com/article/universities-should-encourage-scientists-to-speak-out-about-public-issues

Stoknes, P. E. (2015). *What we think about when we try not to think about global warming*. White River Junction, VT: Chelsea Green Publishing.

Sugimoto, C. R., Thelwall, M., Larivière, V., Tsou, A., Mongeon, P., & Macaluso, B. (2013). Scientists popularizing science: Characteristics and impact of TED talk presenters. *PLoS ONE*, *8*(4), e62403. Retrieved from https://doi.org/10.1371/journal.pone.0062403

Vaidyanathan, R. (2016, January 26). Before Hillary Clinton, there was Shirley Chisholm. *BBC News*. Retrieved from www.bbc.com/news/magazine-35057641

Veer Ramjeawon, P., & Rowley, J. (2017). Knowledge management in higher education institutions: Enablers and barriers in Mauritius. *Learning Organization*, *24*(5), 366–377.

Waters, M. (2016). The public shaming of England's first umbrella user. *Atlas Obscura*. Retrieved from www.atlasobscura.com/articles/the-public-shaming-of-englands-first-umbrella-user

Chapter 2

Social Media

If you are like me, you would only recognize a fraction of the names on a list of the world's 100 greatest tennis players of all time. You would know Billie Jean King and Arthur Ashe, who broke barriers; Andre Agassi, who sported a heavy-metal mullet and wore acid-washed jean shorts on the court; Serena and Venus Williams, who wear bold fashions and sometimes purple hair; Anna Kournikova, who starred in her then-boyfriend Enrique Iglesias' music video; and John McEnroe, with his infamous tantrums. These seven are not the very top players, but their image (based on breaking barriers, personality, style, or other markers unrelated to their skill with a tennis racquet) is what makes them so memorable. Agassi even said in a 1989 commercial, "Image is everything."

Image might not be *everything*, but it counts for a lot if you aim to lodge yourself in people's minds. I am not suggesting you wear acid-washed jeans and a mullet to your next research conference (though you would be memorable). I am suggesting you find ways for your online, on paper, and in person profile to help you be perceived and remembered as a go-to expert in your specialty area.

One of the main ways to manage your image is social media. For example, if you submit an article for a high-profile magazine or apply to give a TED Talk, those contemplating your acceptance will Google you to get a sense of your credibility, and they will want to find and judge your consistent social media presence.

Social media is also crucial to sharing your work with all audiences it can benefit. "Publishing good science in scholarly journals is important but what may be even more important is getting the scientific information into everyday communication streams. Today that is social media" (McGrath & Brandon, 2016, p. 245).

Some readers will want to develop all the tools discussed in this chapter, whereas others might only want a bio or a single social media account. It is fine to start with only those tools you know to be vital to your immediate goals. You can always build more of these tools later as you see fit. Knowing this chapter can be used with such flexibility should prevent you from feeling bogged down with "too much preparation," since it is important to ultimately move on to the prospects discussed in subsequent chapters. Just remember that a more pronounced social media presence will significantly boost efforts to share your discoveries.

RESEARCHERS' PLACE IN SOCIAL MEDIA

We are experiencing a revolution of scholarly communication through social media that represents a shift toward giving research and ideas greater visibility (Sugimoto, Work, Larivière, & Haustein, 2017). For example, "circulating newly published papers [on Twitter] allows for more exposure and has been linked to increased citations. Twitter mentions are an important . . . way of rigorously tracking the non-scholarly attention a paper receives" (Lee, 2019, p. 2). Social networks facilitate fast, easy, and concise communication well-suited to busy researchers.

SCRAPPY TIP

Right before you give a presentation (with your social media sites displayed on a slide), tweet and post a special resource or handout (I use tools covered later to schedule these ahead of time). Ask attendees to take out their cell phones and find your post. Many will use that moment to "follow" you online, whereas they might not have otherwise set themselves up to stay updated on your work via social networks.

You do not have to be a massive organization or celebrity to reach many viewers. LinkedIn's Top Voices list of 2018, which used varied metrics to determine whose posts engaged professionals and got them talking, included researchers from a variety of fields (data science, economics, education, healthcare, and more) (Roth, 2018).

Academics increasingly are sharing and discussing research on social media platforms such as Twitter rather than in the faculty lounge (Priem, 2013). LinkedIn is used by 65% of researchers for professional purposes, and scholarly articles are mentioned on social networks and other online sites once every 7 seconds (Elsevier, 2018). Using social media helps researchers combat the isolation common in their field while increasing the impact of their work (Reeve & Partridge, 2017).

"The old adage 'publish or perish' could soon go digital as 'clicks or canned'" (Brown, 2017, p. 1). Social networks are changing the way academics disseminate research, and academics are expected to have a professional online presence, which is increasingly recognized in determining tenure and promotions (Espinoza Vasquez & Caicedo Bastidas, 2015; Gruzd, Staves, & Wilk, 2011). Reddick (2016) announces his new publications through Facebook and Twitter and notes, "As a scholar wedded to seeing my research impact people in the communities that I research, it is imperative that I spread the word outside the ivy walls of academe" (p. 60).

Social media tools are important for those who author books, papers, or other works. "As an author, you are the face of your work, and the information you share on social media can help you gain exposure, convey crucial information in real-time, and foster genuine, direct connections with your readers" (Routledge, Taylor & Francis Group, 2017).

SCRAPPY TIP

When viewing your profile in Twitter, click "Lists" and then click to see which lists count you as a "Member." These are lists other people have created so they can click on the list when they want to view only tweets from select people (like you). Scanning the names of lists people have put you on will give you an idea of the types of tweets you mainly send and the brand message you are maintaining. You can then make informed changes to your social media habits, such as tweeting more frequently about an area on which your expertise seems to be off the lists' radar.

I cannot stress enough the value of establishing a presence on social media and using it to

- Share your expertise (directing traffic to your papers, presentations, etc.) with academics and non-academics,
- Connect with others, and
- Learn of valuable opportunities (not to mention all of the other things you will learn: new research strategies, links to newly released studies, and more are waiting for you on social networks).

SCRAPPY TIP

Keep an eye out for the expertise-sharing opportunities regularly announced on social media. When I landed a recurring opportunity as lecturer of the PostDoc Masterclass at University of Cambridge, one of my career highlights, it was made possible by social media. I saw a Twitter post about the position, and that post linked to the class's Facebook page, where I found the University of Cambridge's application instructions.

BRANDING

When you think of the company Apple, you might imagine its products (like a MacBook or iPhone) or its logo (an apple), but its "brand" relates to the feelings and impressions you associate with Apple. Common associations with Apple's brand include cutting-edge technology, creativity, underdog, streamlined design, and thinking differently. This association is proliferated by what Apple does (its products satisfy people's need for streamlined, effective technology), what others write and say about Apple (which relates to what Apple does), and what Apple tells us about Apple (like the impression its advertising leaves).

Personal branding is similar to branding, except you are proliferating a mental association with a person (you) rather than a product or company. For researchers, your personal brand is the essence of what you offer your profession and those you encounter. As you pursue opportunities to spread your knowledge, efforts to communicate a clear personal brand will help others understand what you can offer them. For example, no one will ask you to speak at a solar energy symposium if your expertise in solar energy, your professionalism, and your polished communication are not known to people. Your website, conduct, handouts, literature, logo, slides—anything you put out into the world—can communicate these kinds of qualities as your brand, as can your social media through what you post and what you include in your profile.

Branding is important to helping you stand out to successfully share your ideas (Arruda, 2016),

DEFINITION OF PERSONAL BRANDING

"Personal branding is essentially what you are known for and what people seek you out for"

(Tannahill-Moran, 2016, p. 1).

but a strong personal brand can also limit you to whatever niche you brand yourself as having (Hartley, 2016). How specific a brand you establish will depend on how sure you are that your specialties will never change.

Determining this is no easy task. I say this as someone whose first website was www.OverTheCounterData.com, one of the focus areas for my first studies and books. Though that concept of sharing data effectively relates to this book's concept of sharing research and strategies effectively, the website was very data-specific.

At the time I thought this emphasis would never change, but it did. My expertise expanded to encompass additional topics unrelated to data. I then had to change my web address, social media account names, details on repeatedly used slides and handouts, business cards, and more to reflect my name instead of a single one of my specialties. This took time away from my work and risked confusing my contacts.

To avoid a similar mistake, err on the side of caution. If you have a long career researching people who are both homeless and disabled, have opened a specialized homeless shelter, and are certain that will remain your specialty, you can establish that clearly (such as with a web domain that bears your shelter's name). However, if you are passionate about your indigenous archaeology specialization right now, but you have always been a renaissance woman with varied interests, proceed as if your expertise will fundamentally change someday to something that might not even be on your radar right now. In this case (and in most cases), I recommend using a website domain and social media account names that simply reflect your name (instead of a topic) and possibly your doctorate. Use a design style that communicates a polished presence (and anything else that matches you as a person), and nods to your current topic without limiting you to it. For example, my logo at www.JennyRankin.com alludes to a bar graph (as my initial expertise I shared with the world was how to best display data), but also suits my additional areas of expertise (the logo hints at growth, since my other niches relate to helping students, educators, and researchers be their best). Let your business card reflect your specialty, but limit your order so future cards can reflect a change in concentration.

Of course, if you start a center, organization, consulting company, or other movement, you can get highly specific branding for a website, social media profiles, and other materials devoted solely to that endeavor. Maintaining two "identities" (your personal branding and that of your endeavor, such as through different websites and social media accounts) can be taxing, so this arrangement works best if more than one person is involved in the movement. This chapter and book apply to the marketing and spreading of your endeavor, just as they apply to sharing your ideas as an individual person; however, see the "Branding for a Movement" text box for additional considerations.

BRANDING FOR A MOVEMENT

There are additional branding considerations if you seek to brand a center, organization, company, or other movement (in other words, something other than a person):

- Consider if you want your brand to also appeal to fields outside your primary field. If you do, select terms (for the organization name and literature) that will be as easily understood in those fields as they are in your typical sector.
- Be sure any terms you use (like "PD") will still be used, current, and recognizable 10 years from now, given how fickle terms and movements can be.
- If picking a concept for your brand, try to find one that lends itself well to a visual. If your brand triggers an image in people's minds, this can help them understand and remember the brand. This also makes it easier to come up with a brand icon or logo.
- Conduct Google searches to be sure no one is already using that term, particularly in any trademarked/copyrighted form. This is especially true if you pick a name for your brand (rather than your own name), like *The Big Bang Theory*'s fictional "Professor Proton." Even if you use your own name as your brand you will want to be sure it is not already in use. If it is, consider a twist on your name or brand to avoid confusion, such as always including your middle name.

Boiling yourself down to a specific concept lets people instantly understand the essence of what you are mainly all about. People are busy, and branding's shorthand helps you to be noticed, included, and remembered. Just keep your brand open enough to evolve (such as with a web address that matches your name). Complete Exercise 2.1 to plan some aspects of your brand.

EXERCISE 2.1: PERSONAL BRAND

1. What are six words or short phrases you want people in the field to associate with your name? These traits or topics should be true to who you are. For example, do not write "good with people" if you are socially awkward. Rather, aim for a brand that reflects your best qualities.

2. Now circle the three most important associations you just wrote. Then place a star next to the single most important. As you judge importance, keep your expertise-sharing goals in mind (for example, do you aspire to shape policy, engage in public debates, or inform experiments from behind the scenes?).

3. Google "modern color schemes" to investigate possible color schemes to use for resources you will produce in the future (such as slides, handouts, websites, logos, etc.). What is the color scheme best suited for you (or where can it be found online)? A consistent palette will aid recognition of your work.

SOCIAL MEDIA USERS

Social networks are dominated by the well-educated, meaning users are better equipped for academic dialogue. Facebook, Instagram, LinkedIn, Pinterest, Twitter, and YouTube all have their greatest number of users in the college graduate category (which also includes postgraduates), as opposed to the "high school or less" and "some college" categories (Pew Research Center, 2018a).

Social networks also provide a direct avenue to the public, where you can inform non-experts on your work. Seventy-one percent of Americans use social media to get news, connect with one another, and share information (Pew Research Center, 2018a). For the first time in history, more adults surveyed report relying on social media for news (20%) than those relying on print newspapers (16%) (Pew Research Center, 2018b). Contrary to popular belief that Millennials dominate social sites, Generation X (ages 35–49) spends the most time on social media (nearly 7 hours per week), and the average for all adults is over 5 hours per week spent on social media (Casey, 2017). By joining dialogue on social networks and sharing links to relevant work, you can help shape the content and tone of field news.

Those based at learning institutions can reach out to students through social networks. Since 52% of Generation Z members use Twitter, the American College Application Campaign ran a social media marketing campaign to inspire students to apply for college; within one week its #WhyApply hashtag reaped 2,367 uses and 5.3 million impressions (Shop, 2017). Nicholas Provenzano (@thenerdyteacher) joined Twitter to promote his educational blog (Pannoni, 2015) and already has well over 63,000 followers. Having more followers means more people are likely to see the updates you share (new findings, opinions, links to articles you have written or admire, etc.) and learn from you to help the world.

WHICH TOOLS TO USE (A PRACTICAL APPROACH)

Even non-techies can find the standard social media tools to be easier to use than they anticipated. However, there are hundreds of social networks, and even a single site could take up every minute of your time. Thus, be selective and conscientious in how you use social media so that you do not sacrifice time from work and life. An easy way to do this follows and is mirrored in Table 2.1, which summarizes my own habits. It involves picking one tool with which to be most active and using the others mainly just for posting.

Set up the following social media accounts (available online and also in application format for use on electronic devices), which are particularly popular amongst researchers and important for your branding. Using tools like Hootsuite and TweetDeck, covered later, will allow you to manage these with ease (such as posting just once to have the post appear in multiple social media accounts simultaneously). Though you can opt to pay for more advanced features, you can use all of the tools (in the ways described in the following list) for free. The tools (and thus where to click) are ever-changing, so Google specific directions on how to achieve what is described.

1. **LinkedIn** (www.linkedin.com). Even if you plan to never spend time on this site perusing posts, you should at least have a professional profile page where people can find you, learn about you, and reach out to you.

Table 2.1 Sample Social Media Use That Takes Minimal Time

Tool	Use Type	Do I regularly peruse this site to learn from others?	Do I post here each time I have a new book, paper, appearance, and the like?	Do I post links here to others' work I admire?
LinkedIn	Professional	No	Yes	Yes
Twitter	Professional	Yes	Yes	Yes
Facebook	Personal for the "page," professional for the "group"	No	No for the "page," yes for the "group"	No for the "page," yes for the "group"
Instagram	Professional	No	Yes	Yes
ASNSs	Professional	No	No (major work only)	No

- **App-specific tip:** For those open to getting more from this site, consider creating a group devoted to your brand or topic of interest. When you post links to your new work or appearances, you can post both on your page and within these special interest groups, which people can join.

2. **Twitter** (www.twitter.com) is where the research field is currently most active. Weibo (www.weibo.com) is a similar tool used widely in China.

   I use Twitter exclusively for professional reasons, whereas I relegate my main Facebook page to personal use, such as keeping in touch with out-of-state cousins (though I cover a professional workaround in the following section). Establishing a single function (professional or personal) for each social media account helps your posts remain appropriate. For example, only my friends can see Facebook photos in which I happen to be in a bathing suit or tell an embarrassing anecdote, whereas I post nothing on Twitter I would not want the professional community to see.

   I dragged my feet when it came to joining Twitter but quickly came to love it. Because of the vast number of researchers and educators who use it—and its 280-character limit (so posts have to get straight to the point)—I quickly learn of new studies that fit my interests, and it takes me less than a minute to share my own work with thousands any time I have a new book, paper, or appearance.

   "The number one reason to be on Twitter? That's where the journalists are—all day, every day—talking to each other" (Badgett, 2016, p. 148). A PBS NewsHour editor took interest in my stance on President Trump's proposal to arm teachers with guns only because I privately messaged her about it on Twitter.

   - **App-specific tip:** As I write this, Twitter is currently reworking its process for verifying accounts, which displays a blue badge beside your name to indicate yours is an authentic account of someone "of public interest." This can enhance your credibility and thus improve people's acceptance of your ideas (like retweeting your comment or asking to interview you). Check https://verification.twitter.com for future verification instructions.

3. **Facebook** (www.facebook.com) has particularly active pages for universities (like www.facebook.com/ULaVerne), specific departments or classes (like www.facebook.com/DepartmentOfComputerScienceUniversityOf Oxford), and academic groups (like www.facebook.com/groups/Society.of.Professors.of.Education). WeChat (https://web.wechat.com) is a similar tool used widely in China.

   - **App-specific tip:** If you already use Facebook for personal reasons, add a "group" to your personal website. This allows you to publicly share your professional content on the group page while keeping your Facebook page personal and private (almost like having two separate accounts, but without the hassle of multiple logins).

4. **Instagram** (www.instagram.com) is not yet used by researchers as commonly as the previously presented sites. However, Instagram is the fastest growing social media tool in use across all age groups and especially by teens and young adults (Ahlquist, 2019). As youth grow into research positions, and as current researchers' Instagram use continues to grow, Instagram could ultimately become the preferred social network for academia, as Twitter is now.

It is thus worth setting up an Instagram site where people can begin to follow you, even if you rarely post. Though I opened my Instagram account for personal reasons, I now use it only for professional use.

- **App-specific tip:** Make your account "business" rather than "personal" and submit a verification request to earn a blue tick beside your account name. Like Twitter's blue badge, this indicates yours is an authentic account "of public interest."

5. **Academic social networking sites (ASNSs)** are social media sites designed specifically for scholars. ASNSs include the following:
   - Academia (www.academia.edu)
   - Bepress (www.bepress.com)
   - Mendeley (www.mendeley.com)
   - ResearchGate (www.researchgate.net)
   - Scholabrate (www.scholabrate.com)
   - Zenodo (www.zenodo.org)

Sites like these allow you to network with other academics and to discover and share new research. ASNSs improve scholarly communication, facilitate collaboration, and facilitate the development of an online academic identity (Jordan, 2014). Whether or not you choose to network in that manner, which takes time, you might at least have a professional profile page where people can find you, learn about you, and reach out to you.

Keep in mind that you do not have to answer the extensive questions about every degree, every accomplishment, and so on when crafting your profile. Simply include a link to your website (or whatever webpage you predominantly keep updated with new biographical information). I choose to not update every ASNS with my latest work (in favor of spending that time elsewhere), but if you find your colleagues are particularly active on a particular ASNS, you might choose to be more active there.

ASNSs often double as research repositories. Using them in that capacity is covered in the "Exposure for Your Other Writing: Research Repositories" section of Chapter 11.

Hundreds more social media options exist. Take note of which ones are used heavily in your field or by stakeholders your work can help and sign up accordingly. For example, TikTok (www.tiktok.com/en) has recently surged in popularity but does not serve most researchers; however, if your work is video-friendly and you seek to engage youth with your work, you might find it worthwhile.

If you make more-regular use of social media than I do, then you increase your chances of reaching more people with your work but sacrifice more time from your work. If you make less use of social media than I do, then you decrease your chances of reaching more people with your work but gain more time for your work.

Whatever balance you strike is a personal choice, but note that it takes very little time to post your work so that, at the very least, social network users can discover it using their favorite tools. The single "Yes" in the third column of Table 2.1 (noting that I regularly peruse Twitter) is the only item on that table that takes some time away from my days (usually time when I am watching TV, waiting in line, or otherwise not positioned to work). Everything else I do on social media takes negligible time yet allows my work to reach thousands of people I likely would not reach without these tools.

ACCOUNT BASICS

For each social media account you set up, keep the following tips in mind. Though they might seem obvious, many academics overlook them.

- **Do not change your name** (such as upon marriage). Using the same name throughout your academic career will improve your citation record (Ebrahim et al., 2013) and make it easier for people to find you.
- **Create a profile that will be easy for others to find.** For example, a good Twitter handle for someone who goes by Maria Cho Patel is @MariaChoPatel. If you already established an account name you regret, you can often change it without losing any of your followers (as is the case for Twitter).

  If possible (noting that sometimes your desired profile name has already been taken by someone else), word your name the same way for each social media tool. For example, if you go by @ChantelJNguyen on Twitter, it is not ideal to use Dr. Nguyen on Instagram and Chantel Jones Nguyen on Facebook.
- **Complete the "bio" field**, which most of these tools have space for, even if it is only to include a link to a website where you keep your biographical information current. If it is a site you use regularly, include a bio that succinctly communicates what you want the world to know about you (such as that you research human genetics, did a TED Talk, teach at Howard University, and do keynote speaking). This will be covered more in the "Personal Branding" section of this chapter.
- **Include a photo of yourself** and use the same photo for all social media accounts (though you might use a different photo for accounts you want

to distinguish as personal). Social media expert Josie Ahlquist (2019) said, "Not having a photo on LinkedIn is like pulling your hand away right before somebody tries to shake it." The same is true of other social networks, too. A photo tells people that you welcome being found.

TOOLS TO SAVE TIME MANAGING POSTS

When you have something new to share, it is time-consuming to log onto each social media account to post the same information one account at a time. Fortunately, the sites and apps listed here make managing multiple accounts less time-consuming.

- Set up a HootSuite (www.hootsuite.com) account or similar tool like Buffer (www.Buffer.com). This tool allows you to post once, in a single place, and have the post simultaneously added to your Facebook (page or group), Instagram, LinkedIn, Twitter, Pinterest (www.pinterest.com), and YouTube (www.youtube.com) accounts. This way, you only have to post something a single time to reach users on all sites, depending on which social media sites you choose to use. HootSuite is free if you only integrate it with up to three of your social accounts. You can also schedule posts ahead of time to appear when your audience is most active or to spread out the posts (since users are prone to unfollow someone who dumps an overwhelming number of posts at once). Once you are comfortable using HootSuite, download the web browser extension Hootlet (www.hootlet. com) for even faster sharing.
- Set up a TweetDeck (www.tweetdeck.com) account. This allows you to monitor multiple Twitter accounts and multiple Twitter searches on a single dashboard. You can also use TweetDeck (for free) to schedule Tweets, in the same manner described for HootSuite.
- When posting to Instagram, you can opt to have the post also go to your Facebook (page or group), Twitter, and Tumblr (covered in Chapter 5) accounts without having to post separately on those sites. Over time additional integrations will likely be possible.

If you are tech-intimidated, you might choose to use each social account on its own for a while before adding the tools presented here to your repertoire.

POSTING GUIDELINES

Posting valuable content brings you more followers, which will cause more people to see your own work when you post about it (such as when you share a link to a study you published). Thus, when you read online field news and research your topics of interest online, it helps to post links to that content. Sharing links to others' work you deem valuable is part of using your voice to better your field and beyond.

With Twitter as an example, these guidelines can increase your tweets' (and your) visibility:

- When sharing others' work, include the author's Twitter handle (example: @RebeccaSkloot) and source's Twitter handle (example: @NYTimes). This often prompts that person or organization to favorite and retweet the tweet, which can bring you new followers. This encourages exposure to the work you want to share.
- Include one or two hashtags (example: #AcWri) per tweet or post. Many people use hashtags to search for content, so hashtags expose people who do not know you to your posts. Tweets with at least one hashtag are retweeted 55% more often and increase post engagement by up to 100% (Cooper, 2013).
- Do not post many times in succession. Posting in bursts increases the chance of others unfollowing your account.
- Engage in Twitter chats related to your topic or field (see www.tweetreports.com/twitter-chat-schedule for examples), explained in Chapter 10. If the conversation fits, include a link to one of your papers or presentations as you post a related comment.
- Stick to professional content, as people you do not know will likely unfollow you if you clutter their news feeds with coverage of *The Real Housewives of Orange County*, photos of your meals, or other subjects in which they are not necessarily interested.

TECH TIP

Some social media provide data analytics. For example, Twitter lets you view "Tweet Activity" to see which of your tweets had the most views and engagements (such as retweets and link clicks). Instagram lets you view "Insights" like how users are interacting with your posts and when your audience is most active on the app. Use such information to inform how you craft future posts.

- Add social media icons to your website and other bio/profile webpages to give people easy access to your accounts. If these pages do not allow you to add icon links, you can add their addresses to your bio.

- Sync your social media accounts. For example, I have synced my accounts with my SquareSpace website, so whenever I post a new blog entry, it automatically appears as a post on each of my social media sites.
- Maintain an open, positive, and constructive tone, as scholars are most likely to engage with tweets that reflect these qualities (Alderton, Brunsell, & Bariexca, 2011). On that note, do not post when you are drinking alcohol or when your emotions flare.
- Add an image to your post when appropriate. Tweets with images get clicked 18% more, liked 89% more, and retweeted 150% more frequently (Smith, 2016).

RESOURCE TIP

Andrew Ibrahim offers free tools to help researchers create visual abstracts for their own studies and tweets (see www.surgeryredesign.com/resources).

- Include a "visual abstract" that summarizes a study's key findings. Tweets with visual abstracts were seen by 7.7 times as many people, retweeted 8.4 times as often, and clicked on (to read the paper) 2.7 times as often (Ibrahim, Lillemoe, Klingensmith, & Dimick, 2017).

As long as you do not let social media time detract from your main work, the more active you are with any social networking tool (posting quality content regularly), the better. Those who made LinkedIn's Top Voices list of 2018 were two times more likely to respond to comments or reply to another member's post, and thus received seven times more comments, 10 times more likes, and five times more shares on their posts (Roth, 2018).

Such posting can expand your audience, allowing your wisdom to benefit more people. The more you post quality findings that can help the world, the more followers are likely to read and learn from them, and the more likely you are to have followers who can benefit from your future shares as well.

EXERCISE 2.2: SOCIAL MEDIA

1. Set up a new social media account using the guidelines presented earlier. If you are already using all of the tools described, skip to step 2.

33

2. Use a social media search field to find people whose work you admire and consider following them.

3. Determine which of the users from step 2 have the most followers. Explore their posts and make note of what they post about, how they post, and how often.

4. After using a social media tool for at least a week, use its analytics features (described in the "Tech Tip" text box) to gain insight into which of your posts garner the most engagement.

5. Post something in a style informed by what you learned from steps 3 and 4.

BIO

You will use a bio repeatedly for social media, and also when applying this book's strategies. A professional bio "is the short summary of relevant background you need to introduce yourself in a variety of settings" (Jacobs, 2014, p. 1). According to brand and marketing strategist Alex Honeysett (2017), it is the most important text you will ever write about yourself. If it is well-crafted, your bio can open a lot of doors for you to share your research.

SAMPLE BIOS

Download the "Sample Bios" eResource to see examples of a single bio written for five different length requirements (including social media). See the "eResources" section near the start of this book for details. Note how the most impressive and pertinent accomplishments show up in all five examples. Common bio details include:

- Full Name (including post-nominal letters, like PhD)
- Job Title
- Place of Employment
- Past Roles of Note
- Major Awards and Honors
- Website (leading the reader to your online resume or CV)

TIME-SAVING TIP

As you adjust your bio for different lengths and purposes over time, save all your bios in a single place, ordered by word count. This will save you time when you pull bios to meet different needs in the future.

You will also use these bios for opportunities shared in this book. What you include in your bio (see the "Sample Bios" text box for details) will be shaped by how many words you are allotted, but longer is not always better. Your bio should drive home who you are and why someone should pay attention to you . . . and, thus, what you share. Complete Exercise 2.3 to play with some ideas.

SCRAPPY TIP

Tailor your bio to the environment where it appears. For example, when I wrote *First Aid for Teacher Burnout: How You Can Find Peace and Success* (2017), my back-of-book bio mentions I won a Teacher of the Year award, which would appeal to my audience of teachers. However, when I wrote *Designing Data Reports that Work: A Guide for Creating Data Systems in Schools and Districts* (2016), I instead used this space to note my previous role as chief education and research officer (CERO) of an educational technology data systems company, which would appeal more to my audience of edtech and data specialists.

EXERCISE 2.3: BIO

1. List four to eight key details (like a specific award you won) that should appear in your own bio for a use of your choosing (such as at the end of a magazine article you wrote).

2. Craft a short bio in which you include these details.

3. Now write the same bio for two other word counts (such as condensing it and/or lengthening it with more details).

CURRICULUM VITAE (CV)

Some social media sites—particularly ASNSs—have fields in which to enter resume and CV information. Your complete CV should be available somewhere online, so you might utilize an ASNS or your own website to list all major accomplishments. An "online CV increases researchers' output visibility to the academic community" (Ebrahim et al., 2013, p. 97).

TIME-SAVING TIP

Even if you will not need a CV to show others, maintaining a CV for your own purposes will be a huge time saver. You can just electronically copy information from its various sections whenever providing such information is required to secure an opportunity. For example, when a conference organizer wants you to list all your previous speaking engagements before she books you for a keynote, you will not have to dig through old files to find each date, location, session title, etc. It is much easier to simply save these details on a CV as each new accomplishment occurs.

I maintain a longer-than-recommended CV (www.JennyRankin.com/bio) because I often use it to copy/paste requested information (as captured in the "Time-Saving Tip" text box), and I can easily remove less-vital sections before submitting the CV to someone in static form. Choosing your own CV's length will be an act of weighing pros and cons to determine what best suits your needs.

Institutions in some fields frequently use the same CV housing tool (such as www.chroniclevitae.com, used extensively in higher education). Consider whether maintaining your CV on such a site is worthwhile for you (such as whether you will use it regularly for a job hunt).

SCRAPPY TIP

If you are actively on course to complete an achievement (such as earning your doctorate), it is ethical and advisable to mention this. For example, you could list your PhD in the Education section of your CV with its expected completion date (just be sure its "To Be Completed" nature is clear, and that you are realistic about the expected date).

I put together my CV for the first time (having previously only needed a resume) when I started looking for a university teaching job. I was surprised to find it was just as useful for non-university contacts. Often when I am communicating with someone about my work or a collaboration, I give this person the link to my CV.

CV TEMPLATE

Download the "CV Template" eResource for a Word document you can use to build your own CV. See the "eResources" section near the start of this book for details on accessing and using the template. Common CV segments include:

- Bio (added to the beginning if the CV gets large and unruly so your proudest moments stand out)
- Employment
- Education
- Awards and Honors (if you have many honors within a specific category – like grants – consider making that its own segment)
- Volunteering
- Publications
- Media Interviews
- Presentations and Seminars
- Research
- Professional Affiliations and Memberships
- Technical Proficiencies (applicable for some specializations)
- Social Media
- Resume (to include a link to your resume, if you also maintain one)

When I began my academic career, I was mortified by how few awards, publications, and the like I had to include on my CV at the time, even after a long career as an educator. However, using the strategies shared elsewhere in this book, my CV looked fantastic within its first year. If you feel disheartened by your achievements when crafting your first CV draft, know that this book's tips will lead you to all sorts of accomplishments in a matter of weeks or months, depending on your efforts. Complete Exercise 2.4 to start building your own CV if you do not yet have one.

EXERCISE 2.4: CV

1. Pre-plan your CV. Referring to the CV Template text box, list the categories that will make strong segments on your CV (like if you have won many impressive awards, you will include the "Awards" category). When you start putting together your CV, start with these categories.

2. Referring to the CV Template text box, note the categories within which you have few or no accomplishments. As you pursue the opportunities featured in this book, try improving some of these areas first.

3. Using the "CV Template" eResource (or other tool), start building your own CV. Your CV is meant to make you look your best, so modify it to suit your expertise. For example:
   - If your education is more impressive than your employment history, put your CV's "Education" section before the "Employment" section.
   - If you are new to research and have not volunteered, take out the "Volunteering" and "Research" sections.

. . . and so on. When you have a website (discussed later), post your CV online.

EMAIL SIGNATURE

Add a link to your most-used social media accounts to your automatic email signature (something easily set up in most email providers). This helps your contacts see what you are sharing there and follow you for future posts.

Email Signature

Jenny Grant Rankin, Ph.D.
Facebook / Instagram / LinkedIn / Twitter
Books / Latest Book
Bio & CV / Press / Media Kit

My email signature looks like this (see text box); each underlined word can be clicked to acquire the item mentioned. If appropriate, include your title and affiliation after your name.

Upon breaking into the email service industry, Hotmail automatically added a short message and link to the bottom of every email its users sent anyone. Berger (2013) credits this practice with causing Hotmail to acquire 8.5 million subscribers in just over a year. In other words, people pay attention to the information at the bottoms of emails and follow the links there.

WEBSITE

A website offers people an easy way to find you and your work in one centralized location. It also helps you establish your brand. If you are in an early stage of your career, a website can help people understand you are serious about communicating your ideas. "Crafting an online scholarly identity . . . exposes you to a level of public engagement with your ideas that simply is not feasible through other modes of dissemination" (Stewart, 2016, p. 81).

Some people use one of their social media accounts as their primary website (particularly LinkedIn). Others manage their own domain. You have many website and webpage options. Regardless of which you choose, the site should allow you access to personally edit and add extensive and varied content. The guide mentioned here will help you establish the best webpage for you.

GUIDE TO CREATING A WEBSITE

See the "eResources" section near the start of this book for details on accessing the "Guide to Creating a Website". Two different approaches for your web presence are detailed in the guide: hosting your own website (Option 1) or maintaining a web*page* within an existing website (Option 2), such as one hosted by your institution, organization, company, or publisher. Think carefully about which will work best for you. If you choose Option 1, however, you should *also* utilize Option 2 whenever the scenario is available to you. The guide offers a shortcut that makes it fast and easy to maintain multiple webpages.

HEADSHOT

Select a single headshot to use for everything (your social media sites, website, "about the author" portion of articles, etc.). Some researchers I know hired a professional photographer for beautiful headshots.

39

Consider these tips for whatever photograph you select:

- A beefy border (such as the surrounding foliage in my headshot) will give you more cropping options when different sites have different proportion requirements for your headshot.
- The background should either be blank or free of distractions (for example, the foliage behind me in my headshot is blurred) or should highlight a key accomplishment. For example, some educators are able to fit in the lectern or signage of a noteworthy event at which they are speaking. As long as the photo leaves enough room to make your face clear, these images can help communicate your merit.
- Are you known for being happy and energetic, or for being serious and intense? Your headshot should reflect your nature.
- The photo should clearly look like you. It is tempting to pick a photo taken when you were younger or fitter, or a photo in which you look stunning but not your usual self, but such images will not aid your recognition as you mingle at conferences and forge connections.

REFERENCES

Ahlquist, J. (2019, March 28). Engaging the digital generation. *Elsevier's 2019 Education Leadership Forum*. Presentation conducted from the NOPSI Hotel, New Orleans, LA.

Alderton, E., Brunsell, E., & Bariexca, D. (2011, September). The end of isolation. *Journal of Online Learning and Teaching*, 7(3), 1–14.

Arruda, W. (2016, April 26). Effective branding is in the details. *Forbes*. Retrieved from www.forbes.com/sites/williamarruda/2016/04/26/effective-branding-is-in-the-details/#5a54f9fd4a6a

Badgett, M. V. L. (2016). *The public professor: How to use your research to change the world.* New York, NY: NYU Press.

Berger, J. (2013). *Contagious: Why things catch on.* New York, NY: Simon & Schuster.

Brown, J. L. (2017, August 1). Will 'publish or perish' become 'clicks or canned'? The rise of academic social networks. *EdSurge*. Retrieved from www.edsurge.com/news/2017-08-01-will-publish-or-perish-become-clicks-or-canned-the-rise-of-academic-social-networks

Casey, S. (2017, January 17). *2016 Nielsen social media report*. Retrieved from www.nielsen.com/us/en/insights/reports/2017/2016-nielsen-social-media-report.html

Cooper, S. (2013, October 17). Big mistake: Making fun of hashtags instead of using them. *Forbes*. Retrieved from www.forbes.com/sites/stevecooper/2013/10/17/big-mistake-making-fun-of-hashtags-instead-of-using-them/#548ed65928f0

Ebrahim, A. N., Salehi, H., Embi, M. A., Habibi Tanha, F., Gholizadeh, H., Motahar, S. M., & Ordi, A. (2013, October 23). Effective strategies for increasing citation frequency. *International Education Studies*, *6*(11), 93–99.

Elsevier. (2018). *Get noticed: Increase the impact of your research*. Retrieved from www. elsevier.com/__data/assets/pdf_file/0014/201326/GetNoticed_A4_factsheet_2017.pdf

Espinoza Vasquez, F. K., & Caicedo Bastidas, C. E. (2015). Academic social networking sites: A comparative analysis of their services and tools. In *iConference 2015 Proceedings*, 1–6.

Gruzd, A., Staves, K., & Wilk, A. (2011). Tenure and promotion in the age of online social media. *Proceedings of the American Society for Information Science and Technology*, *48*(1), 1–9.

Hartley, D. (2016, May 20). Stop trying to build your "personal brand": Trust me – I'm in marketing. *Psychology Today*. Retrieved from www.psychologytoday.com/blog/machiavellians-gulling-the-rubes/201605/stop-trying-build-your-personal-brand

Honeysett, A. (2017, January 26). The professional bio template that makes everyone sound accomplished. *Forbes*. Retrieved from www.forbes.com/sites/daily muse/2017/01/26/the-professional-bio-template-that-makes-everyone-sound-accomplished/#3c2198ba7cb2

Ibrahim, A. M., Lillemoe, K. D., Klingensmith, M. E., & Dimick, J. B. (2017, August 1). Visual abstracts to disseminate research on social media: A prospective, case-control crossover study. *Annals of Surgery*, [Epub ahead of print]. doi:10.1097/SLA.0000000000002277

Jacobs, D. L. (2014, June 3). What to do when you need a bio, rather than a résumé. *Forbes*. Retrieved from www.forbes.com/sites/deborahljacobs/2014/06/03/what-to-do-when-you-need-a-bio-rather-than-a-resume/#7307fc8b284f

Jordan, K. (2014, November 3). Academics and their online networks: Exploring the role of academic social networking sites. *First Monday: Peer Reviewed Journal on the Internet*, *19*(11), http://dx.doi.org/10.5210/fm.v19i11.4937

Lee, J. M. (2019, February 8). How to use Twitter to further your research career. *Nature*. Retrieved from www.nature.com/articles/d41586-019-00535-w

McGrath, J. M., & Brandon, D. (2016, August). Scholarly publication and social media: Do they have something in common? *Advances in Neonatal Care*, *16*(4), 245–248. doi:10.1097/ANC.0000000000000319

Pannoni, A. (2015). High school educators share how they became Twitter rock stars. *U.S. News*. Retrieved from www.usnews.com/education/blogs/high-school-notes/2015/07/06/high-school-educators-share-how-they-became-twitter-rock-stars

Pew Research Center. (2018a, March). *Social media use in 2018*. Retrieved from www. pewinternet.org/2018/03/01/social-media-use-2018-appendix-a-detailed-table

Pew Research Center. (2018b, December). *Americans still prefer watching to reading the news—and mostly still through television.* Retrieved from www.journalism.org/wp-content/uploads/sites/8/2018/12/PJ_2018.12.03_read-watch-listen_FINAL1.pdf

Priem, J. (2013, March 28). Scholarship: Beyond the paper. *Nature: International Weekly Journal of Science, 495*(7442), 437–440. doi:10.1038/495437a

Reddick, R. J. (2016). Using social media to promote scholarship. In M. Gasman (Ed.), *Academics going public: How to write and speak beyond academe* (pp. 55–70). New York, NY: Routledge, Taylor & Francis.

Reeve, M. A., & Partridge, M. (2017, September 6). The use of social media to combat research-isolation. *Annals of the Entomological Society of America, 110*(5), 449–456. doi:10.1093/aesa/sax051

Roth, D. (2018, November 13). *LinkedIn top voices 2018: Meet the all-stars who get the professional world talking.* Retrieved from www.linkedin.com/pulse/linkedin-top-voices-2018-meet-all-stars-who-get-world-daniel-roth

Routledge, Taylor & Francis Group. (2017). *Author directions: Navigating your success in social media: 5 key tips for authors using social media.* Boca Raton, FL: CRC Press.

Shop, A. (2017, November 29). How the 6 'e's of social can get more traction to your tweets. *EdSurge.* Retrieved from www.edsurge.com/news/2017-11-29-how-the-6-e-s-of-social-can-get-more-traction-to-your-tweets

Smith, K. (2016, May 17). 44 Twitter statistics for 2016. *Brandwatch.* Retrieved from www.brandwatch.com/blog/44-twitter-stats-2016

Stewart, D. (2016). Crafting an online scholarly identity. In M. Gasman (Ed.), *Academics going public: How to write and speak beyond academe* (pp. 71–85). New York, NY: Routledge, Taylor & Francis.

Sugimoto, C. R., Work, S., Larivière, V., & Haustein, S. (2017). Scholarly use of social media and altmetrics: A review of the literature. *Journal of the Association for Information Science and Technology, 68*(2017), 2037–2062. doi:10.1002/asi.23833

Tannahill-Moran, D. (2016, September 23). 3 examples of great personal branding. *Work It Daily.* Retrieved from www.workitdaily.com/personal-branding-examples/#!RWk7E

Chapter 3

Message and Press

Imagine I called on you, right now, to stand up in front of a crowd and share your most important findings within 20 minutes. Unprepared, you would probably share a lot of key information until your time ran out. But the delivery might be disjointed, or you might elaborate on one key point (that is not necessarily the most important point) at the expense of others.

It is hard to deliver your most crucial message if you have not first identified that message and the best ways to deliver it. This chapter will help you do just that. It will also help you partner with the press/media to share your message widely.

FIND YOUR MESSAGE

Sharing your findings with the world is easier when you have a strong message to share. For example, you might know everything there is to know about nicotine, but your most important message might be a discovery that quitting "cold turkey" is the most effective way to stop vaping.

Before you elaborate on your ideas, identify your core message. Heath and Heath (2008) found that a concept is more memorable when it is simple and has been stripped down to its core, making the message as compact as possible. Identifying your primary message will help you ensure that it stands out when you communicate findings.

> **DEFINITION OF MESSAGE**
>
> Your message is the main finding, fact, idea, strategy, topic, perspective, or other "thing" you want to share.

Your message can be an important lesson or idea you wish to share with others, or even just an area of work within which you have expertise to offer. See the "Sample Messages" text box for examples.

> ## SAMPLE MESSAGES
>
> - List-making makes it easier for adults to fall asleep.
> - The [name of program] is closing economic gaps between different races.
> - Trauma researchers should gather data from doctors volunteering abroad.
> - Bats use fascinating hunting strategies.

When you ultimately share your message through writing and speaking, you can have more specific messages for those particular appearances. This is sometimes referred to as a thread or a through line: a connecting theme that runs through the entire work. For this chapter, focus on a message you want to spread throughout the world: the message that fills you with the most passion. As you progress through the book and work on specific sharing opportunities, you can adjust your message for particular opportunities so that it specifically suits those audiences, venues, and so on.

Options

Notice that not all of the messages presented here have world-saving implications. Discovering something sure to help others, such as a cancer cure, makes excellent message material. However, something with less-obvious applications is still worth sharing. For example, someone who hears your bats message (see text box) might stick around to hear echolocation findings that may ultimately improve his deep-sea exploration, inspire an astrophysics study unrelated to bats, or help with bat protection efforts. Any message that fills you with passion is worth sharing.

The message will likely not be built exclusively on your own findings. As Brian Stacy of the U.S. Department of Agriculture shared, "It is very rare for a single study to conclusively resolve an important research question, but many times the results of a study are reported as if they do" (Belluz, Plumer, & Resnick, 2016). "You could say, 'Well to be an objective scientist, you just talk about what you found,' but that's sort of a sin of omission if you don't tell people why you chose that topic" (Jackson & Besley, 2018). You are aware of more than just your own findings. If you have conducted literature reviews and followed field discoveries for years, you have knowledge beyond your own work, such as those upon which your work builds. Consider all of these when determining your main message.

The message can also be your opinion. As researchers we are schooled to remove subjectivity from our studies, and we tread lightly writing recommendations. However, just because your studies must remain impartial doesn't mean you lose your right to have and share opinions, ideas, or hypotheses in your outreach efforts. For example, sharing a hypothesis publicly can reach the ears of foundation members who then give you funding to test that hypothesis, something necessary to reach a theory that becomes your future message. So, if your experience leads you to hold an opinion on trauma researchers (see text box), share that message. Just be clear about which of your comments are evidence-based, and consider how remarks will impact your reputation.

Simplicity

Also note that messages (see text box) are simple. The researcher sharing one of these ideas likely has many ideas related to it and many important aspects of the message to share. However, a long paragraph or list conveying the idea (not to mention a multipage discourse) would not be neatly packaged to pass to someone else.

Imagine we are playing the telephone game, in which someone whispers a message in someone else's ear, who then whispers the same message in the next person's ear, and so on, until we all get to hear what the last person in line heard whispered. If the message were, "I am on fire," that message would likely pass perfectly to the last person unchanged. However, if the message were, "My pant leg came into contact with a bonfire, and now the flames have consumed my pants and are burning me," the message would likely morph in ways its originator cannot control.

The shorter and less convoluted your message, the better. Whittle your ideas down to their essence.

Inspiration

When considering what your message might be, draw inspiration from any of the following:

- Research findings from a study you conducted or were part of.
- Knowledge or insight you have obtained from extensive literature review.
- A major accomplishment (like launching a new type of spacecraft).
- A new movement you are part of (like the student entrepreneurship movement).
- A new technology or tool you incorporate into your practice (like virtual reality).
- A unique perspective you have (for example, if you conducted a study while living in a war-torn region).
- Whatever your colleagues ask (or should ask) for your help about.

- A problem you are trying to solve (such as children of color being under-represented in college preparatory courses).
- A cause about which you are passionate (such as getting more women involved in meteorology).
- A special collaboration you are part of.
- A unique population you work with.
- A think tank or group you are part of.
- Your organization's mission statement.
- How your topic intersects with what you hear or see in the news.
- A common misunderstanding to offset.

Whatever your message, it should be something about which you feel passion. If you do not feel excitement about what you have to share, it is unlikely others will. Finding and maintaining that passion is easier when you know the answers to the questions in Exercise 3.1, so spend some time thinking about (and then writing) the answers when you reach that po`1int in the chapter.

Special Considerations

Some possibilities to be wary of when determining your primary message include:

- **Your research area intersects with controversy.** For example, maybe your research can inform whether or not Brexit was a good idea or whether active euthanasia should be legalized. For 26 years, Nicolaus Copernicus refused to publish his discovery that the earth revolves around the sun because he feared ridicule. His discovery was only published when someone submitted the work just before Copernicus's death. Astronomy was stagnated when Copernicus held back from sharing, but it is arguably worse if you suppress a message that could help actual lives. Determine whether you want to take a public stance on an issue or whether you want to share your findings without pairing them with your opinion. Either way, you can find an impactful message with which you feel comfortable.
- **Your research area intersects with a common misconception.** Even if you have many important findings, you might choose to emphasize those that counter widespread misinformation. For example, "Most commonly, people believe that people with dyslexia transpose or invert letters when reading, when actually it's a sound-based processing disorder," and many teachers share this misconception (Korbey, 2019, p. 2). Thus, a dyslexia researcher might choose to prioritize debunking the myth over a message covering the finer points his research addresses.
- **You are not yet sure of an outcome.** "Scientific findings often represent work in progress, are applicable only to particular contexts or populations,

or are unsettled about questions to which the public wants clear answers" (National Academies of Sciences, Engineering, and Medicine, 2017, p. 27). Even if answers are pending, you can still share the importance of unraveling the mystery (like "answering this question will lead to better protective gear for firefighters") or craft a message based on findings determined along the way.

If any of these circumstances intersect with your area of study, consider how they might impact your message. How you choose to navigate these issues is a personal matter.

Shared Message

Note your message might be the same as that of others. For example, maybe you are part of a non-profit that unites you and your colleagues behind a shared mission.

Sharing the same message others have is fine. In fact, people's acceptance of new messages improves when they hear the same message different times and in different ways. Charles Darwin sat on his theory of natural selection for two decades, not publishing for fear of backlash, before Alfred Wallace shared his similar discoveries with Darwin. They published both of their papers together in 1858, and each naturalist's ideas bolstered acceptance of the other's to where the theory of evolution by natural selection became widely accepted.

We should treat the research arena as a collaboration rather than a competition. Touting the same message as others does nothing to hurt our causes.

Number

You might have more than one message (like if you research different topics). If you have a few messages, you might use a different message for each hour in a course you teach, or for different book segments or articles you write.

Another option is to frame a single message in different ways for different audiences. For example, imagine your message is that we know too little about the long-term impact of genetically modified organisms (GMOs) to allow widespread consumption. You might frame your GMO message in terms of social progress and quality of life for one audience, but then focus on consumers' right to know and public accountability for another audience, though the effectiveness of intentional framing depends heavily on your message (National Academies of Sciences, Engineering, and Medicine, 2017).

For this chapter's exercises, think of your message as the main piece of news you want to share with the world, as the main thing you would want to get across if you were interviewed in a 30-second radio clip or had a chance to make a quick impression on someone. For example, my latest message is: "Researchers should share findings extensively and effectively to widen their impact on the world."

This whole book is focused on that main message, but you will still notice more specific points made within each chapter.

Pick one message and your most typical audience to complete Exercise 3.1. This will help you get to know your focus and its merits.

EXERCISE 3.1: MESSAGE

1. Start thinking about your message in generalities. Write down some words or phrases that relate to your message.

2. What might your message be?

3. What is so special about your message? It can help to consider how your work is unique or addresses something traditionally overlooked.

4. Why should people care about your message? It can help to consider how your work has a massive impact or offers important benefits.

5. How will people be able to apply what you share? Messages become more powerful when benefits can be replicated.

Evolution

As you share your message with others, let it evolve based on what resonates with people. One reason for *The Daily Show*'s success is that co-creator Lizz Winstead tweets possible jokes on Twitter and posts longer bits on Facebook, then sees which ones get a lot of likes (Grant, 2016). As you share your message widely, pay attention to what phrasing and context seem to work best. Likewise, your message can evolve as awareness of your message evolves over time in the field, media, and public.

CRAFT YOUR ELEVATOR PITCH

Sharing your message with the world is easier when you have narrowed it down to one sentence that both

- Summarizes your main message and
- Communicates its merit.

You might think of this as your *elevator pitch*, meaning: If you had someone's attention for the span of an elevator ride, how would you get that person to believe in your concept?

Here is a sample pitch based on a sample message provided in the previous section:

- Writing a "to-do" list makes adults fall asleep 15 minutes more quickly.

> ## DEFINITION OF ELEVATOR PITCH
>
> An intriguing statement that summarizes your primary message and communicates its merit.

As with your message, you might opt to develop different pitches for different audiences. Reflect on your core message from Exercise 3.1. Then draft and shape your pitch using Exercise 3.2 until you have a concise, compelling sentence.

> ## EXERCISE 3.2: ELEVATOR PITCH
>
> 1. What is your "elevator pitch" that summarizes your message and its merit?
>
> 2. Can you make your pitch more concise and compelling? Rework it until each word has maximum impact and superfluous words are absent.

If your pitch does not thrill you, keep reworking it until it sounds stronger. If you still feel underwhelmed, return to this book's "Find Your Message" section to consider a different starting point. You might want to investigate how your research intersects with current issues.

Your *message* will remain the heart of what you want to share (for example, upon completing a speech or publication you will think, "I hope I got my message across"). Your *pitch* serves as the way you will communicate your message when you have limited time or space, with the hope this leads to a chance to share more (you will think, "Since I only have this person's attention for seconds right now, I will share my pitch"). Future chapters will cover longer pitches you might use when proposing a story to journalists.

CRAFT TALKING POINTS

As you successfully share your pitch, you will earn the luxury of saying more (such as when a journalist likes your pitch and wants to hear details, or when a presentation submission leads to giving a speech, or when your article proposal is accepted). At those points you will want to be ready with two to eight key talking points that support your message. Just as you did with your message and pitch, strip these points down to the key information you need to get across.

Assign a general rank to your points (maybe it is most important to share points 1–3, and to share points 4–6 if time or space allows). Sometimes this rank will depend on your audience (for example, I share points 1–3 when I speak to parents, whereas I share points 1, 2, and 4 when I speak to policymakers).

> **DEFINITION OF TALKING POINTS**
>
> Important statements that support and elaborate on your pitch.

You might already have talking points on hand, or you might jump straight into opportunities covered later in this book (such as speeches or articles) and glean talking points from the work you develop then. Either way, Exercise 3.3 can help you keep a list of important points close at hand. As you write numerous works, deliver numerous speeches, get interviewed in numerous broadcasts, and more, you will apply these talking points in different ways to sway different audiences.

EXERCISE 3.3: TALKING POINTS

1. What are key points you will communicate to drive home your message or pitch? Write two to eight talking points.

2. With your primary audience in mind, rewrite (or else renumber) your points in order of importance.

CRAFT YOUR MEDIA PITCH

Getting someone to share your words with others on your behalf (such as in a newspaper, popular column, radio show, television news show, or other venue) often involves submitting a pitch: a succinct description of a piece you would like the outlet to run. Like the elevator pitch, your media pitch involves knowing your idea's succinct and compelling core, but here you must also convince someone to publish or air your message.

You must also get to the point and capture journalists' interest quickly. Most news outlets have fewer resources than in the past and reporters are busier than ever. In fact, 42% of journalists work on their stories a minimum of one day in advance, and "more than 1/3 of journalists globally publish more than seven articles a week" (Cision, 2019a, p. 10).

Recommendations for a compelling media pitch include:

- Be timely and insert yourself into the news of the day (such as a hot topic or upcoming event).

- Offer something unique: new information or a new perspective on an existing topic.
- Familiarize yourself with the outlet and pitch something appropriate for it and its audience.

When Cision (2019a) surveyed 1,999 journalists from 10 countries, the most common theme was that pitches need to be more relevant: "75% of journalists say fewer than a quarter of the pitches they receive are relevant or useful" (p. 17). This can be avoided by better understanding the contacted reporter's target audience and what it finds interesting.

Many readers or viewers will not be as familiar with your topic as you are. Even if they are, there will not be enough time in a typical segment to cover all you know about a topic. Thus, when you pitch a story for a news outlet, find an angle with mass appeal for the reporter's audience and communicate clearly (no jargon).

See the text box for an example of how a successful story pitch

- Couches the topic in an intriguing, newsworthy way (here this is done in the subject line, the opening sentence, and the facts); a story's newsworthy aspect or angle is known as a "news peg;"
- Shares the topic and my purpose in writing immediately;
- Shares a timely problem in the first sentence (example: teacher burnout just reached an all-time high), as neither a news story nor its pitch should bury the lede under a load of text;
- Is angled to appeal to an outlet's specific audience (example: ways the public can help with teacher burnout);
- Is actionable and arms readers to combat the problem shared; and
- Includes a link to a key term (example: teacher burnout) so more information can be accessed if needed without cluttering the pitch.

Try couching your expertise within a story you imagine interesting viewers or readers, which can involve relating your expertise to current hot topics. Aim to offer something new, such as a new finding or a new perspective on an existing topic.

SAMPLE PITCH TO PRODUCERS THAT LED TO AIRTIME

Subject: Teacher Burnout is a Pandemic

Hi [Contact's Name],

I would love to see you produce a segment on **teacher burnout,** which just reached an all-time high.

FACTS:

- 15% of teachers leave the profession every year (20% in low-income neighborhoods, meaning historically underserved students are hurt most).
- Nearly half of teachers leave the profession within 5 years of starting, and teacher attrition is rising.
- Teacher turnover costs the U.S. $2.2 million every year.
- There are two pages of cited stats like these in my recent, award-winning book *First Aid for Teacher Burnout*.

Teaching is a society-changing profession in need of the **public's help**. There is much that parents and community members can do to better support their neighborhood schoolteachers.

I can provide the **names** and contact information of people in the U.S., U.K., and Africa (as this is an international problem) who are taking steps to protect teachers' well-being. Please let me know if you would like a free **copy of my book** for support in your investigation, and if there is anything else I can do to support a story.

Thank you,

Dr. Jenny Grant Rankin
Press/media kit: www.jennyrankin.com/press
Cell: [#]

Academic writing has taught you to be formal, but that has no place here. For example:

- You would not normally start a sentence with a number, but "15% of teachers . . ." is more succinct than "Approximately 15% of teachers . . ."
- You would normally write out the word "five" because it is less than 10, but "5" stands out more and makes skimming easier.
- You would not normally make some words bold to stand out, but this helps ensure the reporter does not miss key details.

Also, subtle informality communicates confidence.

A simple pitch like this can be adjusted to suit different opportunities. For example, see the variation in Chapter 8 used to book a conference keynote and note how that version includes speaking background.

Many networks are driven by ratings and air stories that tap into fear, shock, or another sensation, but this is not always the case. Even if you do supply the statistics and case studies to catch an audience's attention through worry, I encourage you to also provide details (including contacts reporters can use) on current efforts to solve a problem and where hope can be found. If a problem-based story rattles an audience but doesn't point anyone in the right direction, it is less beneficial.

Some networks stand out in their prioritization of a story's merit over ratings. For example, *60 Minutes* does not select its segments based on ratings, public demand, or whether most viewers will side with them; rather, the show relies on good stories that give the audience something interesting and important (Dommerholt, 2012). The approach is working. *60 Minutes* regularly ranks as the #5 show or better on Nielsen's weekly Top 10 List and averages 12.4 million viewers (CBS Interactive Inc., 2018).

Likewise, Public Broadcasting Service (PBS) is prone to shows that celebrate and explore topics. For example, the public is not necessarily asking for a documentary about a Missouri man who reinvented himself as a musician from India, or an episode on how orcas hunt seals, or a show on the spirit of multicultural Los Angeles, but PBS presents such content in ways that are engaging for anyone.

Picking an outlet you respect and watch, listen to, or read will help you understand what its producers want. The "Newspaper" section of Chapter 5 and the "News Media and Television" section of Chapter 9 offer additional insight. Later in this chapter you will learn ways to get the press to come to you, and you will want to have ready your media pitch and possible idea packaging (covered next).

EXERCISE 3.4: MEDIA PITCH

1. Select a particular outlet (such as a television program, podcast, or newspaper) where your message would make an appropriate story. What is your media pitch that summarizes your message and its merit?

2. Review the "Craft Your Media Pitch" section (presented previously) and check to see if every recommendation there has been applied to your pitch. Revise as necessary.

2. Can you make your pitch more concise and compelling? Rework it until each word has maximum impact and superfluous words are absent. Remember, a pitch need not adhere to the rules of academic writing.

CONSIDER PACKAGING

For the 2016 U.S. presidential election, former Secretary of State Hillary Clinton's slogan was "I'm with Her," and President Donald Trump's slogan was

"Make America Great Again." Both candidates had bumper stickers, signage, commercials, many appearances, and more to spread these slogans. A phrase just as memorable at the time, however, came from First Lady Michelle Obama in a single speech at the 2016 Democratic National Convention. She talked about raising her daughters to not stoop to the level of a bully, including any public figure who uses hateful language. After leading up to the moment with rich storytelling, Obama shared her family's now-famous motto, which is: "When they go low, we go high." Though also used for her family, this aphorism perfectly captured what Obama was implying about the presidential candidates (one going low and one going high in the moral sense), and reporters continued to reference this unforgettable phrase following the speech. Obama didn't need bumper stickers, signage, commercials, or frequent appearances to spread her "slogan;" rather, the statement was so perfect that it spread all on its own and might have helped Clinton win the popular vote. Two years later I even heard the aphorism used in an episode of *Will & Grace*.

We often see concepts packaged in creative ways when remembering them means life or death. We know to "stop, drop, and roll" if we catch fire, without having to remember a full essay on what to do in that emergency. We merely recall the acronym CAB to remember the order in which to perform cardiopulmonary resuscitation steps: compressions, airway, and breathing.

Just reading a list of talking points will do little to move an audience. The way you put together and present your ideas will determine whether or not they engage listeners and readers, whether or not they are memorable, and whether or not the ideas spread from one person to another to increase their benefit. This book's "Writing" and "Speaking" chapters cover many ways to effectively share your ideas, such as through storytelling. However, as you apply those chapters' strategies, it can also help to neatly package your message within a term, image, classification, or description. That package can then drop into whatever way you choose to frame your message for different audiences.

Consider whether one of this section's packaging approaches will help you communicate an idea as you pursue speaking and writing. We will look at ways other researchers have packaged their discoveries to help them resonate with people and spread (approaches and examples follow). If none of these are appropriate for communicating your concept, that is fine. Packaging is simply an option to consider.

Terminology

Which of the following terms do you encounter most frequently?

A. Climate change
B. Global warming
C. Inadvertent climate modification

I am guessing you answered A or B or were torn between the two. Though the three terms have nuances of meaning (*global warming* concerns the planet's rising average surface temperature, whereas *climate change* encompasses global warming along with other environmental problems like rising sea levels) they are closely related.

Yet *inadvertent climate modification* was originally the most popular term. It accurately described the issue, but scientists like Broecker (1975) and Charney of National Academy of Sciences (1979) were smart to favor *climate change* and *global warming* instead (choosing which of the two terms to use based on which specific phenomena was being described).

Climate change or *global warming* is three to four syllables, whereas *inadvertent climate modification* is 11. That is quite a mouthful, and mouthfuls are less likely to be remembered and repeated than their snappier cousins. *Climate change* or *global warming* takes up just 14 characters in a newspaper headline, whereas *inadvertent climate modification* takes up 32. Journalists would rather top their stories with something direct.

Although scientists can use a host of distinct terms in their own discourse, concise and explicit phrasing better injects a concept into the media, public conversation, and political agendas (which are interdependent) to increase findings' odds of making an impact. We are all familiar with talk of *climate change* and *global warming* today, whereas awareness of *inadvertent climate modification* might have continued to limp along the fringes of mainstream awareness.

Some fields are notorious for embracing new terminology, often when new terms are unnecessary. Giving an old discovery a novel name as if it is new or giving a strategy a confusing name when a single word could have captured it well are undesirable pet peeves in industries and a disservice to the concept you want to convey.

The time for selecting a term to describe something is in either of the following circumstances:

- Your concept is new to people (such as discovering a new species of insect).
- Your concept is complicated (such as a multi-step process or a specific combination of factors).

In either case, it should be when your idea has never been captured with a simple phrase or term before.

In these cases, finding a term that gets to the heart of a concept's essence and clearly evokes its meaning (bringing an image to mind for those who hear it) can assist understanding, memorability, and communication. For example, FrameWorks Institute helps nonprofits inform public opinion and move important issues through Congress by crafting buzzwords that clarify messages, such as coining the term "heat-trapping blanket" to help the Environmental Protection Agency impart an easy-to-visualize image of global warming (Joslyn, 2016).

Carefully selected terms also make concepts easier to spread. For example, *climate change* and *global warming* evoke the heart their issue (and even indicate the terms' individual nuances) in a way that is easy to grasp and communicate to others. This helps these concepts reach more people, and increased awareness is necessary to prompt action. You will still want to explain the terminology you use, but your audience will walk away with a succinct way (this neatly packaged term) to call to mind what you have taught them.

Note that some terms survive because the movements they describe are major, historical, or controversy-rich and thus spread as "hot topics," but the terms themselves tell us nothing of what they describe. As poor examples, *affirmative action* (U.S. term) and *positive action* (U.K. term) are weak terms that would have been easily forgotten if they had not described a major proposal. Think about it: if you had not previously learned those terms' meaning, you would have no idea what kind of action they described.

The term *affirmative action* was pulled from executive orders signed by John F. Kennedy and Lyndon B. Johnson and lacked the design considerations that go into a term meant to stand alone. Any term you design to spread—whether you are capturing the findings themselves or a movement you want your findings to trigger—should be well-thought-out and should reveal something about what it describes.

Images

The visual cortex in the back of the brain is extremely fast and efficient, whereas cognition (handled primarily by the cerebral cortex in the brain's front) is much slower and not as efficient. Thus, visualizing information takes fuller advantage of the brain's abilities (Few, 2014). In a Stanford University study on cognitive methods for information visualization, Kessel (2008) found that visualizing information enhanced cognition, schematized and reduced complexity, assisted problem solving, enhanced memory, and facilitated discovery—but only if the visualizations were applied effectively.

TECH TIP

If you use Microsoft Word or PowerPoint, use the SmartArt function (versions differ, but you can typically click "Insert" and then "SmartArt") to see the multitude of arrangements available to express your ideas.

This section of the book concerns a single image, such as a graphic organizer, that neatly packages your entire concept (as opposed to the multiple images used in slides to communicate various talking points). Some researchers are known largely by the images packaging their core findings.

For Abraham Maslow's (1943) Hierarchy of Needs, the mere description of human motivation patterns was not as neatly packaged as the pyramid that has been used to portray the human needs' hierarchy (see Figure 3.1). Even though experts have since suggested changes to Maslow's hierarchy (Heath & Heath, 2008; Villarica, 2011), they can easily communicate their revisions by applying them to this visual construct (such as by renaming the pyramid levels or redrawing them as overlapping waves). We remember the needs within a hierarchy because the visual arrangement embeds itself in our memories, in line with Kessel's findings. The pyramid visual makes Maslow's whole concept easier to understand, easier to remember, and easier to share with others.

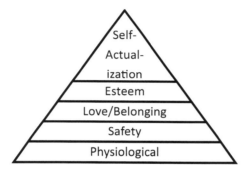

Figure 3.1 Maslow's Hierarchy of Needs

Classification

Simplifying ideas as a list or hierarchy, or further arranging the ideas into groups or within a chart, is a useful way to communicate a large amount of information in an easy-to-process way (the Microsoft Word SmartArt tool can help here as well). Some well-known classifications are:

- Periodic table of elements
- Food pyramid
- Global Business Standards (GBS) Codex
- Bloom's Taxonomy of educational objectives
- Genus and species

Despite the merit of discoveries that contributed to these classifications, the big picture and relationships among the elements would be cumbersome to digest and impart to others if the information had not been packaged so neatly. Take genus and species as an example: "After organisms were cleverly classified, relations between them and among them became more obvious" (Moulton, 2004, p. 107) than they would have if the information had remained solely in a host of papers or awash in field jargon.

One needs to investigate each concept further, of course, to know more than the summary each classification holds. However, people are *drawn in* to read more because they have a tool that classifies the ideas so clearly.

Consider how these elements have assisted the spreading of the previously presented classifications:

- A taxonomy often fits on a single page, making it an inviting read and easy to hand to someone.
- People can quickly and easily understand the classification's nature, its basics, and how to apply it.
- The document can easily be translated into varied languages.
- Academics can easily communicate their criticisms or revisions in simple terms (like "swap the top tier with the tier below it," as has been suggested for Bloom's Taxonomy), which also spread easily.

When I conducted one of my studies on how to best communicate data, the research "paper" was so big it was published as a book. If I wanted all data providers and leaders to follow these standards, I could not just sit back and expect them all to read the 50,000 words within the book (see Rankin, 2016). I thus created a simple packet of standards (see www.jennyrankin.com/s/OTCDStandards.pdf) that data providers and communicators can follow to make data easy to use. Though the book can be read to better understand the standards and the research behind them, the packet can function well on its own as a checklist of best practices to follow when displaying data. Since most of the book's readers are researchers and educators, the standards also give these readers something to hand to data system vendors who are less likely to encounter the research-heavy book.

When you need to communicate a long list of best practices or other information, standards and other classifying formats allow you to convey the meat of your ideas. The grouping also gives readers a straightforward framework to understand how the ideas relate and differ. Furthermore, if you rid your standards of jargon or at least define any field-specific terms used, then you expand the variety of audiences that can understand your ideas.

Descriptions

Anecdotes, analogies, metaphors and other literary constructs hold lots of potential to make concepts resonate with audiences. Such words can evoke associations and emotional responses that make ideas more memorable, as long as the description is highly appropriate to the concepts you seek to communicate. For example, an anecdote used to introduce a research question enhances memorability as long as it is closely related to the paper's actual topic (otherwise the reader struggles to recall what the anecdote related to, even though he recalls the anecdote well) (Madan, 2015).

I research, write, and talk about the need to better display data so it is easier to use appropriately. Yet that idea (and the best practices that go with it) might not resonate strongly or memorably with readers. Consider the following less-than-striking delivery of this idea:

> When data is displayed better, people are able to better understand and use the data. In a study of more than 300 studies and texts from experts in related fields, best practices for the reporting of data were identified. These best practices were synthesized as a set of 60 standards to which data visualizations and reports can adhere. These 60 standards call for:
> - Better **labeling** on data displays (like annotations that succinctly explain data and warn of common misunderstandings),
> - Accompanying data with **supplemental documentation** (such as reference guides that offer details about the reported data and illustrate what to look for in data displays),
> - Access to an online **help system** (with easy-to-follow lessons that help users access and interpret data),
> - Better **display** (like clearer data visualization, and display formats that encourage proper interpretation), and
> - Effective **content** (offering users the exact data they need, without superfluous content, in a timely fashion).

This explanation is informative but dry and forgettable. I solve this by explaining these same best practices in conjunction with the "over-the-counter" concept that inspired my research. Imagine if the previous text were replaced by the following analogy:

> You would never take flu medicine from a container merely reading, "Flu," with no indication of how to best use the contents. You would be left to wonder, "How many pills should I take and when? Of what possible side effects and dangers should I be warned? What kind of flu (stomach or cold) does this treat?" Such a lack of support from the product would be dangerous, and thus we do not see unmarked medicine containers on drugstore shelves.
>
> Rather, you are able to use over-the-counter medicine properly on your own because a **label** tells you exactly what you need to know. If you require further explanation, you can reference **supplemental documentation** tucked inside the box, or search online for a **help system** like www.WebMD.com. You can also guess a product's nature from its packaging and **display** (for example, a colorful label with a crayon drawing of a smiling child indicates

59

medicine appropriate for children to take, and that label would be grossly misleading if the product was only for adults). Also key to the medicine's success is appropriate **content** (your flu symptoms would not get better if the medicine only contained sugar and food coloring, or if a year had passed since the expiration date).

Just like medicine, data can help or hurt lives—depending on the efficacy of its use. Yet most data displays lack embedded supports to make the data's use easy. These inadequate visualizations and reports can be dangerous to the lives of those impacted by data-informed decisions, just as unmarked medicine containers would be. Imagine if we made data "over-the-counter" for those using data to inform decisions. The 60 research-based best practices known as Over-the-Counter Data Standards improve data displays with

- **Labeling** that explains the data's implications,
- **Supplemental documentation** that walks users through the use of each data report,
- An online **help system** with lessons on interpreting data,
- Effective **display** (like data visualization that encourages proper interpretation), and
- Appropriate **content** (that helps data reports do what they are meant to do).

This way people can use data properly and easily, without a data expert needing to be present. . . . just as you do not need a medical expert standing beside you when you take over-the-counter medicine.

This comparison helps the audience recognize how ridiculous and dangerous it would be to give people data without over-the-counter supports. This helps the audience understand the importance of the standards and the research behind them. Organizing the best practices (in this case, the study findings) within succinct standards makes the knowledge accessible, easy to share, and easy to apply. Calling these Over-the-Counter Data Standards helps the audience remember the over-the-counter concept (and with it the importance of the standards) without having to provide this lengthy description every time.

The description is also efficient in that it taps into people's preexisting knowledge (of what it means to be over-the-counter), so less description is needed. When it comes to selecting words while trying to remain succinct, Heath and Heath (2008) suggest the strategy of using a concept people already know: "You tap the existing memory terrain of your audience. You use what's already there" (p. 52). For example, they could describe the various attributes of a pomelo to help you understand what a pomelo is, or they could instead tell you a pomelo is like a supersized grapefruit. The latter description builds on what you already know and is far more potent, just as "horseless carriage" helped people understand what an automobile was in the late nineteenth century.

Selecting a Package

Your pitched concept might be served by a term, image, classification, or figurative description. Consider how you might package your concepts to make them digestible and memorable. What specific language will make your information easy to understand, remember, and share with others? Complete Exercise 3.5 to play with some ideas.

Remember: the whole purpose of packaging is to make it *easier* for people to understand and spread your concept. If you expect people to remember "The 16 C's of Company Culture: comradery, cooperation, collaboration, etc.," you will be let down. That package is too long, too complicated, and with too many possible variations. Forgo packaging unless it makes your concept easy to grasp, remember, and share with others.

EXERCISE 3.5: PACKAGING

It could be that your concept requires no special packaging, so do not feel forced into using whatever you develop in this exercise. However, it is worth playing around with some ideas to see if clever packaging can help your findings spread.

1. Reflect on your elevator pitch from Exercise 3.2 and the concept you are hoping to share. Which of the following are likely to be your concept's biggest challenges?
   • Easy to understand
   • Memorable
   • Easy for anyone to share

   Effective packaging helps with all of these challenges. Keep these in mind as you complete the rest of this exercise.

2. Write some terms that succinctly capture your concept. Read the "Terms" subsection of this chapter for assistance (and to determine if a special term will work well).

3. Draw an image or begin a classification that could make your concept clear. Read the "Images" and "Classification" subsections of this chapter for assistance.

4. Write a description or phrase that could cleverly capture your concept. Read the "Description" subsection of this chapter for assistance.

5. Consider if using one of these packaging ideas will help your ideas have impact. If so, place a star next to it and use it as you apply this book's concepts.

BE PRESS-ACCESSIBLE

Your social media, website, publications, and appearances could possibly catch the eyes of reporters. However, there are additional ways you can position yourself for journalists to take notice. Doing so is not about self-promotion; it is about seizing a more visible platform to share information that can help humanity.

Press/Media Page and Press/Media Kit

Add an obvious link to the top of your website that leads to a Press/Media webpage (I will use the terms "press" and "media" interchangeably here, though some prefer to distinguish between them). If you do not have that capability—like if you only have a page on someone else's website—a downloadable "Press/Media" file can suffice. Journalists look for the information these contain, but they also look for these pages as an indication you are quote-worthy and used to working with the media. Seeing a list of previous press experience on a devoted webpage will help assure them of this. This page should also make it easy for reporters to contact you.

Your press/media webpage can contain:

- Your easy-to-spot email address and/or phone number.
- Short list of topics you specialize in.
- Brief bio summarizing your most impressive and relevant qualifications.
- Links to your full bio and CV, appearances, and publications.
- List of your media interviews, expert quotes, and more.
- "Media Assets" (photos of you that the press can download and use).

If you are a published book author, a more elaborate press kit will get you into book festivals and more. To keep things streamlined and accessible, I maintain my press kit online as my press page. Visit www.jennyrankin.com/press to see my press kit and how I handled each of the following sections:

- Contact Information
- One-Sheet [this is an industry norm that is expected]

- Bio
- Media Appearances
- Press Release for Latest Book
- Excerpt from Latest Book
- Marketing Plan for Latest Book
- Reviews of Latest Book
- Request Copy of Book for Review
- Previous Publications
- Sample Author Q&A
- Suggested Interview Questions
- Media Assets (e.g., Headshot)
- Social Media

Registered Source

Register with Public Insight Network (PIN) (www.publicinsightnetwork.org) as a source for information for journalists. PIN is used extensively by TV stations and networks (like PBS), public radio stations (including NPR), commercial news organizations (like *The Washington Post*), and universities (Briggs, 2016). Also register with field-related databases (like www.ewa.org/sourcesearch) where those who report specifically on your field search for sources. Some additional databases are included in the next section.

Reporter Queries

While some journalists search for sources (such as within the previously described databases), others use tools to blast their queries out to possible sources. For example, more than 35,000 journalists use Help a Reporter Out (HARO) (www.helpareporter.com) to share requests with experts like you via email, and ResponseSource (www.responsesource.com) emails over 32,000 such media inquiries per year. My brief responses to reporters' calls for soundbites swiftly resulted in my being interviewed on outlets like *HuffPost*, *NBC News*, *Newsweek*, *O: The Oprah Magazine*, *Reader's Digest*, *U.S. News & World Report*, *The Washington Post*, and many others to reach mainstream audiences.

See Table 3.1 and register to receive emails that curate journalists' calls for input (most of these are free). Although searching through all the queries sent to you is too time-consuming for most researchers, you can circumvent that problem by following the suggestions in the textbox.

Some of these sites also offer databases reporters can search to find you (like those described in the previous section), or databases of reporters that you can search to pitch your story to journalists, as well as added functions you can opt to pay for. Similar services include Agility PR Solutions (www.agilitypr. com), Anewstip (www.anewstip.com), Bitesize PR (www.bitesizepr.com),

Table 3.1 To Receive Free Reporter Queries by Emails

Service	Website	Main Country Reached
Help a Reporter Out (HARO)	www.helpareporter.com	U.S.
JournoRequests	www.journorequests.com	U.K.
ResponseSource	www.responsesource.com	U.K.
SourceBottle	www.sourcebottle.com	Australia

Cision Gorkana (www.gorkana.com), KITI (www.thekiti.com), MyBlogU (www.myblogu.com), ProfNet (https://profnet.prnewswire.com), and ResponseSource (www.responsesource.com).

TIME-SAVING TIP

Sifting through every journalist query to find those pertaining to you is too time-consuming. Use some of these strategies to allow only pertinent queries to appear in your inbox:

1. Add filters to your email account that only allow mail (from the reporter query suppliers) to reach your inbox when it also contains keywords that align with your area of study.
2. Sign up for a free account with HotKettle Alerts (www.hotkettle.com) and enter filters (such as your research topic). The service will only email you the HARO and SourceBottle alerts (and occasionally other query sources) that fit your criteria.
3. If you do sign up for HARO (www.helpareporter.com) and SourceBottle (www.sourcebottle.com) to get journalist queries, you can select a single subject area (like "Education") to only receive alerts pertaining to that subject.
4. If you work somewhere with a marketing department or PR team, arrange for someone there to follow the query sources in Table 3.1. This way he or she can send pertinent alerts to those with pertinent areas of study.

When responding to a query, give the reporter what he asked for. For example, include each asked question with your succinct answer below it. Do not require the reporter to contact you for more information; rather, write in sound-bites so that journalists can quote directly from your response. I often do not know I am being quoted in a story until it is published, because a reporter on deadline does not always have time to let sources know their responses are being used until the piece is written—if they make the time at all.

Tight deadlines are also the reason you should respond to a query as soon as possible. Most journalists have already determined which sources they will cite within one hour of the query's release (Cision, 2019b).

BE PRESS-FRIENDLY

Since publications have slashed staffing in order to survive, journalists are under more pressure than ever and thus have less time than ever (Stein, 2016). If you do not make things easy on the press, journalists are likely to pass you over to cover news elsewhere. Being press-friendly will help you get your ideas out into the world where they can have impact.

When interacting with press, be:

- **Timely.** Return a call or email immediately. Even if you do not have time to talk that day, note you are available to talk that night (or at other specific times) so you can be counted on as a contributor. Editor Jaschik (2016) wrote, "Reporters remember who called back promptly—and few things are more likely to make you a regular than responsiveness. You can win a Nobel Prize and, if you don't call back, you won't get the calls" (p. 14) from press again.
- **Helpful**. If you are not qualified to address what a journalist is looking for, e-introduce her to someone you know who is. This is a great way to ensure quality information is shared by the press while simultaneously helping others in the field. This approach also encourages reporters to see you as their "go to" person.
- **Precise and understandable**. Being misquoted by journalists is a problem spanning centuries. Even Abraham Lincoln, in the wake of his 1858 "House Divided" speech, visited the newspaper office to personally check the galley proofs because he worried the newspaper would inaccurately print the copy he gave reporters.

  The press will typically not share your level of expertise in relation to your topic. Reporters will try to condense and summarize anything elaborate you say, so be very succinct and very clear (avoiding jargon). Unlike those of President Lincoln, "your words" will typically be published without your having a chance to approve a journalist's version of them, so offer verbiage the press is sure to understand. Following pitch guidelines (covered earlier) will help you achieve coherence when reporters accept pitches.

- **Committed to a stance on issues**. A major reason an expert never makes it onto NPR or other media outlets is that the media want either of the following combinations of guests: one opposed to the discussed issue and one in favor, or one conservative and one liberal (Etzioni, 2010). If you waver back and forth between two opposite stances, you are often deemed a less-desirable guest.
- **Listening carefully to what your journalist's story will focus on** so you can offer a response that will fit well within the piece (or speak up if the angle is misinformed). For example, most news publications focus on a consumer perspective, so journalists are more likely to ask an academic about something like whether parents can expect their children to get into top colleges than something like whether the state university system is equitable (Jaschik, 2016). In those cases, if you consider ways your topic relates to the general public, you can find access points to share with press. In the case of live interviews, some reporters are willing to provide you with questions (or at least topics) beforehand.
- **Amiable**. Thank the reporter for the opportunity to share, do not be condescending, and so on.
- **Wary**. Assume nothing is "off the record."

PUT PARTS TOGETHER

In the "Writing" and "Speaking" parts of this book, you will learn much more about making your findings attention-grabbing, interesting, and memorable. However, all sharing endeavors should be built around what you learned in this chapter.

- Remember your primary **message**.
- Deliver your message in a concrete **elevator pitch** when you have only a moment to interest or sway someone.
- Share compelling **talking points** when you have the space or time to drive your message home.
- Deliver your personalized **media pitch** to convince a journalist or producer to feature you in a story.
- Cleverly **package** your whole message or key findings if it will help your ideas resonate and spread.
- Set yourself up to be **easy for press to reach** so your chances of coverage increase.

Keep this core information ready. It will give you a solid starting point any time or way you seek to share your research.

REFERENCES

Belluz, J., Plumer, B., & Resnick, B. (2016, September 7). The 7 biggest problems facing science, according to 270 scientists. *Vox*. Retrieved from www.vox.com/2016/7/14/12016710/science-challeges-research-funding-peer-review-process

Briggs, M. (2016). *Journalism next: A practical guide to digital reporting and publishing*. Los Angeles, CA: Sage.

Broecker, W. (1975, August 8). Climatic change: Are we on the brink of a pronounced global warming? *Science, 189*(4201), 460–463.

CBS Interactive Inc. (2018). *About us: 60 minutes airs Sundays at 7 p.m. ET/PT*. Retrieved from www.cbsnews.com/60-minutes/about-us

Cision. (2019a). *Cision's 2019 global state of the media report*. Chicago, IL: Cision.

Cision. (2019b). HARO best practices. *Cision*. Retrieved from www.cision.com/us/resources/tip-sheets/haro-practices

Dommerholt, T. (2012, January 17). *60 Minutes: An inside look with producer Shari Finkelstein*. Retrieved from www.wjpitch.com/print/2012/01/17/60-minutes-an-inside-look-with-producer-shari-finkelstein

Etzioni, A. (2010). Reflections of a sometime-public intellectual. *PS: Political Science and Politics, 43*(4), 651–655. Retrieved from www.jstor.org/stable/40927030

Few, S. (2014). Data visualization for human perception. In M. Soegaard & R. F. Dam (Eds.), *The encyclopedia of human-computer interaction* (2nd ed.). Aarhus, Denmark: The Interaction Design Foundation. Retrieved from www.interaction-design.org/encyclopedia/data_visualization_for_human_perception.html

Grant, A. (2016). *Originals: How non-conformists move the world*. New York, NY: Penguin Books.

Heath, C., & Heath, D. (2008). *Made to stick: Why some ideas survive and others die*. New York, NY: Random House.

Jackson, C., & Besley, J. (2018, February 18). The public mostly trusts science. So why are scientists worried? *Science*. Retrieved from www.sciencemag.org/news/2018/02/public-mostly-trusts-science-so-why-are-scientists-worried. doi:10.1126/science.aat3580

Jaschik, S. (2016). Professors and the press. In M. Gasman (Ed.), *Academics going public: How to write and speak beyond academe* (pp. 9–19). New York, NY: Routledge, Taylor & Francis.

Joslyn, H. (2016). Words that change minds. *Chronicle of Philanthropy, 2016*(9), 20–24. Retrieved from www.frameworksinstitute.org/assets/files/PDF/chroniclephilanthropy_wordsthatchangeminds_2016.pdf

Kessell, A. M. (2008). *Cognitive methods for information visualization: Linear and cyclical events* (Doctoral dissertation). Retrieved from ProQuest Dissertations and Theses. (3313597)

Korbey, H. (2019, May 21). Unraveling the myths around reading and dyslexia. *Edutopia*. Retrieved from www.edutopia.org/article/unraveling-myths-around-reading-and-dyslexia

Madan, C. R. (2015). Every scientist is a memory researcher: Suggestions for making research more memorable. *F1000Research 2015*, *4*(19). doi:10.12688/f1000 research.6053.1

Maslow, A. H. (1943). A theory of human motivation. *Psychological Review*, *50*(4), 370–396.

Moulton, G. E. (2004). *The complete idiot's guide to biology*. New York, NY: Penguin Group.

National Academy of Sciences. (1979) *Carbon dioxide and climate: A scientific assessment*. Washington, DC: Climate Research Board.

National Academies of Sciences, Engineering, and Medicine. (2017). *Communicating science effectively: A research agenda*. Washington, DC: The National Academies Press. doi:10.17226/23674

Rankin, J. G. (2016). *Standards for reporting data to educators: What educational leaders should know and demand*. New York, NY: Routledge/Taylor & Francis.

Stein, K. (2016). How to write an influential press release. In M. Gasman (Ed.), *Academics going public: How to write and speak beyond academe* (pp. 105–117). New York, NY: Routledge, Taylor & Francis.

Villarica, H. (2011, August 17). Maslow 2.0: A new and improved recipe for happiness. *The Atlantic*. Retrieved from www.theatlantic.com/health/archive/2011/08/maslow-20-a-new-and-improved-recipe-for-happiness/243486

Part II

Writing

Chapter 4

Writing Anything

In *On Writing: A Memoir of the Craft*, Stephen King (2010) wrote, "The scariest moment is always just before you start. After that, things can only get better" (p. 269). The blank page or screen can be daunting for anyone. Fortunately, as researchers, we have a compelling reason to push through any hesitations: the more we write, the more we share important findings and change this world for the better.

Writing leads to speaking gigs and other opportunities you will not want to miss. For example, one of my early keynote presentations resulted from the conference organizer reading my book and then finding me online. He invited me to deliver a keynote on my book's topic at his organization's next conference, allowing me to reach an audience of 1,200. Even if you do not want to write a full-length book, there are many and varied outlets for your writing, and any one of them could lead to prospects for greater impact.

The more you write, the better your ideas (and your communication of them) will be, and that means increased benefit to society. "The most prolific people . . . generate their most original output during the periods in which they produce the largest volume" (Grant, 2016, p. 37); for example, Albert Einstein wrote 248 publications, Thomas Edison filed 1,093 patents, and Martin Luther King, Jr. wrote over 350 speeches in the single year of his most iconic speech. It is a matter of statistics: the more darts you throw, the more likely you are to hit bullseye. Your bullseye can be an idea, publication, or speech that shifts the whole field or related behavior for the better.

In addition to volume, your work will be especially impactful if you write for different audiences and different types of publications, as you will cast a wider net and reach people through one avenue who you might not have reached through another avenue.

Consider dating. If you were single and visited the same bar once per month hoping to meet a quality partner, you could easily remain dateless. If you began visiting that bar every single night, you would likely meet more prospects, but you still might not find that special someone. However, if you recognized there were all sorts of places to meet people (the dog park, yoga class, a National Geographic cruise, a friend's party, etc.) and "got out there" more, you would meet a wide range of people, some of whom possessed the qualities of a partner you were hoping to find.

The same is true when sharing your expertise via writing: "get out there." Write plenty and vary your writing outlets. The three chapters in this "Writing" part of the book will provide you with many, varied opportunities to pursue. Even if writing displeases or even scares you (which the next chapter addresses), options abound.

HOW THIS CHAPTER WORKS

(YOU NEED IT FOR THE NEXT TWO CHAPTERS)

Although this chapter's title "Writing Anything" is hyperbolic, it means this chapter will provide you with the fundamental guidelines that apply to all writing opportunities described in this book. For example, considering one's audience (meaning the reader, along with his role, frame of reference, and background) is just as important when crafting a blog post as it is when writing a journal paper. Depending on what you need to submit prior to publication, you may follow some parts of this chapter out of order.

The subsequent two chapters in this "Writing" part of the book will offer additional guidelines specific only to certain types of writing. For example, you will need to write an abstract if you write a journal paper, but not when you craft a magazine article. Though this chapter is broken into subsections ("Before Writing Anything," "While Writing Anything," etc.), it is most beneficial to read the entire chapter before your next writing project and then return to it throughout your writing endeavors.

This chapter contains no exercises. Instead, the next two chapters feature exercises in which you can apply what you learn in this chapter, combined with what you learn in those chapters. Those chapters will also lead you to choose publications to write for, which you will want to have in mind as you consider your audience, purpose, and other aspects introduced in this chapter.

SCRAPPY FAST TRACK

If you want to ascend quickly to authorship (for example, you have no published writing experience but are anxious to author a published book), I recommend you use the information in the "Writing" chapters of this book (including their eResources to find opportunities) to take this route:

Step 1. Though you can skip ahead to Step 3, this first step will help you achieve Steps 3 and 4. Submit articles to short-form publications. Begin with outlets you frequently read (your familiarity with them will make it easier to write an appropriate piece). When you ultimately complete a book proposal, it will help to be able to list multiple publications on your CV. When you ultimately write the 2-3 book chapters that typically accompany a book proposal, you can use these articles' ideas as a starting point (using new verbiage to form chapters in your book). If you have conducted a study or academic literature review *and* you plan to write an academic book, it can help to have some journal publications under your belt. However, be aware of Step 3 before submitting all your papers to journals.

Step 2. Use Chapter 2's "Resume and CV" section to make your CV as impressive as possible and show off your published writing. Your CV will accompany your chapter and book proposals. Begin pursuing an assortment of this book's opportunities (media interviews, TED Talks, etc.), which will increase your appeal as a potential author, and continue to pursue those opportunities as you move on to the next steps.

Step 3. The same paper that could appear in a journal could instead become a book chapter; see the "Book Chapters" section of this chapter and submit a chapter. When that book is published, you will be a published author, which will look great on your proposal for a full-length book to a publisher. If the book is sold through popular vendors, the book can also appear on your "author page" with these booksellers (like the author page you will reach if you visit www.Amazon. com, search for me, and then click my name when it appears as a link beside my books). This means that even if you have not written an entire published book, you can still set up an author page (book proposals look better when you provide proof of a strong online presence).

Step 4. Submit a proposal to write a full-length book (the "List of Book Publishers" eResource discussed later provides web links for submissions). For two expedited ways to produce a book (such as a short book or monograph), see the next chapter's "If You Hate Writing" section.

BEFORE WRITING ANYTHING

Have you ever bought a gift for someone you didn't know very well? Maybe it was a hostess gift for your partner's friend, a holiday gift for your new mother-in-law, or a birthday gift for an estranged sibling's kid. It is hard to pick great gifts for people you do not know well. The chances they will like the presents are slimmer, and they are more likely to want to return the gifts that do not meet their needs.

This is because knowing people and circumstances up front, and using that understanding to shape what you select and deliver, gives you a major edge on success. The same is true of writing. Considering your audience, circumstances, and submission norms up front will help you select words and shape your work so it best meets your audience's and publisher's needs, as well as your own.

Determine Circumstances

To know the writing waters in which you are about to sail so you can plan accordingly, do the following:

- **Plan to write for publications that will land in the hands of the right audiences.** Think of who is in a position to *do something* with what you teach her and target those audiences first and primarily (add others over time). This perspective will help you maximize your impact (it is not writing the words that matters; it is how many lives are helped as a result of your writing).

For example, if I am writing about ways teachers can prevent bullying, I will submit to publications like *Teaching Tolerance* that are read by teachers seeking to establish a culture of respect in their classrooms. When I write about decisions made at the multi-school level to improve how data is shared with staff, however, I will submit to publications like *The District* that are read by superintendents and their office staff.

- **Plan to write for publications that match your purpose and message.** The websites of journals, magazines, and publishing houses typically have an "About" section where you can learn about their intent and get a feel for their priorities. Knowing this information can also help you craft more personalized pitches and proposals.

- **Read your chosen publication's current articles.** Note published pieces' topics, voice, tone, style, format, and more. Note which of these aspects vary from one article to the next, versus which aspects seem to be the publication's established norm. Crafting a piece that "fits in" as it covers something new will increase your odds of acceptance and make your piece more digestible for readers, whose expectations have been shaped by previous experiences with the publication.

SCRAPPY TIP

You might see "deadline extended" for an opportunity (like submitting a paper for a special journal issue, a chapter for a multi-author book, or an application to present a paper at a conference). This often means not many people applied, or not enough of those who did apply were deemed worthy of selection. In such cases, it is likely there will be reduced competition if you apply, which increases your odds of being selected and thus reaching new readers.

- **Consider time of year.** When I was eager to share findings from a book I had just written on teacher burnout, I considered how the topic related to what stage schools were right about to encounter. Since summer was just ending, I wrote an op-ed that approached the topic of teacher burnout through a back-to-school lens and submitted it to the *Los Angeles Times*.

My op-ed was published so immediately that I learned of its publication from its readers on social media before even hearing back from the editor. If I had not applied my concept to the time of year, the piece might not have received the same consideration or speedy publication.

- **Consider publication theme.** Many writing venues, particularly magazines, designate themes for issues well in advance of their release. National Science Teachers Association's *Science and Children* magazine (www.nsta. org/elementaryschool/call-sc.aspx) exemplifies this practice. Even journals sometimes have special issues devoted to particular topics.

    Before writing for a publication, learn whether or not themes are established. If they are, cater your submission to clearly address a theme that suits your ideas. Submit well before that issue's deadline and clearly state the piece is intended for that issue.

- **Consider current events.** In 2017 when the world was plagued with unusually numerous and severe natural disasters, I wrote a piece for ASCD's *Inservice* blog on how gifted students are affected by trauma in unique ways. If I had submitted a piece on an aspect of giftedness unrelated to the time's most current events, its publication would have been less likely.

    You can also relate your concept to upcoming events, holidays, or anniversaries of historical events. "Media outlets like to run advance opinion articles that help set up an upcoming event, or alternatively, op-ed pieces that are released in parallel with breaking news stories" (Heller, 2016, p. 26). The same applies to other types of articles, such as those sharing factual information that helps readers understand an upcoming occasion.

SCRAPPY TIP

Due to the holiday season, December deadlines are notoriously hard for people to meet. If you can apply for an opportunity (writing, speaking, or otherwise) that has a December deadline, you might benefit from reduced competition. This means better odds for getting your ideas out there.

- **Plan to contribute something new**. You should provide new information to the field, even if this means communicating an established concept in a novel and improved way. Search a range of field literature to see if your concept has already been covered and how. Be sure your submission stands out from these. A piece is not likely to be selected for publication if it covers an issue that was already covered extensively or if it is similar to a column that was already run (Heller, 2016).

    The newness requirement is particularly rigid in the scholarly arena (such as for journal submissions). In this case, you will need to argue (with cited support) in the work itself that you are filling a gap in field literature with findings of significance. Pitching your concept to experts in your area of specialty can help you identify whether your direction is a new one.

Consider Your Audience

As with planning a speech, before you write you should contemplate your audience. Your vocabulary, examples, explanations, style, and more will cater to the type of person reading your work. For example, will most of your readers have doctorates and be familiar with any research lingo you want to use? If they will not, you will adjust your delivery so as not to confuse or intimidate them. Estimate what your audience members already know, what they might need to know, and how they might be helped to understand.

Identify whether your audience is likely to resist your message for such reasons as political persuasion, religious beliefs, identification with a group opposing your findings, bias, past experience, skepticism, traditions, or values. Consider strategies in the textbox and apply them as needed throughout your writing process.

STRATEGIES FOR OVERCOMING MESSAGE RESISTANCE

- Listen to understand people's views and ask open-ended questions so you can address concerns and cater to values.
- Establish commonalities, such as if you used to be a skeptic or you share the same religion or political party.
- As long as it will not look contrived, dress similar to your audience.
- Leverage storytelling to make people care.
- Tap into people's emotions while appealing to their sense of identity. For example, the Parkland students speaking in tears about school shootings will not move a National Rifle Association extremist to vote for more gun control, but a decorated Marine or country music star sharing a moving moment might.
- Repeat a one-sentence "takeaway" of your message that the audience is most likely to accept (even if it initially rejects others parts of the message). This can serve as a tipping point to break resistance.
- Engage people's scientific curiosity.
- Instead of scary facts or images, share positive images and fun ways for people to contribute.
- Deliver the message through a variety of venues so people are exposed to it more frequently and dissimilarly.

- Utilize a spokesperson the audience identifies with or admires.
- Try moral reframing that caters to your audience's values, such as indicating that supporting working mothers is good for the economy rather than simply "the right thing to do."
- Use language that promotes commonality and understanding.
- Use simple graphs to share data as evidence, but also humanize the data with a moving story.
- Share relatable impact, such as how a practice will improve the audience's daily lives rather than reduce nationwide obesity or lower the cost of the country's healthcare system.
- Collaborate with the group's biggest naysayer or instead focus on those most open to change.
- See the "Beware the Shoulder Chip" section for more.
- Enlist persuasive oratory tactics (entire books are written on this).

Determining who your primary audience is makes subsequent writing steps easier. It is ideal to have one main audience (such as the emergency room nurses who will apply your recommendations), but you can certainly reach a highly mixed audience: determine main groups and plan to relate your recommendations and examples to them all, or else cater to each in different points of the piece.

Determine Purpose

Your purpose will drive the way you frame your message. Now that you know your audience, determine your purpose in writing something. For example, maybe your primary purpose is to inform policymakers about a multifaceted problem, but your secondary purpose is to prompt them to improve their field-impacting decisions. Identifying all of your key purposes will help you write and revise with your goal in mind. In the example just provided, these purposes would encourage you to include facts and stories that inform and would also remind you to include a call to action for policymakers.

Determine Message

What is the main finding, fact, idea, strategy, perspective, or other "thing" you want to share? This message is sometimes referred to as a thread or a through-line: a connecting theme that runs through the entire work. This could be your main message as a researcher (the one you identified in Chapter 3) but make any adjustments that will make a particular piece of writing better suited to your audience and purpose.

Draft a Title

Draft a title, knowing you can rework this during and after writing your piece. The title is your best chance to grab a reader's attention. Your audience will largely base its first impression of your work on the title. Whether or not your title intrigues people enough to read the rest of your piece impacts whether or not they learn what is contained there, but it also impacts whether or not future readers—brought in by citations and recommendations that initial readers spread of your work—learn what you have to share.

Consider an article on school shootings. For its title you might ask a compelling question:

- *Do We Love Our Children Enough to Stop School Shootings?* by Dan Weisberg; note that articles with question titles tend to be downloaded more yet cited less than titles without question marks (Ebrahim et al., 2013);

    . . . or pique readers' curiosity or fears:

- *Thresholds of Violence: How School Shootings Catch On* by Malcolm Gladwell;

    . . . or promise to break things down simply:

- *Four Truths About the Florida School Shooting* by Adam Gopnik; "many of the most viral articles on *The New York Times* and other websites have a similar structure . . . short lists focused around a key topic" (Berger, 2013, p. 174);

    . . . or say something unexpected:

- *Teachers Are Already Armed* (the media was awash in responses to President Trump's suggestion to arm teachers with guns as a solution to school shootings; in this article for *Psychology Today* I argued teachers are already armed to the hilt . . . with compassion, knowledge, grit, etc.—a surprising twist on what the article could have implied—and too overloaded with current responsibilities to add guns to their arsenals).

Each of these is far more intriguing than "Findings from Quantitative and Qualitative Studies on School Site Gun Use Inform New Policies to Protect Students and Staff." The trick is to catch viewers' attention and make them want to keep reading. Saying something unexpected draws people in, but it also cements your idea in their memory (Heath & Heath, 2008). Get inspiration from Mental Floss's clever titles (www.mentalfloss.com); most make you realize there's a tidbit of intriguing information you do not know, and a quick read will quench your kindled curiosity.

Your title can evolve through the writing process, but you still want to begin with something that captures the heart of what you want to say. This way you will have a guidepost during the writing process. Outlet-specific tips (such as crafting journal paper titles) follow in subsequent chapters.

Determine Solutions to Share

Plan to share solutions, not just problems. Your readers should not finish your article or book with a mere understanding of a problem. They should put down your work understanding one of the following:

- How to apply (or at least *about*) specific strategies to combat the problem.
- What causes the problem (so causes can be targeted).
- Leading theories on solutions.
- Recommendations for future research.
- What stakeholders should *not* do.

Otherwise, what is the point? Your larger purpose in sharing your work should involve helping the planet, and solutions make that possible.

Dream Up Magic (Emotion, Stories, and More)

Do not start outlining just yet. Once you outline a written piece, you end up with clear sections and direction. However, it can then be hard to insert some magic (defined in the text box) into something already planned. Instead, give your writing ideas time to marinate. I like to dream up ideas for a piece when I exercise, shower, walk the dog, and try to fall asleep.

Dream up some magic "wow" segments that support your message and the way you have chosen to frame it to achieve your purpose. These moments help readers connect to your content and are typically the parts they remember most. Magic moments also make your ideas more likely to spread.

DEFINITION OF HOOK VS. MAGIC

A hook is meant to grab your audience's attention, introduce your topic, and set the tone of your speech or written work. I dislike the term "hook" because it is often portrayed as only occurring at the start of a piece. This implies that once you initially catch someone's attention you need not worry about losing it, just as a fish can't easily get off a hook.

In fact, attentions are actually slippery escape artists. We are well-served to plan multiple ways to catch and hold attention throughout the course of our delivery.

This is where magic comes in. "Magic" conveys more power and wonder than a hook. Truly magic segments ignite readers' imaginations, make your audience care about what you have to say, make concepts come to life and connections snap into place, and take your readers on an unforgettable ride.

80

When ideas are communicated in a way that is interesting, surprising, or entertaining, people are more likely to tell others about them (like social currency) (Berger, 2013).

The Deficit Model of research communication—in which findings are accepted by audiences if the researcher merely thoroughly informs them—has been debunked. Instead, frame your message in ways that will be irresistible to your particular audience where your particular topic is concerned. Magic moments (many of which employ the emotion-tapping and storytelling strategies shared in this book) will help you achieve this specialized delivery, as will understanding your audiences and their particular conflicts with your topic or stance. For example, remember earlier examples of effective ways to frame climate research for different audiences:

- **Emotional or behavioral resistance:** Instead of scary facts or images, sharing positive images and fun ways for people to reduce carbon footprints prompts people to conserve resources and curtail climate change.
- **Religious opposition:** Appealing to the environment's impact on humanity can move evangelicals.
- **Political opposition:** Priming people's scientific curiosity overcomes political predispositions against such findings.

Magic moments can support whatever approach you select to increase your piece's impact if you weave it around the more matter-of-fact necessities. For example, there are plenty of areas in this book where straightforward strategies must be listed, but note that the magic that begins or pops up within every chapter to make content more digestible and memorable. If you have a lot of information to communicate (such as the many strategies in this book), you can't afford to bury every tip in magic, but you can identify key concepts or moments that can use magic's added boost. If you determine some of these magic moments up front, you can then produce an outline that incorporates them.

You can devise additional magic moments when your writing process is in full swing. You can add, remove, or change magic portions during that stage with an eye to what will best serve your purpose and your readers' needs. You might also revisit the "Consider Packaging" section of Chapter 3 for inspiration; clever packaging of the lessons you give readers can certainly inject magic into your work. You can think of these memorable moments as hooks, but only if you remember that they can occur throughout your work (not just near the beginning), such as each time you introduce a new concept within your piece.

You will notice that many types of magic segments can also be characterized as stories. Embedding stories throughout your work is a great way to hold the audience's attention and make your message memorable. It is far easier for people to remember stories than facts because the human brain processes experiences we are told about in practically the same way it processes experiences that really happen to us (Gillett, 2014).

You will notice magic often also taps into an audience's emotions. Whether the emotions are positive or negative, emotions make people more likely to consider and act on information. Emotion also makes people more likely to remember and tell others about what they learn or experience. Events like the birth of a child, a college graduation, and a marriage proposal are easily remembered because they were full of joy. Getting grounded as a teenager, getting turned down for a date, or getting in a car accident are also easily remembered because they were full of sadness or fear. Whether negative or positive, experiencing a strong emotion causes people to remember that something better. In particular, concepts are more likely to spread (meaning people will remember and tell others about them) when they provoke arousal emotions like awe, amusement, excitement, anxiety, or anger (Berger, 2013).

Ideas for explaining concepts in magic ways (as long as each clearly illustrates your idea) are detailed in the following table. See Table 4.1 to inspire magic for your own work before writing, and also when you reach the outline and template stages shared later in this chapter. Most of the magic examples in Chapter 7 can also be adapted well for writing.

Also determine how you will make your study's impact resonate with readers. For example, if you argue that refugee camps should facilitate a way for those who attended university to continue their degree programs, how will you convey how doing so (or not doing so) affects how displaced persons feel about themselves, connect with their field and peers, perform, or find financial stability, or other measure?

Sharing the impact on lives (keeping identities private where appropriate, such as with minors) is highly effective. The reason why charities mail us photos of individual children, and why the single photo of a dead toddler moved previously-unmoved countries and donors to help Syrian refugees, is that

> Identifying a single victim of a tragedy arouses us more than faceless multitudes do. We'll be concerned by the plight of the girl trapped at the bottom of a well, but give far less thought to millions of children dying of hunger or caught up in genocide.
>
> (Alda, 2017, p. 129)

Heath and Heath (2008) note statistics—even relating to the suffering of millions—shift people into an analytical and non-emotional frame of mind, whereas describing a single person's plight primes people to care about, remember, and act on a concept. Whether or not you classify a particular finding as a tragedy, a win, or somewhere in between, sharing its impact on a single life can help readers care about the many more lives it impacts.

Table 4.1 Ways to Insert Magic into Your Writing

Magic/Hook	*Example*
Analogy, Metaphor, or Simile	In Chapter 3 I described how I package the idea that data needs to be displayed in easy-to-use ways. If I simply make this statement, people tend to think, "Sure, data should be well displayed. That is easy to accept, so I am sure it is already being done." If I simply share statistics indicating most people misunderstand most data they view, even after expert-recommended training, people often erroneously assume this is some failing of the data users. People *really* understand the concept, however, when I compare data to over-the-counter medicine: You would never take medicine from an unmarked container. For over-the-counter medicine to be used properly and help lives, it contains specific supports like a label offering directions and warnings, packaging that accurately indicates its nature, supplemental documentation for instructions that will not fit on the label, etc. Meanwhile, we give people data graphs that lack all of these supports: graphs with no other annotations than the title, poor graphing (i.e., poor packaging) that doesn't encourage accurate interpretation of the data, no supplemental documentation to walk teachers through the meaning of data displays, etc. Such a lack of support is dangerous for those whose lives are affected by data-*mis*informed decisions, just as ingesting medicine from an unmarked container is dangerous. We need to make data "over-the-counter" (thoroughly labeled, etc.) for the those using it. Consider how metaphors or extended analogies can illuminate a concept you present. Accompanying your writing with a related image can clarify the relationship (such as between data and a medicine bottle) and make it memorable.
Case Study or Confession	In the book *Yes, You Can!: Advice for Teachers Who Want a Great Start and a Great Finish with Their Students of Color*, Gail and Rufus Thompson (2014) introduced new issues with sections like "Meet Michaela: A Frustrated New Teacher" (p. 2), "Meet Jamel: A Troubled Student" (p. 72), and "Meet the Parent(s) Part 4: A Single Mother's Dilemma" (p. 135). These sections told true stories that help the reader step inside the lives of varied stakeholders, including teachers with whom she might identify. These experiences help the reader drop her defenses so the book's lessons could take root in the reader's heart and mind.

(*Continued*)

Table 4.1 Continued

Magic/Hook	*Example*
	I began each chapter of the book *First Aid for Teacher Burnout* with one or two real teacher confessions related to the problem each chapter would help solve. This helped readers relate to chapter topics and illustrated problems the chapter would address. The stories also disarmed the reader as she learned of other teachers who shared the same private fears and thoughts that she might. Consider how case studies or confessions might help your reader understand different perspectives and circumstances.
Comparison	Comparisons can humanize concepts to make them more tangible. For example, Stephen Covey (2004) describes *Harris Poll* industry findings indicating problems in companies, but the statistics are overwhelming until he writes, "If, say, a soccer team had these same scores, only four of the eleven players on the field would know which goal is theirs. Only two of the eleven would care. Only two of the eleven would know what position they play and know exactly what they are supposed to do. And all but two players would, in some way, be competing against their own team members rather than the opponent" (p. 3). Heath and Heath (2008) analyze this quote and note it joins the abstract statistics with a human comparison (drawing on our understanding of soccer teams), which make the statistics much more vivid and powerful. When writing, feel free to relate a scenario to something outside your field. The world is rife with comparisons people can connect to, and taking your reader outside the field for a moment can help her recognize something within the field for the first time.
Contrast	When writing about the importance of displaying data appropriately, I told stories of how effective data displays ended a cholera epidemic and won the Crimean War. Then I told the story of how faulty data displays are blamed for a poor decision to launch the Challenger Space Shuttle despite rocket defects. The shuttle exploded, killing all crew members. Contrasting how appropriate data displays saved lives with how poor data displays likely lost lives established the gravity of the topic so readers would embrace the research-based recommendations that followed. Contrast can highlight differences and give readers added insight.
Example	Eng (2017) wrote about scholars' tendency to overestimate what their audience knows. He provided a clear example of how unfamiliar terms impact an audience: Think of it like giving directions. I think I'm being clear when I tell a tourist on the New York City subway to "go to the other side of the platform and take the downtown R train to SoHo." Yet the other person's probably thinking, *First of all, what do you mean by "the other side?" Does the R train only go downtown or are all downtown trains R trains? What stop is SoHo?* (p. 19)

(*Continued*)

Table 4.1 Continued

Magic/Hook	Example
	Empathizing with the confused tourist helps us embrace the need to baseline assumptions about our audience's prior knowledge. Notice we could also consider this example a comparison or simile; magic can fit more than one of this table's categories.
Fable or Parable	A fable or parable can demonstrate a relevant moral or norm that draws the reader in while simultaneously helping the author make a point. For example, consider this introduction to a piece on self-control. Stone (2014) shared the parable of a farmer who drank all night and woke up sick, yet by the next evening he had become increasingly in favor of drinking again. The fable illustrated "preference reversal," in which the value of one option (drinking) grew at a different rate than the value of another option (not being sick). This primed the reader for the rest of the article.
Humor	To underscore lab research shortcomings, Slavin (2018) shares the joke where one scientist says to another: "'Your treatment worked very well in practice, but how will it work in the lab?' (Or ' ... in theory?')" (p. 1). This leads well into Slavin's point that brief, small, artificial lab studies produce large effect sizes with little relevance to practice. Consider how a joke, funny story, or other humor might disarm and enlighten your readers.
Mystery	In a study of books written by academics for non-academics, Cialdini (2005) found of the books that were most successful: "Each began with a mystery story. The authors described a state of affairs that seemed to make no sense and then invited the reader into the subsequent material as a way of solving the mystery" (p. 23). This approach can be adapted successfully for other forms of writing as well.
	When I was an assistant principal, I often corresponded with others about how my students' financial hardships affected their ability to attend school regularly, remain at the same school consistently, and succeed while there. I could rattle off stats like our students' use of the National School Lunch Program for free lunches, but I got my message across more memorably with this story (I have changed names to protect privacy):
	It was mid-year when Ms. New's two sons were newly enrolled at our junior high school. She came to our front office with one of these sons (Max) to get their school schedules and take care of other logistics. When her other son (Dale) was mentioned, Ms. New sent Max from the office, and Dale entered the office in his place a couple of minutes later. A bit later some questions pertaining to Max were raised, so Ms. New sent Dale from the office, and Max entered the office in his place a couple of minutes later. This pattern persisted in which only one son at a time was directed to be with us in the office. Ms. New shook off our inquiries, clearly uncomfortable explaining why she would send one son

Table 4.1 Continued

Magic/Hook	Example
	away before the other could join us. My colleague learned what was going on when he left the building. He saw Max and Dale in the school parking lot as they traded places . . . and a single pair of shoes. The family only owned one pair of boys' shoes, so Max and Dale had to take turns wearing them, which Ms. New felt they must do to be properly dressed in the school office.
	What challenges might Max and Dale face when it came to attending school regularly, remaining at the same school consistently, and succeeding while there? Rather than hit you over the head with facts, this mystery puts you in my place to guess, as the story progresses, why the boys kept trading places. When listeners realize there is a gap in their knowledge—which a story can deliver—they tend to be hooked until that gap is filled (Heath & Heath, 2008). This story also humanizes the families behind the statistics; Ms. New's insistence that her sons not break propriety when on school grounds reminds listeners to treat underprivileged families with dignity.
	Those sharing research or practitioner findings can often benefit from a mystery. By introducing the problem you were trying to solve in your study or in your institution, you can put the reader in your shoes to discover the solution "with" you. This invests the reader in your topic while also communicating its nature.
Personal Anecdote	Before I describe the five components to making data over-the-counter, I sometimes tell of the experience that inspired my study. My daughter got sick with a flu. She didn't need a doctor, but she did need over-the-counter medicine. I was able to easily understand which medicine was appropriate for her, the medicine's nature, and how to use the medicine safely due to components that allow medicine to be used effectively (explanatory label, clear packaging, effective content, etc.). I then detail how these same components can be easily applied to the way data is displayed. Through this anecdote, the reader acquires an understanding of the term "over-the-counter" and how it applies to data, and the reader recognizes the life-or-death importance of each component explained.
	Personal anecdotes, such as the human struggle or mental journey behind one of your findings or efforts, humanizes concepts to help audiences connect with them. Such anecdotes can also be about others. Consider this title of an NPR story:
	• Dolly Parton Gives the Gift of Literacy: A Library Of 100 Million Books (Pao, 2018, p. 1).

(*Continued*)

Table 4.1 Continued

Magic/Hook	*Example*
	That is impressive but not relatable. However, consider how much more inviting the story is when a personal anecdote is introduced, even short enough to fit in this tweet: • "Dolly Parton's father never learned to read. She started her nonprofit, Imagination Library, to give children what he didn't have: early access to books" (NPR's Education Team, 2018, p. 1). Although the title likely touches you on an analytical level, the tweeted anecdote likely touches you on an emotional level. Touching people on an emotional level is more likely to make them connect, care, remember, and act than touching them on an analytical level will (Heath & Heath, 2008).
Quiz	I began one article like this: Grab a pen or pencil and fill in the blanks: • Less than 15% of _____ would recommend their profession to others. • 91% of _____ suffer from stress. • 15% of _____ leave the profession each year (this statistic rises to 20% for those working in high-poverty areas). • More than 41% of _____ leave their jobs within five years of starting. If you stopped people on the street and gave them this quiz, they might guess things like *police officers, emergency room nurses, attorneys,* or *warzone doctors.* Who else could be shouldering such pressure and fleeing the profession in droves? However, if you're an educator, you probably know the answer because you lived it. The professionals who serve as the quiz answer to complete all four of the above sentences are *teachers.* (Rankin, 2018, p. 1) Quizzes actively involve the reader and help her feel invested in what you share. Imagine if this passage had instead spoon-fed the statements to the reader as facts. That reader would have taken on a much more passive role. Even if a reader gets the whole quiz wrong, you have actively involved her in your content and instilled a desire for the correct answers.
Relate Material to the Reader	Although second-person point of view (using words like "you" and "your") is typically discouraged for scholarly writing, as in journal papers, it is more welcome in less-formal publications and can be highly effective. Writing "you" helps readers imagine that you are conversing with them more intimately and allows them to step into your written world.

(*Continued*)

Table 4.1 Continued

Magic/Hook	*Example*
	Consider this opening to a book on the brain (something very clinical) and how it draws you in as the reader:
	The oddest thing is that you're not quite the same person as you were a few minutes ago. You have a memory of picking up this book, and this memory has joined others held somewhere in your biology: how you came to be here today, who you are and even how to read these words. Something must change amongst the atoms and molecules of your body for you to learn and remember these things.
	(Howard-Jones, 2018, p. 1)
	Try replacing words like "people" and "someone's" with "you" and "your" to see if your written piece improves.
Story	Though "story" has a single row in this table, storytelling is mentioned throughout this book as a powerful tool that is often involved when leveraging other research-sharing strategies. Stories can heighten audiences' attention to scientific findings, make the research easier for them to understand and remember, and have an especially strong influence on audiences with lower numeric skills (National Academies of Sciences, Engineering, and Medicine, 2017).
	Alda (2017) of the Center for Communicating Science tells an alarming-yet-funny tale of a dentist's malpractice on his mouth. Miscommunication led to the operation, which removed Alda's ability to smile until a follow-up surgery. The story is highly memorable (it is hard to forget a botched dental job) and helps readers understand the value of communicating and listening (Alda's topics). People are more likely to tell others about a concept when it is an integral component of a specific story people will want to tell; 70% of story details get lost after five or six retellings, but the main point sharpens (Berger, 2013). If people are able to tell your "cool story" without including your crucial message, then it is not the right story for you to tell.
	The world is full of gripping stories. Tales of survival, triumph, or overcoming adversity all introduce a human element that helps readers connect with your content and grasp its gravity.
	If you want to find an *inspiring* story to use, Heath and Heath (2008) suggest looking for three key plot types, depending on your purpose: "Challenge (to overcome obstacles), Connection (to get along or reconnect), [or] Creativity (to inspire a new way of thinking)" (p. 289). The stories you choose to share should convey your message and should be short enough to maintain the reader's attention and leave room for your related points.

(*Continued*)

Table 4.1 Continued

Magic/Hook	Example
Surprising Statistic or Fascinating Fact	A surprising statistic or fact can seize a reader's interest if it is unusual (such as a little-known aspect of a well-known event), extreme, emotional, or hard to believe. For example, in an article explaining ossification, a means of bone development, Shannon-Karasik (2018) writes, "Humans are born with nearly 300 bones, but most adults have around 206" (p. 1). Babies have nearly 100 "extra" bones when they are born! That is too unexpected and interesting a fact to ignore. We are positioned to care about the details shared in the rest of the article.
Voices of Those Involved	Our recommendations are often meant to help vulnerable populations (such as those who are poor, disenfranchised, oppressed, or children), but their voices are frequently missing from academic conversations. Consider including quotes from those whom you research to communicate your message. For example, rather than claim that your new program helps students learn to read, include quotes from three students describing how this phenomenon happened for them. See the Education Writers Association's reporting guide to interviewing children (www.ewa.org/sites/main/files/file-attachments/ewa-reporter-guide-interviewing-children.pdf) for legal guidance in quoting minors, and use sensitive language when speaking of disabilities, nontraditional lifestyles, or other population qualities.

Consider how you can add such stories to your writing. You might focus on one person as an introduction or devote a few-sentence account to a different life each time you describe a new facet of your idea. If you also share statistics or wide-sweeping facts, try doing so after you have primed your reader with a more personal story. Scholarly writing is not off-limits for such stories, which can illustrate whatever concepts your reader must understand.

Create a Template

Setting up an organized structure for your words will make writing easier, whether your brilliance spills rapidly onto the page or you struggle to drag the words out. A template can even be the place where you craft your original outline.

Open a new page/file in your word processing software (I prefer Microsoft Word) and type any headings you are required to include. Add your title (knowing it can change), name, affiliation, bio, and other staples. Format the pages to match any publisher specifications (common for journal submissions). If there are no format requirements, you can aim for a standard approach (double-spaced lines with size-12 Times New Roman font) or use a format that matches what your targeted venue uses for published work (for example, electronically copy text from an online article, paste it onto your template, and use its font and spacing for your work).

Having a template will protect your writing flow. If you are working on the Introduction and think of something you do not want to forget to include in the Conclusion, you can quickly throw a reminder (just a few words, without elaborating) into the Conclusion section and get right back to what you were writing in the Intro.

Outline

You can then outline (list brief notes and ideas in the order you plan to write about them) directly on your template. Just be sure you have already spent time dreaming up compelling ways to share your ideas (covered earlier in this section). Otherwise, if you try to outline before you spend time daydreaming, you might find yourself locked into a lackluster delivery.

Reflect on your audience, purpose, and message. Record key talking points on your outline in the order you plan to share them. Fill in needed information and transitions you will need to make. Do not feel the need to get too specific in your outline (sometimes that limits you once you are in the flow of writing, whereas you want to be able to follow your gut as you write when it tells you what is needed).

SCRAPPY TIP

Getting discouraged by rejections? Look at the CV or publication list of someone whose career you admire and note which publications were her earliest. Early-career publications sometimes signify venues that are easier to break into, and the author you admire obviously got accepted there *before* all of her later successes. Consider which of those magazines, radio shows, etc. fit your work and then apply there.

WHILE WRITING ANYTHING

Now you can flesh out your outline directly on your template, turning ideas into complete sentences and working your magic. In other words, it is time to write.

Little Things That Add Up

Keep the following tips in mind as you work. They might seem like little things, but missing any one of them can throw a wrench into your process or product.

- **Adhere strictly to submission guidelines.** Publications often provide clear parameters for the following:
  - The submission (word count, line spacing, section subheadings like "theoretical framework" to include, bio location and length, etc.).
  - The submission process (what the subject field of your email should state, what questions you should answer in your cover letter, how your submission's electronic file should be named, etc.).

    Yet ignoring publishers' requirements is a common submitter's mistake. For example, "Some [journal] publishers report that one paper in five does not follow the style and format requirements of the target journal" (Shaikh, 2016, p. 3).

    Follow all guidelines closely. Though you can ask for clarification if you are unsure about something, you can avoid bothering editors in many cases by reviewing pieces they already published and mirroring the format you find there.
- **Establish order through formatting.** Headings, subheadings, text-boxes, bullets, checkboxes, and other formatting conventions can help you organize material in a way that is easier for readers to digest.
- **Do not get bogged down with precision** (spelling, edits, etc.) while writing your initial draft. If you used the word "trajectory" but do not think it fits quite right, just put "@@" in front of the word for now. That will be your signal to investigate and correct something later ("@@" is easy to spot, and an electronic search for those two characters side-by-side will bring up a list of places you need to revisit), so you can continue writing.
- **Do not be afraid to write out of order.** If you are eager to flesh out examples of your theory's application in real settings before writing your Introduction, seize that excitement and skip ahead. You can write sections in any order and can catch any transition or cohesion problems during revision.
- **Use an appropriate and consistent style.** Do you want your piece to read like you are speaking to the reader in a familiar, casual way? Do you want to be humorous? Do you want to be blunt or formal? The answer to questions like these is a very personal one. Think hard about what you want your writing voice to sound like, and use a style that will fit your nature, audience, and purpose.

Beware the Shoulder Chip

Some of your audience members will have preexisting grievances that cause them to look for particular weaknesses or claims in your work . . . and to find those weaknesses or claims, whether or not they actually exist in your work. This can trigger confusing reactions to your writing, such as someone accusing you of a stance you do not have.

Grievances have often developed because someone feels disrespected on a regular basis or sees a topic mishandled frequently. By anticipating shoulder chips some readers might have, you can be sure your work clearly sidesteps related misunderstandings so your real message can be heard. Table 4.2 provides examples of how you can do this, though your piece's purpose and space allowance will impact which of these are appropriate.

Table 4.2 Problems for Which Readers Search

Reader's Grievance	Ways to Prevent Grievance or Misunderstanding
You are blaming or belittling a particular stakeholder.	• Beginning in your introduction, use language that applauds the stakeholder and acknowledges the difficulties and impact of her role. • If appropriate, mention (early) your own experience in the stakeholder's role.
Your findings are not backed up by sound research, or you are jumping to conclusions (like you claim causation when there is only correlation).	• Detail how you arrived at a conclusion. • Cite others' research (not just your own). • Detail how you accounted for secondary variables (such as how you know that it wasn't income that accounted for a group's success). • If space doesn't allow for these details, provide a link or web address that readers can follow to get them.
You are misusing terms.	• If there is common confusion surrounding a term, define the term early. • As an alternative, provide a footnote with explanation. For example, when I write "data is" I commonly add a footnote explaining how data can be used as a singular or plural noun (otherwise I will lose readers who mistake the former tense as grammatically incorrect, since the term's singularity did not used to be universally accepted). This might seem excessive, but some people go a little crazy when they think they spot an error.

(Continued)

Table 4.2 Continued

Reader's Grievance	Ways to Prevent Grievance or Misunderstanding
You are implying researchers know more about a topic than those practicing "on the front lines."	• Detail how input from those in different roles was an integral part of your process and reasoning. • Acknowledge on-the-job variables. For example, if you recommend professors give each student personalized feedback, give examples of how a professor with 600 students manages this.
You are treating an old movement or discovery as if it is something brand new.	• Acknowledge related movements of the past and describe how the new movement builds upon these. • Explain the specific ways in which the new movement differs from the old.
You are ignoring major variables (for example, success in a health program in which participants must pass a rigorous physical test to join will have limitations translating to other programs).	• Be upfront about pertinent characteristics (such as those of the facility where a study took place, those of participants whose feedback you collected, etc.). • Address how your findings might apply to other environments and underscore important conditions.
Your recommendation is flawed or unrealistic.	• Spend time outside your own place of work to understand the constraints involved. For example, a recommendation that each disaster victim receive 30 minutes of uninterrupted one-on-one time with a relief worker to reduce trauma is unrealistic for a relief worker who must tend to 10–50 victims of varied condition simultaneously. • Recall or speak with very different stakeholders. Consider how your recommendation would apply to and help all involved. Adjust your recommendations as necessary, or stipulate limitations (example: the strategy only works well with participants who exhibit high intrinsic motivation).
No one else is saying what you are saying, so you must be wrong.	• Demonstrate how your theory is a natural extension of past research or movements. • Emphasize concrete evidence supporting your stance. • If replying to this criticism, politely mention that many norms accepted in the field today were initially deemed preposterous (like the fact that the earth revolves around the sun).

Address Inequity

Unless you are writing a very short piece, there will be room to address the equity aspects that impact your topic. Most topics involving humanity merit addressing how some populations are underrepresented or underserved in order to also provide strategies to combat the disparity.

For example, if you write about grooming future scientists, you will be writing only on behalf of boys if you do not address how girls' interest and confidence in science plummets the longer they are in school. If you write about how to end economic disparity, you will be ignoring major barriers if you do not address the huge discrepancies between different races, ethnicities, and socioeconomic statuses of students being enrolled in college preparatory classes. Let these insights shape the solutions you recommend so your writing works to close gaps in our society.

Too often, scholars fail to address disparity unless they are writing exclusively about that topic. White, male, and straight people worry they will say "the wrong thing" when promoting equity for those in groups other than their own. But that fear stands in the way of dialogue that can improve fields and advance lives, whereas you can educate yourself to avoid pitfalls like treating someone as a "native informant" (see Quaye, Griffin, & Museus, 2015) or using racial terms without understanding their complex context (see Patton, Harris, Ranero-Ramirez, Villacampa, & Lui, 2015).

At the same research symposium, I heard an invited speaker argue against desegregation efforts (reasoning that they communicate one's neighborhood has nothing worthy to offer, as she had felt being transplanted in a faraway school as a child, rather than focusing on improving local schools), and immediately after that I heard another invited speaker argue that school desegregation is the single most important answer to ending racial inequity in our nation. Both speakers were highly regarded experts, both speakers were Black women, and both deemed the other presenter's stance as wrong. But only by hearing these views were we, as an audience, informed of the complexities involved in this issue and more invested in finding the best solution while mitigating its shortcomings.

Do not act like you have all the answers (a rich, straight, White, Christian, male American should not claim he knows as much about experiencing discrimination as those in traditionally marginalized groups, and someone in a traditionally marginalized group should not assume that group has a single perspective on everything), but share the diversity facts and ideas you have investigated so we can all move our understanding forward through vital discourse. Knowing you do not have all the answers is a blessing when it comes to equity, because it keeps you studying and speaking with others to continually advance your understanding. Can you imagine if every researcher took ownership of the quest to end disparity in our world? It is a powerful goal, and it makes coverage of other topics more comprehensive in the process.

Whatever topic you have chosen, I challenge you to find where equity intersects it. If you struggle in this endeavor, see Chapter 7 for added support.

Do Not Lose Your Core Message

Remember your pitch from Chapter 3? Be sure it stands out clearly in your work. Sometimes we get so busy explaining something in detail that we forget to drive home statements that capture the essence of what we are saying. Summarizing your points in single sentences will make your message clear and also make it easier for others to cite direct quotes from your work.

Be Very Clear

Only 23% of Americans questioned understood what it meant to study something scientifically, and 51% understood how an experiment might work (National Science Board, 2016). While research itself confuses people, field-specific terms and phenomena add additional chances for misunderstanding. Although clarity is crucial for nonacademic audiences, even fellow researchers will be confused if your point or prose is unclear.

Craft straightforward sentences, use jargon sparingly, establish context (for example, when you say "leaders" in your abstract, do you mean C-level executives?), and define terms to avoid confusion. Although sentences like "The study's purpose was. . . " might seem clunky or mundane, their straightforwardness is actually helpful for the reader.

Sentence structure also impacts clarity. I could have written the previous sentence as *How clear something is can be affected by the way that sentences within it are structured*, but that would not be as straightforward or clear. Trim unnecessary words and rearrange overly complicated sentences.

Those used to academic writing, in particular, struggle with clarity. See Pinker (2014) for the many reasons for this. Scholars tend to pad sentences with qualifiers that weaken prose, and with jargon that complicates prose. The more difficult the sentences are for the reader to process, the more they produce *cognitive strain*, which is a state involving discomfort, lack of trust, and disbelief in what you are saying (Kahneman, 2011).

If field or research terms cannot be avoided in a mainstream piece, then explain their meaning. When discussing a link between abortion and declining crime in the book *Freakonomics*, Levitt and Dubner (2009) had to address causation to make their point. Though causation and correlation are terms used regularly researcher to researcher, they are not familiar to every mainstream reader. The authors thus walked readers through the process of how they considered different data in relation to causation and correlation throughout their investigation. As their process unfolds, the reader learns the meaning of these terms while learning how a causal relationship was established.

95

> ## RESOURCE TIP
>
> For free, downloadable tools to help you make scientific findings accessible for any audience, I recommend:
>
> 1. National Academies of Sciences, Engineering, and Medicine's *Communicating Science Effectively: A Research Agenda* (www.nap.edu/catalog/23674/communicating-science-effectively-a-research-agenda), which covers quandaries like how to best communicate numerical probabilities.
> 2. National Science Board's *Science and Engineering Indicators Report* (www.nsf.gov/statistics/2016/nsb2 0161) offers insight into the public's understanding of science and engineering that can inform your writing style and language.
> 3. U.S. Department of Education's *Going Public: Writing About Research in Everyday Language* (https://files.eric.ed.gov/fulltext/ED545224.pdf), which includes a glossary pairing research terms with revised usage, so you can make complex concepts simpler without losing accuracy.

Worse than the crimes of jargon and complicated prose, however, is what many experts call The Curse of Knowledge. This curse involves forgetting what it was like to not know something we now know. The audience reads something to gain something new, yet we often forget the audience does not already share our knowledge or perspective. If left unchecked, The Curse of Knowledge makes us use terms while erroneously assuming the reader already knows what they mean, or we explain how to apply an idea without fleshing out what the idea is made of and what it looks like (Pinker, 2014). To trump The Curse of Knowledge, we must maintain awareness (throughout the planning, writing, and revision processes) of our audience's nature and needs.

Part of clarity is establishing context. Once when I read an article on writing an effective proposal, it wasn't until six paragraphs in that I could begin to guess the author meant a business proposal—though nowhere in the entire article was the phrase "business proposal" ever used. The meaning of "proposal" could have alternately been a book proposal, an op-ed proposal to a problem, a marriage proposal, a grant proposal, or something else. Ideally, your reader should know your piece's focus from your title, and your introduction should unequivocally communicate what the written work will be about.

We get used to the shorthand we use with our closest colleagues. Yet we cannot presume our audience accepts our terms to mean the same thing we do. Like "proposal," words can mean different things in different contexts. Even if your readers understand a term can be used in a particular way, they need confirmation that is the way you are using the term.

When you write for an international audience, be extra wary of misunderstandings. For example, in the U.S., the leader of a school for children is commonly called the principal, whereas in England this person is commonly called the headteacher. Editor-in-chief Hugh McLaughlin notes, "We get people who write from America who assume everyone knows the American system—and the same happens with U.K. writers. Because we're an international journal, we need writers to include that international context" (Higher Education Network, 2015, p. 3).

Consider your range of readers and provide context clues and definitions as needed. Online, terms can feature hyperlinks that lead to definitions, and longer forms like books can include a glossary, definition textbox, or an explanation of terms that appears in the book's introduction.

Write Confidently

Do not use phrases like "I think . . ." or "In my opinion . . ." that qualify your statements. First of all, your name is on the piece as its author, so the reader already knows these ideas are coming from you as opposed to someone else. Second of all, you are an expert. You are backing your statements up with citations, case studies, examples, concrete facts, and other supports. Verbiage that makes you sound unsure or alone in your beliefs undermines your message.

However, check self-absorption at the door. Being confident does not mean mistaking a writing project as an opportunity to ramble about yourself. I am shocked by how many academics cross the "let us talk about me" line.

Providing examples from your own experiences is helpful for readers and highly recommended. What *is not* helpful or recommended is devoting large sections to things like, "Let me tell you my history . . ." or "My list of accomplishments . . ." There are exceptions (such as the "Meet the Author" section of a book, an author bio accompanying an article, or stories that illustrate strategies or findings). Otherwise, focusing predominantly on yourself for multiple paragraphs is self-indulgent, off-topic, and wastes space that could be spent informing and engaging your reader.

When sharing your own experiences, only include the pieces that propel your message about your topic. If your piece reads like a memoir, consider reworking it.

Do Not Overload Your Reader

We are experts on the topics we write about, so there is *much* we can share. We often get carried away in our excitement: "Ooh—since I mentioned ___, I should also mention ___! I have so many great examples of ___ I can throw in, too!" But readers can only take so much. Even if they are interested in your topic, readers can miss your core message amid excess verbiage.

In describing what the Center for Communicating Science wants from scientists sharing information, Alda (2017) writes, "Sometimes, telling us just enough to make us want to know more is exactly the right amount. We gag on force-feeding. We're uncomfortable feeling like geese getting our livers fattened" (p. 73). This is especially true of short-form writing, whereas readers are expecting more information in a book.

When stopping short of overload, you can always point readers to resources for more information when they are ready. Online articles can include links to more information, and printed pieces can feature web addresses and other details for those interested.

Cite Recent Work

As a general rule, all sources should be from within the last six years, with few exceptions. If you do cite older work, there should be a reason for it. For example, something like, "In a seminal study," "In an often-cited paper," or "established the foundation for" can help justify the source's inclusion. Pair the finding with any follow-up evidence that helped advance the previous source's merit.

AFTER WRITING ANYTHING

- **Proof and edit meticulously**. Use your word processing software's spell check and grammar check tools. Print your piece and proofread it for errors, clarity, and recommendations given in this chapter and others. Turn the submission requirements into a checklist (I add a to-be-checked box next to each required item) and ensure you have met every demand.
- **Step into your audience's shoes.** Are the "big picture" and your message conveyed? Does the flow work for readers? Are you sure your sentences and explanations are clear? Are you too wordy or do your descriptions ramble? View your work with an open mind and fix fumbles.
- **Check with people you mention** in relation to personal experience (as opposed to repeating what you see in print), as there's a chance you will get details wrong. Whenever I mention someone I know or someone for whom I am unsure of a detail, I share the verbiage with her (prior to submission and publication) to ensure details are accurate. Sometimes I hear back, "Actually, I am leaving that position this week; here's my new job title. . . " or "That is great, but did you know I also. . . ." I have had my qualifications and words misprinted plenty of times, whereas this practice keeps my sharing of others' information accurate.

The people I contact are usually excited to be mentioned and want me to keep them posted when the piece is published. They often become the biggest sharers of those works, which helps me reach more readers. Folks you mention will likely do the same.

- **Revisit and finesse your title.** Revisit the "Before Writing Anything: Draft a Title" section of this chapter and ensure your title will capture readers' attention and draw them into reading the rest of your piece.

  Also, make sure your piece delivers on what the title promises. If not, you can either rework your title or rework your piece. Otherwise, your title primes readers with expectations of what they believe your writing will deliver, and a piece that fails to deliver this will disappoint. Your reader will be distracted by thoughts like, "When is he going to cover __?" Though the "Writing for Journals" section of this chapter pertains to journal papers, its segment on titles offers many tips you can apply to other forms of writing, too.

- **Write compelling cover letters/emails and proposals.** These should stick to the publisher's specifications (does he want a cover letter or cover *email*?), avoid jargon (many editors are not experts in the field and their understanding of your topic is likely less deep than yours), and win over the editor or journalist. Have at least one item that will make your proposal jump out from the rest (for example, if you assisted President Obama in addressing your topic, you better slip in that fact).

  In order to be succinct, an email or its attachment can use hyperlinks that lead to more information. I did this on the sample cover email shown here (each underlined word was a link the editors could click), which resulted in acceptance.

  One approach is to craft your cover letters and proposals before writing your actual submissions, which can help you identify your purpose before tackling the writing process. Whenever you wrote your cover email or proposal, review what you prepared and be sure the cover letter or proposal accurately reflects the written work you are submitting. Edit each item as needed until these two pieces are well-matched.

SAMPLE COVER EMAIL THAT LED TO A PUBLICATION

Dear *Los Angeles Times* Editorial Team,

I have attached a timely 612-word submission for the Commentary section. The op-ed relates to this "back-to-school" time of year and the pandemic of <u>teacher burnout</u>.

I live in Southern California writing <u>books</u> for researchers and educators. My perspective on this submission's topic stems from being a former teacher (honored by the U.S. White House for my dedication to students), assistant principal, school district administrator, and chief education and research officer. My CV and bio (with long list of publications) can be found at <u>www.JennyRankin/bio</u>.

Thank you very much for your consideration.
Sincerely,
Dr. Jenny Grant Rankin

- **Provide (or consider providing) images.** In most cases, you will not be expected to provide images to illustrate your work, but editors often appreciate being offered a copyright-free image they can consider using. See the "Guide to Slide Design" eResource (described in Chapter 7) for assistance in preparing or selecting copyright-free images.

AFTER RECEIVING VERDICT

Your work will typically be reviewed prior to its publication, and you will often receive reviewers' and editors' feedback, to which you are expected to respond. Sometimes this process is handled in a formal way (for example: "Review comments on the Reviewer Feedback Form and use the form's last column to respond to each line item, indicating how you will change your work to reflect a suggestion"), and sometimes the process is as informal as fielding a few suggestions or questions from an editor. No matter the conditions, this section's tips can help you make the most of this stage so that each written piece is shaped into its best possible self.

Consider Feedback

You could receive reviewer feedback whether or not your work is accepted. Acceptance might hinge on the condition that you respond to the reviewer's feedback and make requested changes.

Usually there is something to learn from each piece of feedback, and some change to make whenever a change is requested. This need not be the same change that was requested, but it should be a change that solves the problem at the root of the feedback. For example:

- The reviewer writes, "The qualitative aspects of the paper were communicated, but the quantitative aspects were not addressed."
- You immediately think, "That reviewer is crazy! My paper wasn't a mixed methods study. It was only a qualitative study and thus there were no quantitative aspects to address."
- After further consideration you think, "The reviewer misunderstood that my paper was mixed methods. I will revise the abstract, introduction, and methodology sections of the paper to make it clear this is a qualitative study." You can incorporate this reasoning into your response to the reviewer's comment and describe the change you made. Thus, you are making a change that solves the true problem (confusion) that triggered the reviewer's response.

If your initial impression of the feedback is outrage or a feeling the reviewers "got it wrong," return to that feedback later when you feel calmer. Even if a reviewer is off-base, this usually means he was confused in some way. You can at least consider ways to make your concept clearer (such as by making its context clearer) so future readers do not get lost.

Clarify Changes

Indicate exactly where you made changes (for example: "Second sentence in the first paragraph of the 'Recommendations' section") so editors do not have to hunt for them. When editors embed feedback directly on the draft (such as by using Word or Adobe Acrobat's comment features), use that same system to add your responses.

When a piece is extensive, such as a dissertation, and its feedback is provided in a separate document, use a system that makes it clear you are addressing every comment. In these cases, I create a table with a row for each request. Requests go in the first column, my explanations of resultant changes go in the second column, and descriptions of the exact location of each change go in the third.

Once I left out such details and it cost me a project. I had spent a year of back-and-forth with changing editors (whose requests contradicted one another) on an article for a publication known for mistreating freelance contributors. In my final email to the newest editor, I noted I made her requested changes but—for the first time—did not detail where they lay. What I got back was a curt, late-night email from the editor that she could not spot the changes, my article had become "too much work," and she was canceling its scheduled publication. This constituted a waste of my time and the potential good that could have come from the piece, all because I did not provide details I could have easily offered.

101

Speak Up

Speak up early if major problems are brewing. Egido (2018) found that during the feedback stage, the reviewed may not feel at ease and are uncomfortable expressing their thoughts to the reviewer, yet open exchange is necessary to arrive upon the best decisions for work. While you want to be agreeable to work with, your main priority must be the quality of your work, as this will shape its impact.

One of my books (not with this publisher) was assigned a copy editor I later learned was brand new to the publishing house and to the genre. For her first round of feedback, she edited my draft without turning on the "track changes" feature in Word (which shows where edits were made), and she only told me of a fraction of her changes to the manuscript. Once I spotted some alterations and additions she had not mentioned, which misused field terminology and would have embarrassed me if published, I talked to her about how vital this feature was and why I needed to know about changes being made (I also reread the whole book from scratch to catch her other changes). She used the feature from that point forward and ended up doing a great job. If I had remained silent about this major problem, however, we would not have worked successfully together and the book (along with its impact) would have suffered.

Thrive Despite Rejection

Learn from a rejection. Reviewers' comments and the justification for your rejection can be golden pieces of information. They can help you improve your paper, achieve acceptance on your next try, and improve future work. In an international survey of more than 4,000 paper writers and reviewers, 91% of authors indicated the peer review process improved their papers (Mulligan, Hall, & Raphael, 2012). In fact, being previously rejected from a publication increases a paper's eventual citations and impact (Ball, 2012).

Though helpful, reviews are also subjective. You might even find reviewers sometimes contradict one another. Consider the highest-grossing movie of 1985, *Back to the Future*. Disney passed on the script because it was "too sexually perverse," whereas Columbia Pictures rejected the script because it was not "sexual enough" (Conradt, 2016, pp. 4–5). Madeleine L'Engle's *A Wrinkle in Time* is one of the most frequently banned books as it is sometimes perceived as being "anti-Christian," yet other critics argue the award-winning book is "too religious" (Parr, 2018, p. 7).

Different reviewers have different backgrounds, goals, and impressions. Do your best to glean helpful recommendations from the feedback you receive, even if it means finding alternate ways to improve the work (like an approach more likely to meet the needs of all readers), and your work will benefit.

Also, remember that rejection is common. Academics list and talk about their published books, elite periodicals, and journal articles, but they rarely reveal the longer list of rejections they received on their journey. Rejection is part of the publication process and does not mean you or your ideas are unworthy.

I have found there to be a domino effect when it comes to getting published: the more I got published, the more "previous publications" I got to mention when submitting new pieces to get published elsewhere, and then it seemed like I had an easier time breaking in to new publications than I had when I was new to all this. So, have heart: acceptance will get easier!

Be proud of your courage and initiative in putting yourself out there. Though rejection stings, it is worth braving discomfort for the sake of bettering the world with your findings. You owe it to yourself (and those you can help) to dust yourself off, rework your piece, and submit again.

REFERENCES

Alda, A. (2017). *If I understood you, would I have this look on my face?: My adventures in the art and science of relating and communicating.* New York, NY: Random House.

Ball, P. (2012, October 11). Rejection improves eventual impact of manuscripts. *Nature.* Retrieved from www.nature.com/news/rejection-improves-eventual-impact-of-manuscripts-1.11583

Berger, J. (2013). *Contagious: Why things catch on.* New York, NY: Simon & Schuster.

Cialdini, R. B. (2005). What's the best secret device for engaging student interest? The answer is in the title. *Journal of Social and Clinical Psychology, 24*(1), 22–29.

Conradt, S. (2016, April 30). 8 hit movies that were originally rejected by studios. *Mental Floss.* Retrieved from http://mentalfloss.com/article/79197/8-hit-movies-were-originally-rejected-studios

Covey, S. (2004). *The 8th habit: From effectiveness to greatness.* New York, NY: Free Press/ Simon & Schuster.

Ebrahim, A. N., Salehi, H., Embi, M. A., Habibi Tanha, F., Gholizadeh, H., Motahar, S. M., & Ordi, A. (2013, October 23). Effective strategies for increasing citation frequency. *International Education Studies, 6*(11), 93–99.

Egido, A. A. (2018). *Students' presupposition, prejudice, and discrimination in an English language class.* Londrina, Brazil: State University of Londrina.

Eng, N. (2017). *Teaching college: The ultimate guide to lecturing, presenting, and engaging students.* New York, NY: Author.

Gillett, R. (2014, September 18). Why we're more likely to remember content with images and video (infographic). *Fast Company.* Retrieved from www.fastcompany.com/3035856/why-were-more-likely-to-remember-content-with-images-and-video-infogr

Grant, A. (2016). *Originals: How non-conformists move the world.* New York, NY: Penguin Books.

Heath, C., & Heath, D. (2008). *Made to stick: Why some ideas survive and others die.* New York, NY: Random House.

Heller, D. E. (2016). Writing opinion articles. In M. Gasman (Ed.), *Academics going public: How to write and speak beyond academe* (pp. 21–37). New York, NY: Routledge, Taylor & Francis.

Higher Education Network. (2015, January 3). How to get published in an academic journal: Top tips from editors. *The Guardian.* Retrieved from www.theguardian.com/education/2015/jan/03/how-to-get-published-in-an-academic-journal-top-tips-from-editors

Howard-Jones, P. (2018). *Evolution of the learning brain: Or how you got to be so smart.* New York, NY: Routledge/Taylor & Francis.

Kahneman, D. (2011). *Thinking, fast and slow.* New York, NY: Farrar, Straus and Giroux.

King, S. (2010). *On writing: A memoir of the craft: 10th anniversary edition.* New York, NY: Simon & Schuster, Inc.

Levitt, S. D., & Dubner, S. J. (2009). *Freakonomics: A rogue economist explores the hidden side of everything.* New York, NY: HarperCollins.

Mulligan, A., Hall, L., & Raphael, E. (2012, December 4). Peer review in a changing world: An international study measuring the attitudes of researchers. *Journal of the Association for Information Science and Technology, 64*(1), 132–161.

National Academies of Sciences, Engineering, and Medicine. (2017). *Communicating science effectively: A research agenda.* Washington, DC: The National Academies Press. doi:10.17226/23674

National Science Board. (2016). Chapter 7: Science and technology: Public attitudes and understanding. In *Science and engineering indicators 2016.* Arlington, VA: National Science Foundation.

NPR's Education Team. [@npr_ed]. (2018, March 1). *Dolly Parton's father never learned to read. She started her nonprofit, imagination library, to give children what he didn't have: Early access to books.* [Twitter moment]. Retrieved from https://twitter.com/npr_ed

Pao, M. (2018, March 1). Dolly Parton gives the gift of literacy: A library of 100 million books. *NPR Ed.* Retrieved from www.npr.org/sections/ed/2018/03/01/589912466/dolly-parton-gives-the-gift-of-literacy-a-library-of-100-million-books

Parr, A. (2018, February 27). 12 fantastic facts about A Wrinkle in Time. *Mental Floss.* Retrieved from http://mentalfloss.com/article/62736/12-fantastic-facts-about-wrinkle-time

Patton, L. D., Harris, J. C., Ranero-Ramirez, J., Villacampa, I., & Lui, J. (2015). Engaging undergraduate women of color. In S. J. Quaye & S. H. Harper (Eds.), *Student engagement in higher education: Theoretical perspectives and practical approaches for diverse populations* (pp. 15–35). New York, NY: Routledge.

Pinker, S. (2014, September 26). Why academics stink at writing. *The Chronical of Higher Education*. Retrieved from https://stevenpinker.com/files/pinker/files/why_academics_stink_at_writing.pdf

Quaye, S. J., Griffin, K. A., & Museus, S. D. (2015). Engaging students of color. In S. J. Quaye & S. H. Harper (Eds.), *Student engagement in higher education: Theoretical perspectives and practical approaches for diverse populations* (pp. 15–35). New York, NY: Routledge.

Rankin, J. (2018, Summer). How administrators can help teachers win the burnout war. *Educational Leadership*, 75(9), 1–6.

Shaikh, A. A. (2016, April 4). 7 steps to publishing in a scientific journal: Before you hit "submit," here's a checklist (and pitfalls to avoid). *Elsevier*. Retrieved from www.elsevier.com/connect/7-steps-to-publishing-in-a-scientific-journal

Shannon-Karasik, C. (2018, April 13). 7 ways your kid's bones are different from adults & a couple of ways they're exactly the same. *Romper*. Retrieved from www.romper.com/p/7-ways-your-kids-bones-are-different-from-adults-a-couple-of-ways-theyre-exactly-the-same-8780327

Slavin, R. (2018, June 28). "But it worked in the lab!" How lab research misleads educators. *Best Evidence in Brief*. Retrieved from https://robertslavinsblog.wordpress.com/2018/06/28/but-it-worked-in-the-lab-how-lab-research-misleads-educators

Stone, J. (2014, July 1). Why do we procrastinate and cheat on our diets? *Psychology Today*. Retrieved from www.psychologytoday.com/us/blog/clear-organized-and-motivated/201407/why-do-we-procrastinate-and-cheat-our-diets

Thompson, G. L., & Thompson, R. (2014). *Yes, you can!: Advice for teachers who want a great start and a great finish with their students of color*. Thousand Oaks, CA: Corwin.

Chapter 5

Writing Short-Form (Articles, Papers, Etc.)

Quick quiz:

1. Would you rather read a *book* on how Laotian community engagement strategies differ from Thai strategies, or an *article* on the same topic?
2. Would you rather read a *book* on how the brain stem supports cognitive function, or an *article* on the same topic?
3. Would you rather read a *book* on how to speak Dothraki, or an *article* on the same topic? (And if you already speak Dothraki, you are one of the few people in this world nerdier than me; *me nem nesa!*)

Chances are, you selected "article" for most of these questions. I read a lot of books. You probably do, too. But for every book we read, we read countless more articles, papers, online content, or other assortment of short-form writing. We are also more likely to read outside our usual genres and topics when the reading commitment is only a handful of pages. Shorter works' higher consumption rate means you can introduce far more stakeholders to your ideas if you embrace short-form writing. Even if short-form writing limits you to sharing only a taste of a complex topic, that taste leads people to seek the rest you have to share.

Some short pieces are for experts in your field and decision-makers, whereas some are for the general public. The latter group is often neglected by folks like us yet has a huge impact on lives. Julian Tyson decided to write an article for *The Conversation*, a site where professors and researchers write for the general public. The article "reached more readers than the scholar had in *all the preceding decades* of work" (Lynch, 2016, p. 7). Our work is relevant for people outside academia. When we write for specific lay audiences or for the public at large, we can offer these folks information that renders valuable change. Plus, fellow researchers are included among readers of non-field publications, too.

HOW THIS CHAPTER WORKS
(YOU NEED CHAPTER 4)

Chapter 4 provided you with the fundamental guidelines that apply to all the writing opportunities described in this book. The writing guidelines provided in this chapter are supplemental and are meant to be considered *with* the guidelines in Chapter 4.

IF YOU HATE WRITING (OR EVEN IF YOU LOVE IT)

Some of the smartest people I know struggle with writing. Others write well but doing so takes them a lot of time. The following tricks can help those who dread writing but want to publish their work. These tips happen to be useful for those who love writing, as well.

- Submit snippets of text to publications. See the "Reference Sites" and "Short Answers" sections of this chapter for opportunities.
- Co-write with a colleague. If you pull your weight by offering bullet points, disparate snippets of content, sources to cite, and the like, a colleague who writes with ease can pull it all together. If he ends up with the greater workload, place his name before yours in authorship.
- Instead of collaborating on each single piece, create a multi-author blog or column in which you and colleagues take turns posting.

TIME-SAVING TIP

Use a good organizational system for your computer files so you can easily borrow verbiage from things you wrote before (like for a grant proposal, email to a colleague, award submission, etc.) from one area and paste it into content for a publication. Many times what we write without publication in mind can later serve as the foundation of a draft we tweak for publication. I store every statement I cite on its own row of an excel file, which I can sort by date, source, or category.

- Use an interview format for a piece in which someone interviews you about your work. This way you merely answer questions and do not have to worry about the hook, flow, and so on.

- Conversely, you can interview someone else about his work you admire. This way you merely have to draft interview questions and pull them together with an intro, conclusion, and transitions.
- If you are artistic and techy, you can get key points across in an infographic in place of a traditional article. Many online news sources, in particular, give infographics the same treatment as a full-length article.
- Write a chapter in a book, rather than an entire book (when the book is published, you will still be a published author, can likely set up a www. Amazon.com author page, etc.). See the "Book Chapters" section of this chapter for details.
- Submit your work for others to write about it. For example, the *New Media Consortium Horizon Report* series compiled researchers' input every year, and their reports did the same. This chapter covers how to pitch a story idea to journalists who can cover your work.
- Opt to write a short book rather than a full-length book. The Routledge Focus series (as short as 20,000 words) is one example (details at www. routledge.com/resources/authors/how-to-publish-with-us), and other publishers welcome even shorter manuscripts.
- Write the foreword for someone else's book you respect. Forewords give you the chance to frame and add to conversation.
- Create a blog (see the "Blogging" section of this chapter) and invite others, such as your colleagues or students, to write for it. You can curate material and facilitate posts that focus on a set or changing theme.
- Lead a full book project as an editor (this would put your name on the book's cover, allow you to set up an author page on each site where the book is sold, etc.). A great place to start is the IGI Global online proposal form (www.igi-global.com/publish/submit-a-proposal). This would involve reading and editing the submissions. You could opt to edit the book with a colleague to save time, though your reading could double as research for other projects.
- Write book reviews. It is hard to be at a loss for what to say when you are relaying your reaction to something. See the "Book Review" section of this chapter for details.
- Record yourself as you talk about your topic. Most smart phones and newer laptops have an audio recording feature. You can then replay and transcribe your words (or use transcription software, which can help even when you have to clean up its mistakes). This gives you a foundation you can edit to produce a polished draft.
- Dig up your old college essays and other papers. If these were unpublished and share something important, you can polish them up and submit them for publication. Most of your writing will have already been done for you by your past self.

- Consider turning your dissertation into a monograph (specialist book). This way you will not have to start from scratch in writing a book. See Routledge, Taylor & Francis Group (2017) for guidance determining if publishers would consider your work to be commercially viable as a book.
- In November, follow #AcWriMo on social media for encouragement producing content during Academic Writing Month.

If writing just doesn't flow naturally for you, know that if you apply the time it will get easier. Maya Angelou said, "What I try to do is write. . . . It might be just the most boring and awful stuff. But I try. . . . And then it is as if the muse is convinced that I'm serious and says, 'Okay. Okay. I'll come.'" (Heffron, 2011, p. 219).

Do not be too critical of your first draft; just get it onto your paper or screen. The next step—editing that draft—will likely be a much easier process than the initial draft proved.

LIST OF WRITING OPPORTUNITIES (JOURNALS, MAGAZINES, NEWSLETTERS, BLOGS, REFERENCE TOOLS, AND NEWSPAPERS)

LIST OF WRITING OPPORTUNITIES

This book lists hundreds of short-form writing opportunities (such as journal papers, magazine articles, newsletter and e-newsletter pieces, blog posts, short answer and reference sites, and newspaper op-eds and articles) for you in an electronic file that makes it easy to find and pursue writing opportunities. You can sort the file by publication type, visit each website with a simple click, and add additional publications that are specific to your research area and work. The list contains details like publication category and manipulation-friendly fields you can use to track your submissions. A separate list will feature book publishers (covered in the next chapter). See the "eResources" section near the start of this book for details on accessing and using this "List of Writing Opportunities".

REFERENCE SITES

Contribute snippets of text for online reference tools used frequently by those within your field or the general public. Particularly when it comes to informing non-experts about your work, it is important to reach out to people through the tools they use. For example, consider how contributing your knowledge to the following resources will reach different populations:

- A member of the general public could avoid a misunderstanding when referencing Wikipedia (https://en.wikipedia.org).
- A reporter could describe your topic in accurate terms after using Harvard's & Hacks/Hackers' Glossary of Common Terms Used in Digital Journalism (https://journalistsresource.org).
- An educator or researcher new to your topic could sidestep a common misconception when referencing the ERIC Thesaurus (http://eric.ed.gov/?ti=all).

You can lend your expertise to improving the listed resources and more. Open this book's "List of Writing Opportunities" eResource (described earlier) and find listings with "Reference" in the "Category" column for examples. Also search elsewhere for examples limited to your specific field.

Quora

Post answers in online communities like Quora (www.quora.com), covered in the "Guide to Hunting and Harvesting" eResource covered in Chapter 11. Search for questions related to your area of expertise and answer all related questions (not just one). For example, my answers relating to teacher burnout (one of my areas of expertise) rendered 2,422 views in one year (with each post averaging 269 views per year). This average is relatively small (compared to posts on popular topics like dogs); however, answers that address topics within your expertise are read by those who follow and care about those specific topics. Think of the impact your words could have on those readers and those with whom they interact.

ResearchGate

ResearchGate has a question and answer forum (www.researchgate.net/topics) that functions like an academic's version of Quora. You can converse directly with scholars from all over the world and impact their treatment of topics. Use the "Follow" function to remain updated on discussion threads in which you want to continually contribute.

Wikipedia

A reference site deserving special attention is one to which researchers often turn up their noses: Wikipedia. Yet the collaboratively maintained online encyclopedia ranks as the sixth most widely used website in the world, and users view 10 billion pages every month within merely the English version of the site (Simonite, 2013). Even if you deride the site for its susceptibility to inaccuracies,

Wikipedia is used profusely. Why not help remove inaccuracies and improve users' understanding of concepts? Academics and non-academics alike visit the site for an initial, basic understanding of what terms mean (example: "What is qualitative? What is quantitative? How do these differ?"), and some use it to take their understanding deeper.

Including findings on Wikipedia promotes increased citation of your work (Ebrahim et al., 2013). You can add your voice to existing Wikipedia articles (even a sentence or two added to an existing piece can make important points and prevent misunderstandings) and create new articles for concepts not yet covered there. Though you must stick to the community's policies discouraging self-promotion, you may still add references to your pertinent work (for example, cite and add a link to your journal paper) and ensure any page about you (common for authors) is accurate.

Your voice is also needed to broaden the perspectives that shape users' understanding of your field. Men comprise 90% of those running Wikipedia, and founder Jimmy Whales says editor diversity is the biggest issue facing Wikipedia (Simonite, 2013). This impacts the content read during those 10 billion monthly page views. For example, Wagner, Garcia, Jadidi, and Strohmaier (2015) found the Wikipedia editor community's lack of diversity introduces gender bias into Wikipedia content. Imagine obscurities such as these shaping such a large number of users' understanding of concepts related to your studies. Expanding the number and heterogeneity of experts contributing to Wikipedia can help.

SHORT ANSWERS

You can submit short answers, such as in the Comparative and International Education Society's (CIES's) *CIES Perspectives* (for the "Dialogue and Debate" column). This book's "List of Writing Opportunities" eResource (described earlier) contains examples labeled as "Short Answer" in the file's "Category" column.

BLOGGING

The youngest recipient ever of the Nobel Prize, Malala Yousafzai, is known for her crusade for universal education and for being shot in the face by the Taliban at age 15 in response to her activism. What some do not know is that Yousafzai started blogging for the British Broadcasting Corporation (BBC) at age 11. When you blog to share your ideas, the process can also sharpen those ideas and propel your passion.

Blogs offer freedom to share unconventional perspectives and provide great writing practice. Blogging can "hone your writing skills, pushing you to write in a more accessible style and to distill a paper or thought process into a brief, readable blog post" (Author Services, 2017).

Blogging can help you land a book deal, and not just by improving your craft through practice. "Publishers look favorably on blogging: It clearly demonstrates that a scholar is actively engaging with a research community and is interested in promoting their work. It's a marketing tool publishers cannot ignore" (Anyangwe, 2011).

Blogging can also lead to landing a column, speaking engagement, or other opportunity. Ray Salazar (2013) attributes his blog (www.chicagonow.com/white-rhino) as the impetus that opened doors for him on NPR . . . and let us not forget Yousafzai's blogging en route to her Nobel Prize.

TYPE-SAVING TIP

Not a fan of writing but still want to blog? See the "Video Blogging" section of Chapter 9.

You can create your own blog, contribute to someone else's, or both. For example, the blog column I write for *Psychology Today* gets far more hits than my website's blog, but I write pieces for the latter when they are better suited to the site's specific audience. I can also write a piece for my blog and then cross-post it on my *Psychology Today* blog, as well, as long as I add the line "Reprinted with permission from [initial source]" to the bottom (note that your blogs might have different policies for cross-posts). When you control the rights to your posts, you can always allow others to publish them for added readership.

Although many blogs are hardly read, other bloggers gain large followings (meteorologist Anthony Watts is one example: www.wattsupwiththat.com) that lead to speaking engagements, book deals, and more. Academic blogs with high readership tend to fit in at least one of the categories in Table 5.1:

Of course, success can be measured in different ways. You might want to blog simply as a creative outlet, or to help you reflect on your practice, or to support just a handful of practitioners you mentor, or to infuse more diversity into the blogger pool, or to deliver occasional content to those who follow your work. If you deem blogging worthwhile, you can work toward your own definition of success.

Your Own Blog

If you are setting up your own website (see the "Website" section of Chapter 2), that is one place to host your blog. Many web-hosting platforms (like SquareSpace) also allow you to embed a form where visitors can opt to subscribe to your blog. You can then set up a free MailChimp (www.MailChimp.com) account that

Table 5.1 Academic Blogs with High Readership

Trait Encouraging High Readership	Example
Written by someone already highly influential or famous in the field	Bill Nye's Planetary Society Blog (www.planetary.org/blogs/bill-nye)
On a website that is well-known and has a strong following	*Psychology Today* blogs (www.psychologytoday.com/us/blog)
Received high recognition	Won "Best Blog" or Society of Environmental Journalists Award for Reporting on the Environment
Offers high value	Readers think, "Finally, this blogger tells me the specifics of how to educate hard-to-reach populations concerning sexually transmitted infection."
Refreshingly honest, brave, or enlightening	Readers think, "Finally, this blogger is saying what no one else has the guts to say!"
Is unique in some way	The posts provide something new (rather than regurgitate the same content seen frequently online)

automatically emails your blog (in e-newsletter form) to anyone who subscribes, without you having to do anything beyond the usual way you would post your blog. Automatically alerting subscribers to new posts increases your words' chances of being read.

Some services (sometimes free) host blogging sites for anyone, and researchers frequently utilize these. Examples include Blogger (www.blogger.com), Tumblr (www.tumblr.com), and WordPress (www.wordpress.com). You might instead use LinkedIn's "article" feature in a blogging manner. Explore different options to find the setup you prefer.

Other Blogs

Many blogs feature posts from multiple authors, and you can contribute to these (usually without the pressure of providing more). You can open this book's "List of Writing Opportunities" eResource (described earlier) to find examples categorized as "Blog/Site," but you can also find blogs online that are specific to your field or position. Consider contributing to one of these.

If you struggle to get a piece accepted, do not lose heart. Commercial blogs are often particularly eager for expert contributors. If there is a product you use or have studied, consider contacting the company to see if you can write for them. You can also pursue being featured (such as quoted or interviewed) on someone else's blog.

Successful Blogging

In addition to recommendations in the previous chapter, there are additional things to keep in mind when you are writing online content:

- **Lean on the short side**, even if this means limiting what you communicate. Internet users tend to scan written work rather than read it in depth, so . . . the best blogs are generally 1,000 words or fewer (Routledge, 2017). "Given individuals' decreasing attention spans, [a blog post] should be relatively short and easily digestible, so that someone can read it in just a few minutes" (Stewart, 2016, p. 78).

  One of the great things about online content is that it is easy to put links within your writing that lead to more information for those who want it. For example, if in an article for physical therapists you say, "There are also strategies athletes can use," you can make that statement double as a link leading to an article detailing those strategies, rather than go off on a tangent within your post.

- **Include an image.** Online content with relevant images receives 94% more views (Hall, 2015). Images also help readers understand what your post will address, thus helping you communicate your message.

- **Brace yourself for feedback.** Since online content often has comment fields where readers can easily respond immediately to your work, you will hear from more readers than you will when your writing is only printed. Other readers will see these comments, as well, which can result in comment-area dialogue.

  Some writers enjoy this dynamic, as it facilitates discussion. However, it can also be time-consuming. If you find these comment sections taking away from your primary work, consider turning the reader comments feature off, which you can typically do if you manage the blog.

HEARTACHE-SAVING TIP

When readers have a way to voice their reactions to your work, such as through letters to the editor, they can be harsh . . . but the immediacy and potential anonymity of online comment fields can open the door to particularly toxic criticism (racist and sexist comments, ignorant myth-spreading, political ravings, etc.). This is especially true if your work reaches national and international audiences outside your field.

There's no magic tonic to make your online articles and blog posts hostility-proof, but it can save you some heartache to anticipate possible aggression. This will prevent you from being blindsided, help you not to take comments personally (you are doing good work; your merit is not tied to the popularity of your article), and prepare you to respond appropriately (support your case with evidence rather than return insults). If you have the option to turn off the comment field, consider doing so.

- **Use concise and intriguing titles.** Although how to do this was covered in Chapter 4, it needs to be stressed here. Readers who find journal papers and other forms of scholarly writing likely ran searches for something very particular and will base their interest in your work on whether or not it meets what they are looking for, whereas readers of online content are more evasive. Blog posts and online articles need titles that demand to be noticed.

SCRAPPY TIP

In December, note how sites and e-newsletters tout their "Top 10 Articles of the Year", "Must-Read [Field] Stories from 2018", "Most Emailed List," etc. These lists tend to be based on how many people visited the piece online or clicked a share option to spread it to others (easy to determine with web analytics). Reading these lists of titles can offer a sense of what grabbed readers' attention and can help you spice up your own titles and the angles of your content. Remember: more readers can mean more people helped by your expertise.

For example, the most talked-about pieces of Xavier Pavie and Karl Kapp, two of LinkedIn's 2017 Top Voices, were titled "Why Are Innovative Individuals so Loathsome?" (in its English translation) and "Is eLearning Really Dead? Is Instructional Design Dying with It?" (Anders, 2017). This insight could inspire you to try a thought-provoking question as a title.

NEWSPAPERS

Open this book's "List of Writing Opportunities" eResource (described earlier) and find listings with "Newspaper/Outlet" in the "Category" column (some categorized as "Blog/Site," "Magazine," or "Newsletter/eNewsletter" may also be open to commentaries). In addition to following the Chapter 4 strategies, a writer should follow some additional guidelines for newspapers (covered in the following section).

Newspaper Op-Eds and Commentaries

Most newspapers and news sites have their own in-house journalists, but field experts frequently write opinion pieces for news outlets. News sites often post guidelines for op-ed or commentary submissions, like *The New York Times* at www.help.nytimes.com/hc/en-us/articles/115014809107-How-to-submit-an-Op-Ed-essa.

An op-ed was originally "a page of special features usually opposite the editorial page of a newspaper; also, a feature on such a page" (Merriam-Webster, 2019, p. 1), but the term has evolved to mean a commentary (and is sometimes *called* a commentary) in which an author outside of the publication's editorial board argues one viewpoint on an issue that is currently debated and of high interest.

Since op-ed topics are hotly debated, more people are likely to disagree with an op-ed than they would with an informational piece in which shared facts have an obvious, single implication. As you determine how to share your stance, remember that backing up your statements with evidence from your studies and other respectable sources will be especially important. If you write a nationally-published op-ed, "be fully aware that your words, regardless of the evidence that you provide to back up your assertions, will be twisted, manipulated, taken out of context, and used against you by those that disagree with your position on issues" (Gasman, 2016, p. 120).

You will have a word limit (likely 750 words for an op-ed, or 200 words for a letter to the editor). Use it to make your stance obvious from the first paragraph (never try to argue all sides), spend the bulk of the piece arguing your point, and end with a brief summary. Newspapers are generally written for a high-school reading level or below, so use basic language (Heller, 2016).

If you bring up the opposing side, it should only be because it is an elephant in the room readers are likely to be thinking of anyway and only to slam it down immediately with your counterargument. This way, you have briefly acknowledged what readers are likely thinking, but only to knock it down. If you never address a misconception that readers are likely to have, they will read your article thinking, "This op-ed stands on thin ice, because it never addressed a 'fact' [actually a myth] I know that undermines this whole argument."

RESOURCE TIP

The OpEd Project (www.the-opedproject.org) arms women with connections and training to increase the diversity of voices in major commentary forums such as op-eds.

I especially encourage women to write op-eds, since so few currently do. "Nearly 80 percent of the op-eds published in the nation's leading newspapers are written by men, but that number appears to roughly reflect the gender breakdown of submissions" (Lepore, 2013, p. 4). In other words, 80% of submissions are by men. Society has traditionally discouraged women from stepping into conflict-rich environments, so we women need to conscientiously push past any hesitation we have to step into the op-ed fray. Otherwise our voices are not heard in this arena. We have too many important ideas to let that happen.

Newspaper Articles

Most newspapers and news sites rely entirely or predominantly on in-house journalists (and the journalists of partnered news outlets) for their articles. When outside authors *are* considered, follow the specific guidelines on a news source's website. When you ultimately write your article, lead with your core message ("do not bury the lede," as reporters say) and include details only after making your key talking points.

Delivering Your Pitch

Writing for a newspaper often involves submitting a pitch: a succinct description of a piece you would like the publication to run. See "Chapter 3: Preparation" for help writing your media pitch; the chapter includes a sample.

You might intend to write the commentary or article you pitch, but you can also pitch ideas to a journalist who will incorporate them into a piece *he* writes. If you are covered by a news outlet that partners with other news outlets to run its stories, your exposure increases dramatically. For example, The Hechinger Report and Associated Press articles are duplicated by CNN, NPR, *The New York Times*, *The Washington Post*, and many others.

You can follow the news site's pitch submission guidelines, but you can also interact with reporters on social media, comment on their stories where they appear online, and reach out directly to reporters who cover topics related to yours.

MAGAZINES, NEWSLETTERS, WEBSITES, AND OTHER ARTICLE VENUES

Magazines, newsletters, websites, and other article venues offer a chance to share your work in a less formal, highly accessible, and widely read environment. Compared with journal papers, book chapters, and books, articles are shorter and faster to produce. Though editors are typically involved, formal peer review generally is not. This speeds up production time and allows you to quickly get your words into readers' minds.

Strategies covered in Chapter 4 can be applied to an article (remember your audience, be clear, etc.). However, there are additional considerations for an article (see next section), which should be read before pursuing this short-form writing project.

Options

Open this book's "List of Writing Opportunities" eResource (described earlier) and find listings categorized as "Blog/Site," "List (Magazines)," "Magazine," and "Newsletter/eNewsletter," though many venues publish in multiple formats. You can add other target publications to this file (saved to your computer) to track more writing opportunities specific to your field.

For mainstream magazines, do not miss "List of Magazines by Circulation," maintained with current, reputable sources at https://en.wikipedia.org/wiki/List_of_magazines_by_circulation. If you have a message for the elderly, it pays to know that *AARP The Magazine* and *AARP Bulletin* dominate with 23 million U.S. readers apiece (compare this to popular magazines like *Architectural Digest*, *Condé Nast Traveler*, *House Beautiful*, and *Fast Company*, which each have around 800,000 readers). U.K. circulations are smaller but can still reach hundreds of thousands of readers. Though the circulation list includes magazines that are not field-specific, mainstream mags offer the chance to cater our messages to a wide range of stakeholders.

Submission

Find and follow the publication's submission guidelines. Some publications have processes similar to journals, where you submit a complete article to be considered for publication. Others want you to pitch a possible article to them. In these cases, leverage guidance from the "Craft Your Media Pitch" section of Chapter 3.

Keep in mind that 65% of journalists indicate that metrics like audience views and engagement now influence the way they evaluate stories, and they use this data to decide which content to publish (Cision, 2019). This means any story you pitch should hold obvious appeal to the outlet's target audience.

> ## SCRAPPY TIP
>
> When I was guest moderator of an Edutopia (@ Edutopia) Twitter chat, the Edutopia team and I were simultaneously chatting via video conference. During the chat, Edutopia's Online Community Manager remarked on which contributors made comments so insightful that Edutopia should invite them to write some articles for the site. Edutopia, part of the George Lucas Educational Foundation, has a massive following. As this story demonstrates, participating in a Twitter chat can lead to being asked to address a large audience.

Content

Chapter 4 advised you to read your chosen publication's current articles to note published pieces' topics, voice, tone, style, format, and more. For article venues, you have the added chance to consider its top-read articles. Many publications announce "this month's top articles" in emails to subscribers, or at least list the year's most popular pieces. Pay attention to what readers are most interested in or why top titles might have drawn in readers.

Add links (leading from a term to more information on it or leading to a resource readers can use) to online content. Many sites are happy to also include a link to your blog or website, which can earn you followers positioned to read your future work.

WHITEPAPERS AND REPORTS

In academic fields, a whitepaper or report is generally a neatly packaged, in-depth account of a topic, paired with recommendations for improvements in the given area. Similar formats such as lay summaries, briefing notes, and systematic reviews are common depending on the field, but whitepapers and reports should apply to all readers.

Whitepapers and reports can be catalysts in a field. For example, the national report *A Nation at Risk*, commissioned by the Reagan Administration in 1982, is credited with launching our modern era of U.S. education reform (Coggins, 2017) and shifting political conversations away from equity to economic competitiveness (Waisanen, 2018).

Stein (2016) of University of Pennsylvania writes, "Academics in my own organization have begun to realize that . . . presenting findings via a graphically designed report can increase its impact greatly. Rather than being slick and commercial, it is perceived as professional and more credible" (p. 115). Just Google your topic or field, along with the word "whitepaper" or "report" for examples. Notice these vary from long, like the U.K. Department for Exiting the European Union's (2018) Brexit whitepaper, to short, like ExplORer Surgical's (2017) whitepaper on operating-room inefficiencies. For design tips, see "10 Page-Turning White Paper Examples and Design Tips" by Sara McGuire (https://goo.gl/gnfp2J).

JOURNALS

Most of what you learned in Chapter 4 can be applied to a journal or research paper (remember your audience, be clear, etc.). However, there are additional considerations for a paper (see the next section), which should be read before pursuing this very formal writing project. There are especially stringent formats, rules, and expectations for scholarly writing.

Read Top Papers

Before writing your paper, read papers in your targeted journal but also those that have won Outstanding Publication types of awards (these are often available on the award-giver's website). This practice will give you a sense of what successful academic papers look like, how their sections ideally work, and how an effective paper is crafted. Having this context will make other journal-writing guidance easier to understand and apply.

SCRAPPY TIP

An earlier tip involved reviewing lists like "Top 10 Articles of the Year" for a sense of what grabbed readers' attention. Some journals offer similar lists (Google "Most Read Research Articles of 2018" and peruse within-field websites for examples). These can help you identify which titles and abstracts readers find most appealing. Use what you find to improve the appeal of your paper's title and abstract in order to improve your paper's reach.

Group Authorship

Collaborating on work not only benefits the research, it also means more authors to share findings. The more diverse collaborators' affiliations are, the more likely the work is to reach diverse audiences. For example, team-authored papers are cited more, papers with cross-discipline authors are cited more, and papers with international co-authors are cited up to four times more frequently (Ebrahim et al., 2013).

If authoring your piece with a group, aim for diversity. "Peer-reviewed publications with gender-heterogeneous authorship teams received 34% more citations than publications produced by gender-uniform authorship teams. . . . Promoting diversity not only promotes representation and fairness but may lead to higher quality science" (Campbell, Mehtani, Dozier, & Rinehart, 2013). Through a study of 697 volunteers working in teams of two to five, the top three factors determining group success were the presence of women in the group, higher empathy scores (which women had), and the ability for group members to freely participate in discussions (which likely improved with greater empathy) (Alda, 2017). This finding persisted even when the group's communication took place online. In a study of over 2.5 million scientific papers, Freeman and Huang (2014) found that greater ethnic diversity in co-author groups was associated with publication in higher-impact journals and with papers that received more citations than others: "These findings suggest that diversity . . . leads to greater contributions . . . as measured by impact factors and citations" (p. 2).

Though the success of a journal paper is not determined entirely by citations, the degree to which your paper is shared is just one of diverse authorship's perks. Co-authoring a paper with people of different backgrounds involves bringing a wider range of perspectives and ideas likely to improve your project's quality and enhance your understanding of your topic.

Picking Your Journal

Aim to submit to well-read journals. To increase your findings' impact, you will want a publication with a good reputation and wide circulation. Reference the journal rankings at a site like SCImago Journal and Country Rank (www.scima gojr.com/journalrank.php) for help. For more journal ranking sources and an exploration of metrics used, see Walters (2017).

Increased readership is one of the many reasons to submit to an open-access journal, which can be read online by anyone for free. Compared with papers requiring subscription or other form of payment to view, open-access papers are downloaded significantly more and cited significantly more, with the citation advantage ranging by discipline from 36% more in Biology to 600% more in Agricultural Sciences (Tennant et al., 2016).

> **RESOURCE TIP**
>
> If you paste your paper's title and abstract into Elsevier's Journal Finder tool (https://journalfinder.elsevier.com), it will show you which journals are well-suited to publishing that specific paper.

If you do publish in an obscure journal, there is much you can do to promote it (see Chapter 11), particularly if you published it open access, which makes it easier for people to share your work. Share your promotion efforts with the journal editors, as your work to share your paper also helps elevate the journal.

Adhere strictly to your chosen journal's submission guidelines. Note that simultaneous submissions (sending your paper to more than one journal at a time) are usually prohibited.

Style and Format

Read and reference a guide on how to write an effective journal paper. A single section in this book cannot encompass everything you should know, whereas a series of chapters or webpages can walk you through how to appropriately craft every portion of the paper.

See the "Resource Tip" text box for academic writing guides. Since the information in such guides can be overwhelming, read the guide as you work on each stage and section of an actual paper (rather than reading the entire book or hand-out series first and then writing the paper afterwards).

> **RESOURCE TIP**
>
> For free, searchable academic writing assistance:
>
> - Elsevier Researcher Academy (https://researcheracademy.elsevier.com) has learning videos to help you through different stages and types of academic writing (and earns you certificates of completion).
> - Purdue Online Writing Lab (https://owl.english.purdue.edu/owl) has guides for the academic writing process (located under General Writing) and for APA and other citation styles (located under Research and Citation Resources).

Regularly reference a guide on the writing citation style you will be expected to use (for example, the manual found at www.apastyle.org). That style relates not just to citations but also to format and content. In the U.S. it is standard to use American Psychological Association (APA) style, though when I have written for international publications I have been asked to follow other styles, such as Modern Language Association or Chicago Manual of Style. Each journal has a required style. See the "Resource Tip" textbox for style assistance.

Always use the most up-to-date version of a style (unless otherwise directed), since formats evolve over time. For example, APA has just released its seventh edition, which is slightly different from APA version six.

Title

Craft an effective title. "Editors hate titles that make no sense or fail to represent the subject matter adequately" (Borja, 2014, p. 14). Consider what your target reader will search for when trying to find a paper like yours. Aim to be concise while still communicating what the paper will cover. Elsevier publisher Jennifer Franklin told me that 20 words maximum is a good guideline for journal article titles. Avoid abbreviations, jargon, and location unless they are central to the study (such as "Collaboration Across the Berlin Wall").

In his research on journal paper titles, Madan (2015) found the following:

- **Recommended:** Titles that described the study's results or described the research question were met with increased citations. Question-worded titles were more likely to engage readers and increase memorability. Titles that are catchy—for example, ones that are intriguing or suggest innovation—can attract readers, but only if they are also informative. Titles should be clear, informative, concise, and accurate.
- **Mixed:** Some studies found shorter titles rendered higher citation rates, while other studies found longer titles to be cited more often. Some studies found that titles with colons rendered higher citation rates, while other studies found colon-featuring titles to be cited less often.

Once you have drafted a title, search for words you can remove without hurting the title's meaning. For example, consider the following title:

- A Quantitative Study on How Concentrated Poverty Influences the Field of Education as Examined in Randomized Experiments in Michigan's Urban Schools

Your methods ("quantitative study" and "randomized experiments") and location ("Michigan's") can be easily shared in your abstract and introduction. Anyone who finds your paper in a journal or database is already working with content in a given field and doesn't need the "education" reminder in your title. You likely do not need the phrase "concentrated poverty" when "poverty" communicates the general idea. "How" is just clutter. These omissions change our title to:

- Poverty Influences the Field as Examined in Urban Schools

However, this new title doesn't tell us much and is confusing. What does the author mean by "influences the field?" The title's impersonal nature makes the topic seem unimportant, and its generality cuts its chances of being found and read by those who would care about its specific content. Consider this change:

- Poverty Hinders Urban Students' Determination to Graduate

See how different this title is from the version before—and from its original draft—and how much more compelling and revealing it is now. The new title is worded as a statement, but you could also phrase it as a question (Does Poverty Hinder Urban Students' Determination to Graduate?) or reveal a shocking finding (Poor Urban Students Are 50% Less Determined to Graduate). Note you can always add a colon followed by more details, but your core title should be strong enough to woo readers on its own.

Abstract

A defining component of journal papers, conference papers, and research papers is the abstract. The abstract is a 150- to 500-word summary that precedes your article's introduction and is typically displayed like teaser text in the online databases that house your paper.

Potential readers will use your title and abstract to determine whether or not to keep reading the rest of your paper. For your abstract to communicate that such a read is worthwhile:

- Include your purpose, methods, findings, and implications . . . but do not let the novelty and "cool" factor of your ideas get lost in rhetoric. Remember what you have learned in this book about your core message and be sure that message is obvious in your abstract.
- When sharing your paper's ideas in your abstract, it is best to choose up to five on which to focus. Otherwise it is hard to communicate points well, and you end up listing concepts without capturing the nature of your paper.
- Maximize what your sentences say by trimming excess words and being very clear. For example, rather than saying, "The study findings are known to have limited generalizability in some demographic contexts," say something like, "The study findings do not apply to non-urban schools."

Remember: potential readers are hoping to learn about your topic and do not necessarily know the topic jargon or research jargon you might frequently use. Such jargon may sometimes be unavoidable in the body of the paper, but it must be avoided entirely in the title and abstract.

Reading the abstracts of other papers can help you understand what works and what does not. Imagine someone is reading your abstract through the same critical lens and adjust your words as necessary.

Review and Rejection

Question: What do Ernst, Fermi, Gell-Mann, Higgs, Krebs, Mullis, Shechtman, and Yalow all have in common?

Answer: Their papers all won the Nobel Prize . . . after previously being rejected for publication.

"The average acceptance rate for journals is 50%" (Wilson, 2012, p. 12). There is no correlation between a journal's rejection rate and its impact factor (a ratio of citations and citable items from the journal), so even journals with low-impact factors can reject over 90% of papers (Matthews, 2016).

Paper review is a subjective process, and rejection does not mean you or your ideas are unworthy. The "After Receiving Verdict" section of Chapter 4 covers the process of receiving and responding to feedback that is typical for journal submissions, as well as ways in which rejection can strengthen your work.

Review Articles

Consider the value of writing a review article. Though the exact nature of a review article varies between fields, a review article generally summarizes multiple previously published studies on a single topic (as opposed to new findings or analyses) and provides an unbiased account of the studies' validity. This offers readers a survey of the existing body of knowledge without having to find and consume each study separately, which can be especially important for policymakers and media members. Review articles also offer writers a chance to highlight key points, point out common misinterpretations, and make other comments to guide future experiments and shape people's understanding.

RESOURCE TIP

While an impact factor (IF) concerns journals, an *h*-index quantifies the output of individual authors. See what your *h*-index is at SCOPUS (www.scopus.com). An *h*-index of nine requires you to have authored at least nine papers that have each been cited at least nine times.

SHORT-FORM EDITOR

Journals, magazines, newsletters, and other publications regularly need new editors. If you sign up to receive organizations' e-newsletters, you will be alerted to these opportunities. You can also visit publication websites (see those in the "List of Writing Opportunities" eResource and add those in your field) and speak with publication staff to learn of editor prospects.

Publisher support of editors varies, depending on the publication. For example, editing a short newsletter might be on a volunteer basis, whereas editing a major journal could involve financial compensation, training, and staff.

All publishers want good editors. Their wish list of qualifications you should meet will often include:

- Writing published in publications similar to the one for which you want to be editor,
- Editor or reviewer experience,
- Leading expertise on the publication's topic,
- Ability to help the publication with its individual needs (improvise if resources are limited, manage growth if downloads are booming, etc.), and
- Ability to see the big picture ("Does this collection of papers do justice to this issue's theme?") as well as details ("That introduction is a grammatical mess.").

Honing your traits to meet these qualifications will increase your chances of securing an editor position.

PUT PARTS TOGETHER

Chapter 4 provided guidance to write well. This chapter offered added tips as well as multiple opportunities to share your research through short-form writing. Select a publication (use the "List of Writing Opportunities" eResource for suggestions) to which you will submit a written piece. Then complete Exercise 5.1 to plan your submission. Reference sections in this chapter and the previous chapter as you complete the exercise.

EXERCISE 5.1: SHORT-FORM WRITING PLAN

1. What will you be writing?

   - Blog Post
   - Op-Ed/Commentary
   - Article
   - Whitepaper or Report
   - Academic/Journal Paper
   - Other (Describe)

2. To which publication will you submit your piece?

3. Read the publication's submission guidelines. What is the specified word count, formatting, title length, and so on?

4. Note any details that will influence what you write (such as time of year, publication theme, and current newsworthy events).

5. Who is your audience? This can be one main audience or a few key groups.

6. What are your key purposes in writing this piece (what does your audience need from you)?

7. What primary message will run through this entire piece?

8. What new understanding will your audience gain from your piece?

9. What will your audience be able to do after reading your piece?

10. Describe what your style will be (humorous, casual, formal, etc.).

11. What will your piece's title be?

12. What magic will you use to make concepts resonate? Remember Table 4.2.

13. Create a template and use it to outline your piece. Then add to each line item, gradually turning your template into a complete draft.

14. Proof and revise your piece as necessary. Ensure your piece meets submission requirements and criteria described in this chapter and the previous chapter (communicates your core message, is very clear, doesn't overload your reader, etc.).

15. How will you introduce or pitch your piece in your cover letter/email?

REFERENCES

Alda, A. (2017). *If I understood you, would I have this look on my face?: My adventures in the art and science of relating and communicating.* New York, NY: Random House.

Anders, G. (2017, December 12). *LinkedIn top voices 2017: Education.* Retrieved from www.linkedin.com/pulse/linkedin-top-voices-2017-education-george-anders

Anyangwe, E. (2011, August 23). How to get ahead in academic publishing: Q&A best bits. *The Guardian*. Retrieved from www.theguardian.com/higher-education-network/blog/2011/aug/23/academic-publishing-summary

Author Services. (2017). *Blogging: How to make it work*. Retrieved from http://authorservices.taylorandfrancis.com/blogging

Borja, A. (2014, June 24). 11 steps to structuring a science paper editors will take seriously: A seasoned editor gives advice to get your work published in an international journal. *Elsevier*. Retrieved from www.elsevier.com/connect/11-steps-to-structuring-a-science-paper-editors-will-take-seriously

Campbell, L. G., Mehtani, S., Dozier, M. E., & Rinehart, J. (2013). Gender-heterogeneous working groups produce higher quality science. *PLoS ONE, 8*(10), e79147. doi:10.1371/journal.pone.0079147

Cision. (2019). *Cision's 2019 global state of the media report*. Chicago, IL: Cision.

Coggins, C. (2017). *How to be heard: 10 lessons teachers need to advocate for their students and profession*. San Francisco, CA: Jossey-Bass.

Ebrahim, A. N., Salehi, H., Embi, M. A., Habibi Tanha, F., Gholizadeh, H., Motahar, S. M., & Ordi, A. (2013, October 23). Effective strategies for increasing citation frequency. *International Education Studies, 6*(11), 93–99.

ExplORer Surgical. (2017, February 7). *Operating room inefficiencies and costs: A white paper summarizing ExplORer's Findings*. Retrieved from http://explorersurgical.com/wp-content/uploads/2016/10/White-Paper_June-2016.pdf

Freeman, R. B., & Huang, W. (2014). Collaborating with people like me: Ethnic co-authorship within the US (N0. W19905). *National Bureau of Economic Research*. Retrieved from www.nber.org/papers/w19905.pdf

Gasman, M. (2016). *Academics going public: How to write and speak beyond academe*. New York, NY: Routledge, Taylor & Francis.

Hall, D. (2015, April 6). Content with relevant images gets 94% more views. *Social Media Today*. Retrieved from www.socialmediatoday.com/marketing/2015-04-06/content-relevant-images-gets-94-more-views-infographic

Heffron, J. (2011). *The writer's idea book 10th anniversary edition: How to develop great ideas for fiction, nonfiction, poetry, and screenplays*. Ontario, Canada: Writer's Digest Books.

Heller, D. E. (2016). Writing opinion articles. In M. Gasman (Ed.), *Academics going public: How to write and speak beyond academe* (pp. 21–37). New York, NY: Routledge, Taylor & Francis.

Lepore, J. (2013, September 3). The new economy of letters. *The Chronical of Higher Education*. Retrieved from www.chronicle.com/article/The-New-Economy-of-Letters/141291

Lynch, M. (2016, September 23). Should writing for the public count toward tenure? *The Edvocate*. Retrieved from www.theedadvocate.org/writing-public-count-toward-tenure

Madan, C. R. (2015). Every scientist is a memory researcher: Suggestions for making research more memorable. *F1000Research 2015*, *4*(19). doi:10.12688/f1000research.6053.1

Matthews, D. (2016, January 28). High rejection rates by journals 'pointless': Analysis suggests higher selectivity fails to increase journals' impact factors. *Times Higher Education*. Retrieved from www.timeshighereducation.com/news/high-rejection-rates-by-journals-pointless

Merriam-Webster. (2019). *Dictionary: Op-ed*. Retrieved from www.merriam-webster.com/dictionary/op-ed

Routledge. (2017). *Promoting your book*. Retrieved from www.routledge.com/resources/authors/promoting-your-book

Routledge, Taylor & Francis Group. (2017). *Author directions: Navigating your success from PhD to Book: 5 key tips for turning your PhD into a successful monograph*. Boca Raton, FL: CRC Press.

Salazar, R. (2013, May 17). *Top 10 reasons teachers should blog*. Retrieved from www.chicagonow.com/white-rhino/2013/05/top-10-reasons-teachers-should-blog

Simonite, T. (2013, October 22). The decline of Wikipedia. *MIT Technology Review*. Retrieved from www.technologyreview.com/s/520446/the-decline-of-wikipedia

Stein, K. (2016). How to write an influential press release. In M. Gasman (Ed.), *Academics going public: How to write and speak beyond academe* (pp. 105–117). New York, NY: Routledge, Taylor & Francis.

Stewart, D. (2016). Crafting an online scholarly identity. In M. Gasman (Ed.), *Academics going public: How to write and speak beyond academe* (pp. 71–85). New York, NY: Routledge, Taylor & Francis.

Tennant, J. P., Waldner, F., Jacques, D. C., Masuzzo, P., Collister, L. B., & Hartgerink, C. H. J. (2016). The academic, economic and societal impacts of open access: An evidence-based review. *F1000Research*, *5*(632). doi:10.12688/f1000research.8460.3

U.K. Department for Exiting the European Union. (2018, July). *The future relationship between the United Kingdom and the European Union*. London, United Kingdom: HM Government.

Wagner, C., Garcia, D., Jadidi, M., & Strohmaier, M. (2015). *It's a man's Wikipedia? Assessing gender inequality in an online encyclopedia*. https://arxiv.org/abs/1501.06307.

Waisanen, D. (2018). *Education as a civic marketplace: The political rhetoric of Arne Duncan*. Paper presented at the 2018 Annual Meeting of the American Educational Research Association, New York, NY.

Walters, W. H. (2017, October 9). Citation-based journal rankings: Key questions, metrics, and data sources. *IEEE Access*. doi:10.1109/ACCESS.2017.2761400

Wilson, J. (Ed.). (2012). Peer review: The nuts and bolts. *Standing up for Science*, *3*. Retrieved from http://senseaboutscience.org/activities/peer-review-the-nuts-and-bolts

Chapter 6

Writing Books

Theodor Geisel believed the *Dick and Jane* early reading books actually turned kids off to reading because they were so boring. Instead of writing a paper on the books' failings, which might have reached a handful of scholars, he simply wrote a better book, which nearly everyone we know has read: *The Cat in the Hat*, under the pen name Dr. Seuss.

Geisel said, "I have great pride in taking *Dick and Jane* out of most school libraries. That is my greatest satisfaction" (Conradt, 2018, p. 3). The monumental and sustained success of *The Cat in the Hat*—far exceeding that of *Dick and Jane*—suggests that Geisel made an important contribution to turning children into readers.

Is there a topic you see being mishandled by current field literature or a crucial book that doesn't yet exist? Are you someone who could write a book that has a positive impact on your field and our world? If so, write one.

A book's length allows you to dive deeper into topics, explain them more thoroughly, and share more knowledge than shorter formats allow. This gives you an opportunity to educate readers in impactful ways.

Contrary to popular opinion, you do not need to "know people" in high places to land a book deal. I set out to publish my first book without any special introductions or contacts. I simply noted which publisher's books I most respected, looked up the publisher's author submission guidelines online, and mailed in my chapters and proposals. This approach worked for me, and it can work for you, too (but keep reading for a Scrappy Fast Track alternative that increases your odds).

If you do know an editor, definitely approach her about your submission plans, but do not fret if you do not know anyone on the inside. Even now, after my first book has been published and I have an editor, my proposals and manuscripts still have to pass peer review, the publisher's marketing team, and its editorial board. No matter your veteran status in publishing, the most important determinants in your publication are your book proposal and manuscript quality.

This chapter will help you craft a good book, and it will also help you get published. Do not miss the Scrappy Fast Track in Chapter 4, "Write Anything." It contains a formula I have shared with friends, who used it to immediately achieve book publishing success (far faster than they thought possible) with prominent publishers. If you craft a well-written book that amply meets readers' needs, you can be a published book author, too.

HOW THIS CHAPTER WORKS

(You Need Chapter 4)

Chapter 4 provided you with the fundamental guidelines that apply to all writing opportunities described in this book. The writing guidelines provided in this chapter are supplemental and are meant to be considered *with* the guidelines in Chapter 4.

LIST OF BOOK PUBLISHERS

LIST OF BOOK PUBLISHERS

This book lists nearly one hundred book publishers for you in an electronic file that makes it easy to find and pursue academic book authoring opportunities. You can sort the list by publisher type, visit each website with a simple click, and add additional publishers that are specific to your research area and work. The list contains details like publisher websites, categories, and manipulation-friendly fields you can use to track your manuscript and proposal submissions. See the "eResources" section near the start of this book for details on accessing and using this "List of Book Publishers".

BOOK CHAPTERS

You might opt to write a chapter in a book, rather than an entire book. I recommend doing this even if you ultimately want to write a full-length book, as the "published author" status and perks that come with writing a book chapter will ultimately help your full-length book proposal be accepted.

These opportunities are listed as "Book Chapter" in the "Category" column of the "List of Writing Opportunities" eResource (discussed in Chapter 5). One example of these prospects is IGI Global's "Call for Chapter" site (www.igi-global. com/publish/call-for-papers/?dt=book-chapters), where you can find a topic that matches yours and submit a chapter for consideration. Most book chapter opportunities involve scholarly writing and are equivalent in style and length to a journal paper. The "Journals" section of the previous chapter can help you craft these.

However, authors are sometimes invited to write single chapters that are gathered as a collection in a less-formal practitioner book. Consulting Chapter 10 and putting the word out that you want to author books and chapters can expose you to these opportunities.

Writing a single chapter establishes you as an author, even if you still have not written a full-length book. When the book is published, you will officially be a published author and can likely set up an Amazon.com author page and so forth. The "Exposure for Your Books" section of Chapter 11 also applies to your book chapter.

WRITING BOOKS

If you search Amazon.com, the world's biggest online bookseller (Rushton, 2017; Williams, 2018), for texts within your study area or field, you will likely see a demand for scholarly books as well as a niche you can enhance. Your book can join these to shape readers' understanding of important topics.

As the Scrappy Fast Track in Chapter 4 shows, publishing is not the unattainable pipe dream many assume. I meet many researchers who aspire to this goal. Being a strong writer is immensely helpful in this endeavor, but those who are not can grow (pursuing and perfecting short-form writing will help), co-author, or enlist editorial services in order to overcome this hurdle.

Your message could be well-suited to a book if

- Your message is not well communicated by available books (you say something no one else is saying, or say something in a way no one else is saying it), and
- There is a strong *need* for your book.

Note I say "need" rather than "demand," as sometimes stakeholders do not know they need a book until one is written and brought to their attention.

Most of what you learned in Chapter 4 can be applied to a book. However, there are additional considerations for this long-form project (described later), which should be read before writing a book.

Picking a Publisher

It is a good idea to determine your most desired publisher before writing your book (or at least very early in the book writing process, such as after you have crafted a few sections to better understand what kind of book you will write). Though this decision may change as you develop your initial chapters, identifying a likely publisher is necessary to write a book proposal you are likely to use when your chapters are ready for submission.

See the "List of Book Publishers" eResource mentioned earlier for publishers that produce quality academic books. When finding a publisher that is right for you, it can also help to:

- Check who published your favorite books in your area of specialization.
- Visit the publishers' section of a large research conference. This allows you to roam from one publishing house to the next while viewing their latest offerings, chatting with their editors and marketing leads, and sometimes meeting recent authors.
- Present at conferences your desired editors likely attend. "Editors on the lookout for manuscripts become fixtures at academic conferences, and monitor the voices behind conference papers" (Alexander, 2011, p. 1). When I taught a course on my last book's topic at a conference, an editor of an Ivy League university press reached out to me and asked if I would be interested in turning the class into a book (I already planned to publish that book with my current publisher, but if not I would have pursued the other editor's offer). If I had never taught that course, that editor might not have discovered me.
- Consider which publishers sponsor your favorite events and endeavors related to your topic. Knowing Routledge/Taylor and Francis (the publisher of this book) is often the main sponsor of research conferences I admire is one of the many reasons it appeals to me.

TRADITIONAL PUBLISHING VS. SELF-PUBLISHING

Some authors opt to self-publish their books, which means they get their books printed and sold without the involvement of a traditional publishing house. Though self-publishing offers the author a greater share of the book proceeds, a traditional publisher

- Uses more processes (like peer review, editor feedback, and copyediting) that improve the quality of your work;
- Lends credibility to your work (this helps others accept your ideas);
- Uses its own channels to sell your book (this reaches readers you would not reach on your own); and
- Can open doors to sharing opportunities, such as a radio interview in which you discuss your book.

For these reasons, I have always used the traditional publishing route and recommend this route to others.

- Talk to authors you know about their book publishing experiences. If they have editors who could be appropriate matches for your work, ask if an introduction is possible. Editors are more likely to view your project through the lens of possibility if someone they respect has introduced you to them, as opposed to your submission arriving as a stranger's project.
- Look for a publishing house that subjects all potential projects to a rigorous peer review process. Although this might sound counterproductive, this criterion will help you weed out publishing houses with weaker reputations and will also expose you to quality feedback that will improve your work. Your field's acceptance of what you write will be strongly influenced by the reputation of your publisher. As author Martin McQuillan (2014) noted, "In general, the more peer review that your manuscript is subject to, the better it will be. You should immediately be suspicious of a publisher with no peer review process" (p. 3).

Submission Process (Know Before You Write)

The publisher's book submission guidelines will tell you how many chapters you will need to provide up front for an editor's consideration and, if she is interested in your project, to be peer reviewed (a process defined in Chapter 10). Most publishers will want to see only *some* finished chapters (usually the introductory chapter and one or two others that need not be consecutive), as well as a book proposal (which includes descriptions of all chapters) before deciding to publish your book.

Can you imagine laboring over an entire book, only to discover at submission time that you only needed to submit one chapter? I can, because I completed my first two books in their entirety (a related set) before submitting them, simply because I was ignorant about how publishers worked. The good news is that the more complete your entire book is, the better you are able to describe all chapters in the book proposal.

A happy medium is to work on the book until you have a good sense of its direction and can finalize the one to three chapters your publisher will request. While the editors consider your project, and then while the book is being peer reviewed (which can take months), and then while your editor takes a successful submission before his marketing team and editorial board for its final approval . . . you can plug away at finishing the book in the meantime. Even if your book is ultimately rejected, your chapters and proposal will be more refined in case you need to submit elsewhere.

Writing the Book Proposal

Remember "Find Your Message," "Craft Your Pitch," "Craft Talking Points," and "Consider Packaging" from Chapter 3. To write a good book proposal, you first need to identify the core message and purpose of your book, know how to best pitch it, and consider talking points and how you will package concepts (for example, *Never Enough* by Judith Grisel approaches addiction differently than *Dopesick: Dealers, Doctors, and the Drug Company that Addicted America* by Beth Macy).

SCRAPPY TIP

When you list (on your book proposal) already-published manuscripts that are similar to your proposed book, put these in a table where each book has its own row. Then create a column to the right where, for every one of these books, you explain what that book does not provide that your book will. This way those reading your book proposal will not wonder if one of these books already has your project covered.

Start to write a book proposal at the onset of (or very early in) the book writing process. Beginning the proposal this early in the game will help you solidify the audience you are writing for, what your purpose is, what hole in the market you are filling, and so on. For example, a common proposal requirement is to list similar books and describe how your book will differ from these. Can you imagine writing a book without doing this first, only to discover afterwards that someone else has already written and published the book you thought was so original? Answering a book proposal's questions (as best you can) prior to writing will help you avoid missteps and focus your writing.

Reference the proposal requirements (often in an "Author Guidelines" section) on your publisher's website to use the template or specifications provided. The book proposal is typically a list of questions you answer about your intended book. It is OK to go back and forth between crafting the proposal and crafting your book, as your intentions might change as the manuscript develops.

Of course, you will thoroughly perfect the book proposal once your initial book chapters are finalized for submission to a publisher. See Routledge, Taylor & Francis Group (2017) at www.crcpress.com/rsc/downloads/r3-lr_GVCMG1712_Book_Proposal_SS.pdf for a free, online guide that will help you perfect your proposal.

SCRAPPY TIP

If you know a well-known expert in the field who is willing to write a foreword for your book, mention this in your book proposal. This could enhance your credibility in the editors' and reviewers' eyes.

Writing the Book

Just as Chapter 4 covers the need to create a template ahead of time, you will want to create a template for your book. Using a program like Microsoft Word, create an outline (such as listing topics that will become chapters and sections within chapters) based on what you planned in the book proposal. You can then gradually turn that outline into your book as you flesh out each chapter.

Add the title, preface, introduction, author bio, and back cover content at this stage (pasting and reworking content from your book proposal will help). Look at a book like this for a sense of what goes into these parts.

For articles and other short-form writing you will dream up packaging (ways to explain concepts) and magic (such as stories that hook the reader) before you outline. For a book you will craft these throughout each chapter, especially as you introduce or explain new concepts. Table 4.1's magic examples in Chapter 4 can help. As you work, try to keep each chapter roughly the same length, and rearrange content as necessary to ensure concepts are categorized logically and follow a smooth flow.

It is common for publishers to want a reference list at the end of every chapter (rather than all references at the book's end). This allows your publisher to sell individual chapters through academic outlets as an additional source of revenue and reaches readers who will not buy the whole book.

SCRAPPY TIP

Scholarly publishers like a book to serve multiple functions. This increases revenue but also furthers the book's impact. Consider how your book can be read by a single individual, or by a group as part of a book study, or as an accompaniment to professional development (which can incorporate within-book exercises), or by students in college courses. Write your book (and its proposal) with multiple functions in mind.

The recommendation two chapters ago to consider formatting options becomes especially vital for books. Page after page of identical-looking paragraphs can make concepts run together and make key takeaways easy to miss. Consider how headings, subheadings, small text boxes (with tips, definitions, quotes, etc.), bigger text boxes (with case studies, resource lists, vignettes from other experts, etc.), reflection exercises (throughout or ending each chapter), bullets, checkboxes, and more can help you organize material in digestible ways. Also consider how ancillary resources such as downloadable eResources, self-assessments (for one book, I used the free tools Google Forms and Flubaroo to create assessments that emailed results directly to the taker upon completion), courses, and other tools can support readers.

Strategies in the previous two chapters will help with the rest of your writing endeavor. Revisiting academic books you like will give you countless samples of ways to convey ideas.

Contract

Regularly reference your book proposal and contract with your publisher. What did these say about your intended audience, special features, word count, and the like? You do not want to complete your book only to realize it does not fulfill the promise you made to your publisher. If you have not yet secured a publisher, refer to the notes you made in the previous "Writing the Book Proposal" section concerning the intended nature of your book.

Keywords

In addition to your manuscript, your publisher will likely collect keywords and abstracts or descriptions on each chapter you have written. This information will become metadata, which helps online search tools locate your work for appropriate users. See the "Search Engine Optimization" subsection of Chapter 11 to select keywords for your title, abstract or chapter descriptions, and images that make your work show up high on the list when someone Googles related terms.

BOOK EDITOR

Just as you can submit a book proposal for a book you write yourself, you can also propose a book you edit, which contains chapters from different authors. Some of the best books offer chapters from different experts. Gasman's (2016) *Academics Going Public: How to Write and Speak Beyond Academe* is one example.

Editors of collected works typically contribute the preface, introduction, and a single chapter, so you still have the chance to write. Though options abound, one academic book publisher that has expansive reach and allows you to get very specific with your topic is IGI Global (www.igi-global.com/publish/submit-a-proposal). The tips provided earlier in this chapter regarding the submission process and writing the book proposal can be applied to book editor projects, as well.

BOOK REVIEWS

You are likely reading books for your own professional development and study anyway, so why not review them? Rita Platt (graduate course instructor) writes book reviews for MiddleWeb (www.middleweb.com). By doing so, she helps readers in her field and as a bonus, this increases her exposure, which compliments her work as an educational consultant.

If you plan to read a book anyway, committing to reviewing can earn you a free copy and cause you to learn the content more deeply as you craft your response. If you want to review books, check publication pages (the front of a magazine where editorial details are listed in tiny print, or at the end of a book review section) for details on becoming a reviewer, search publication emails and websites for review guidelines, or contact a publication's book review editor to express your interest, succinctly convey your area of expertise, and attach your CV and (if available) a previously published book review. The magazine *Science* (https://blogs.sciencemag.org/books/about-the-editor) exemplifies practitioner-friendly venues that offer clear guidelines for potential reviewers. For other sites on the "List of Writing Opportunities" eResource, like edCircuit (www.edcircuit.com), you will know they accept book reviews when you see reviews on their sites.

Book reviews are not only for practitioner audiences. Journals publish reviews of scholarly texts (books, essays, etc.), and they often actively recruit reviewers. If you want to review books for a journal, check journal pages (in the front and back, as well as the pages housing its current book reviews) for details on book review submission, search journal emails and websites for invitations to review, or contact a journal's book review editor to express your interest in the same manner described earlier. *Coaching: An International Journal of Theory, Research and Practice* (www.tandfonline.com/doi/full/10.1080/17521882.2017.12819 83) and *The Journal of Politics* (www.journals.uchicago.edu/journals/jop/book-reviews) exemplify journals that offer clear guidelines for potential reviewers.

PUT PARTS TOGETHER

Chapter 4 provided guidance to write well. This chapter provided added tips, as well as multiple opportunities to share your studies through a book. Select a publisher (use the "List of Book Publishers" eResource for suggestions) to which you will submit chapters. Then complete Exercise 6.1 to plan your submission. Reference sections in this chapter and Chapter 4 as you complete the exercise.

EXERCISE 6.1: BOOK WRITING PLAN

1. What kind of book will you be writing?
   - Practitioner-Friendly
   - Academic (e.g., monograph)
   - Other (Describe)
2. To which publication will you submit your manuscript?

3. Read the publication's submission guidelines. What is the specified chapter number, formatting, title length, and so on?

4. Who is your audience? This can be one main reader or a few key groups.

5. What is your key purpose (what does your audience need from you)?

6. What primary message will run through the entire book?

7. What new understanding will your audience gain from your book?

8. What will your audience be able to do after reading your book?

9. Complete as much of publisher's book proposal template as you can. What additional details did you establish (similar books already out, your core message, etc.)?

10. Describe what your style will be (humorous, casual, formal, etc.).

11. What will your book's title be?

12. What magic will you use to make some concepts resonate? Remember Table 4.2.

13. Create a template and use it to outline your book. Then add to each chapter, gradually turning your template into a complete draft. When your publisher's required number of chapters are complete, apply the next two steps to those chapters.

14. Proof and revise your chapters as necessary. Ensure your chapters meet submission requirements and criteria described in this chapter and Chapter 4 (communicates your core message, is very clear, does not overload your reader, etc.).

15. Return to your book proposal. Complete and rework your book proposal until it reflects your finished chapters and the book they occupy. You might make changes to your chapters based on your proposal answers, as well.

16. Submit your work. Follow the publisher's submission guidelines carefully. Simultaneous submissions (submitting to more than one publisher simultaneously) are discouraged and some publishers prohibit them.

REFERENCES

Alexander, P. H. (2011, October 17). The less-obvious elements of an effective book proposal. *The Chronical of Higher Education*. Retrieved from www.chronicle.com/article/The-Less-Obvious-Elements-of/129361

Conradt, S. (2018, March 2). The stories behind 10 Dr. Seuss books. *Mental Floss*. Retrieved from http://mentalfloss.com/article/28843/stories-behind-10-dr-seuss-books

Gasman, M. (2016). *Academics going public: How to write and speak beyond academe*. New York, NY: Routledge, Taylor & Francis.

McQuillan, M. (2014, March 6). 10 point guide to dodging publishing pitfalls: Veteran academic authors share their hard-won tips. *Times Higher Education*. Retrieved from www.timeshighereducation.com/features/10-point-guide-to-dodging-publishing-pitfalls/2011808.article

Routledge, Taylor & Francis Group. (2017). *Author directions: Navigating your success in book proposals: Key tips on how to write a successful book proposal*. Boca Raton, FL: CRC Press.

Rushton, K. (2017, September 1). Cut your prices to 99p like we do to sell more books, Amazon tells publishers as furious row erupts. *Daily Mail*. Retrieved from www.dailymail.co.uk/news/article-4845838/Cut-prices-99p-like-Amazon-tells-shops.html

Williams, M. (2018, January 5). Retail apocalypse or retail evolution? Publishers need to help Barnes & Noble evolve—or join it in extinction. *The New Publishing Standard*. Retrieved from www.thenewpublishingstandard.com/retail-apocalypse-or-retail-evolution-publishers-need-to-help-barnes-noble-evolve-or-join-it-in-extinction

Part III

Speaking

Chapter 7

Speaking Anywhere

I am going to tell you something you might not want to hear: you ought to speak (in the formal presentation sense). Even if you are only interested in writing, speaking is a powerful way for your written work to proliferate. For example, when it comes to spreading your discoveries, let us suppose you are only interested in writing books. In that case, speaking engagements would

- Expose you and your work to a wider audience,
- Lead to keynotes that can culminate in book signings,
- Increase your credibility, and
- Expose you to new people (which brings more opportunities for writing and more).

. . . all of which means more book sales, which means more people impacted by your work.

Speaking allows your research to help more people. Conferences, TED Talks, media interviews, podcasts . . . there are many venues through which you can talk about your work. If travel is a problem, you can even present at online conferences from the comfort of your home. While speaking opportunities allow you to share, these occasions also offer chances to connect with other changemakers and to form relationships that open even more doors for sharing your findings with the world.

HOW THIS CHAPTER WORKS

(You Need it for the Next Two Chapters)

As with the earlier "Writing Anything" chapter, this chapter's title "Speaking Anywhere" is hyperbolic: it means this chapter will provide you with the fundamental guidelines that apply to all speaking opportunities described in this book. The subsequent chapters in this "Speaking" part of the book will offer slide help, as well as additional guidelines specific only to certain types of speaking (such as how to plan a TED Talk), but this chapter here will give you the basics you need for speaking at varied venues. Though this chapter is broken into subsections ("Before Presenting Anything," "While Presenting Anything," etc.), it is most beneficial to read the entire chapter before your next writing project and then return to it throughout your writing endeavors.

This chapter and the next contain no exercises. Instead, Chapter 8 and Chapter 9 feature exercises where you can apply what you learn in this chapter and the next, combined with what you learn in those chapters. Those chapters will also lead you to choose events to present at, which you will want to have in mind as you consider your audience, purpose, and other aspects introduced in this chapter.

SCRAPPY FAST TRACK

If you want to skyrocket quickly to speaking to thousands (like if you have no notable speaking experience but are anxious to do keynotes or give a TED Talk), I recommend you use the information in the "Speaking" chapters of this book (including their eResources to find opportunities) to take this route:

Step 1. Apply to speak at many online conferences. As this chapter explains, online conferences are an easy way for beginners to gain speaking experience and obtain recordings of their sessions (required when applying to give a TED Talk).

Step 2. Perfect your slide designs and delivery (covered in the next chapter) and present for at least five live events. At home you can videotape and then watch yourself deliver many speeches to speed up your progress. Also work on your branding (covered in Chapter 2) so the specific expertise you offer is clear. If you produced a resource that captures this expertise (like a book, journal article, etc.) highlight this in your communications, since people selecting speakers like to know they can say things like, "The author of . . ." when announcing and introducing you.

Step 3. Apply to give a TED Talk. If you are familiar with TED Talks and their noteworthy reputation, you might be taken aback by the notion you should apply to give one if you are not yet an icon in your field. In this book I encourage you to be scrappy and aim high. Doing a TED Talk – something that carries mainstream clout – will open countless doors for you. So why not try to give one? As this book covers, there are many TED and TEDx opportunities just waiting for you to apply. When you do, use your online conference recording links whenever an application requests a live recording (unless you have live recordings that show you presenting).

Step 4. Make your TED or TEDx experience obvious to anyone visiting your social media sites, reading your email signature, visiting your website, or reading your CV or bio. If you have another impressive accomplishment, like a bestselling book or appearance on *BBC World News*, that can be used instead (or in addition).

Step 5. Follow the tips in the "Conference Keynote" section to start booking keynotes/plenaries. There are additional scrappy tips in that section.

BEFORE SPEAKING ANYWHERE

Have you ever dressed inappropriately? Maybe you wore a sweater and wool pants without checking the weather forecast, only to spend the day sweltering under a surprisingly sunny sky. Or maybe you wore your rattiest jeans to meet your new partner, only to learn you would also be meeting her family that day. Not determining the conditions and purpose of a situation can lead to discomfort, embarrassment, and a missed opportunity.

The same is true of speaking. Considering your audience, circumstances, and submission norms up-front will help you select words and shape your presentation so that it best meets your audience's and venue's needs, as well as your own.

Determine Circumstances

Considering the circumstances of your speaking venue will help you know the speaking waters you are about to sail so that you can plan accordingly. Is the purpose of the event to get practitioners and researchers to collaborate? Is the conference theme "Advancing Knowledge in the Age of Fake News?" Venue aspects such as these will shape what you propose to present. Identify any venue aspects your presentation should reflect.

Consider Your Audience

Revisit the "Consider Your Audience" section in Chapter 4 to consider aspects of your likely audience. If you have a highly mixed audience, try to determine main groups, and plan to relate your recommendations and examples to them all or else cater to each at different times (based on what will be most effective). Also revisit that section's text box to identify strategies for targeting resistance to your message, for such reasons as political persuasion or religious beliefs.

Determine Purpose

Now that you know your audience, determine your purpose in presenting something. Detailing your purpose will help you frame your message and your plan to provide listeners with what they need, such as information to act upon what they learn about a problem that the audience struggles to solve. This purpose will line you up to. . .

Determine Message

What is the main finding, fact, idea, strategy, perspective, or other "thing" you want to share? This message is sometimes referred to as a thread or a through line: a connecting theme that runs through the entire work. This could be your main message as a researcher (the one you identified in Chapter 3), but make any adjustments that will make a particular speech suited to your audience and purpose.

Finesse Your Title

The title and description must capture viewers' attention, make them want to watch your presentation, and capture the nature of the presentation. Concepts you learned in the "Before Writing Anything: Draft a Title" section of Chapter 4 also apply here.

An unexpected title is far more gripping that the usual headings you hear in academia. For example, I attended a symposium presentation by Kandice Sumner on race. Sumner could have titled her session "The Role That Race Plays in the Institutions that Guide Our Daily Lives" (a line from the session's description).

But that title would have communicated, "This session will have boring bulleted slides and boring delivery, because its title is so bland" . . . whereas Sumner's presentation was anything but bland.

Instead, Sumner wisely titled her session "Race and Other 4-Letter Words." That title gets attendees' attention. It stands out. It says, "I am a different kind of session. I will not mince words—I will shoot straight for what needs to be said."

Note Sumner was able to be efficient with her word use because this title built on what people already know. Remember the "Consider Packaging: Description" section in Chapter 3 about tapping into people's preexisting knowledge (example: a pomelo is like a supersized grapefruit). People have an immediate association with the term "4-Letter Words." That association carries a strong, negative emotion with it (you might utter a four-letter word when you stub your toe or get dangerously cut off in traffic). By tapping into people's pre-existing association, Sumner's title stirred up all that emotion and meaning with a single term. Emotion is memorable and draws people in, as it did for Sumner's standing-room-only presentation.

Berger (2013) found concepts are more likely to spread (meaning people will tell others about them) when they provoke arousal emotions like awe, amusement, excitement, anxiety, or anger. See the "Acceptance" section of Chapter 8 for more tips.

Finesse Your Description

Like the title, your description should capture viewers' attention, make them want to attend your presentation, and capture its nature. In addition, communicate how the session will transform attendees in a valuable way (such as through action-oriented objectives). See the "Acceptance" section of Chapter 8 for more guidance.

Determine Solutions to Share

If you share problems, also share solutions. This can mean listeners learn how to apply (or about) specific strategies to combat the problem, what causes the problem, leading theories on solutions, recommendations for future research, or what stakeholders should not do.

For example, your presentation on "The Roots of Human Trafficking" might begin with stories and statistics that further the audience's understanding of how pervasive slavery continues to be. However, your audience should not leave your presentation merely understanding that human trafficking is a problem that must be overcome. Rather, your audience should leave your presentation knowing specific strategies to combat modern-day slavery, or leading theories on solutions, or different organizations' approaches to solving the problem, or recommendations for future research that can inform solutions, or other ways in which your audience can act.

Plan to Prime the Audience

Priming is an aspect of behavioral economics, which is essentially how our brains strive to make decisions efficiently. Priming involves exposing people to something to trigger specific thoughts and attitudes. For example, people vote significantly more in favor of increased school funding when their voting booths are located in schools, because the schools prime the voters to think and care about schools (Kahneman, 2011).

Exposing an audience to something multiple times also makes information easier to process and accept (Kahneman, 2011), so grounding an audience in the core of your topic from the beginning of your presentation helps prime them to care. Too often we launch into tips, statistics, or research methods without ever acknowledging the very personal story (and value) behind what we have to share. See the "Story" example in Table 7.1 for a story I tell to ground the audience.

Table 7.1 Ways to Insert Magic into Your Speaking

Magic/Hook	Example
Activity *More activity* *examples are* *provided in the* *"Specific Slide* *Types" section* *of the "Guide to* *Slide Design"* *eResource.* .	When I delivered a keynote segment on collaboration, there were over 1,000 attendees and thus not much room to maneuver. However, audience involvement is always possible. I had all audience members stand and face their chairs. I then gave them this series of directions: "As long as it will not physically hurt you, please lift your chair off the ground." Attendees lifted their chairs with ease. "Please put it down but keep standing." "If you are someone who struggles with getting everything done that you want to get done, put one hand behind your back and keep it there." "If there is anything that a colleague is better at than you, put your other hand behind your back and keep it there." "If some days, you are just tired, or feel overworked, lift one leg off the floor and leave it there." "Now, lift your chair." At this point the audience laughed as some struggled to lift chairs with only one of four limbs free. As I invited them to sit again, I asked, "Was it easier to lift before, when we had the use of numerous limbs instead of just one?" The audience called out, "Yes!" I then said, "Somebody tell me, what does this exercise teach us about collaboration?" The responses (such as, "The help of many makes a job easier") provided a perfect introduction to my segment on collaboration, as audience members were fully aware of how important collaboration would be to their jobs. Engaging attendees' bodies adds to lessons' tangibility and memorability.

(Continued)

Table 7.1 Continued

Magic/Hook	Example
Analogy, Metaphor, or Simile	Anyone who watched American TV in 1987 likely remembers the Partnership for a Drug-Free America commercial displaying a close-up of an egg dropped into a frying pan. This is accompanied by a voice-over saying, "This is drugs. This is your brain on drugs. Any questions?" (Rossen, 2017, p. 2). Everyone has a brain, which makes the metaphor personal for all viewers. Whether someone uses drugs or not, and whether someone approves of the ad or not, seeing one's brain being fried is a visceral experience that is hard to forget. The metaphor says much, yet in few words. Analogies and similes can also strengthen a delivery.
Contrast	When I gave a Talk at TEDxTUM on the need to make data easy to use, I told three stories in succession. First, I told how Dr. John Snow ended a cholera outbreak by successfully mapping where deaths occurred (deaths were concentrated around a water pump until its handle was removed). Next, I told how Florence Nightingale used polar area diagrams to convince Britain to fund better health care conditions during the Crimean War, attributed to the drop in the death rate of Allied troops from 42% to 2%. My third story, however, provided contrast. I told of how the Challenger Space Shuttle exploded, killing all crew members, yet many data visualization experts believe the tragedy would have been avoided if the graphs used prior to launch were better designed.

In all three instances, I showed the data visualizations used, and in the case of Challenger I showed how simple improvements to a graph would have made the explosion's culprit (a cold launch temperature) immediately apparent and would have changed the launch decision. Contrasting how good data visualization saved lives with how poor data visualization likely lost lives demonstrated the importance of the topic and the importance of the research-based recommendations I was about to share. |
| Demonstration | To teach a class the meaning of *cultural literacy*, Eng (2017) started calling on students to answer sports questions. He asked things like, "What's the team's overall field goal percentage?" and used terms like "jumper" and "offensive rebounds" (p. 31). He then asked the class if anyone there didn't follow sports, to which 25% raised their hands, and asked if they understood the conversation, which they did not. Eng asked, "But how can that be? We *were* speaking English, no?" (p. 31).

Eng had provided the audience with an experience that enabled them to understand how a lack of familiarity with cultural content prevents one from understanding and assimilating in the culture. This demonstration launched the class into discussing a topic that was now more personal and tangible. |

(*Continued*)

Table 7.1 Continued

Magic/Hook	Example
Example	Alda (2017) described how difficult he found it to explain the complex physics concept of particles, then shared how physicist Brian Greene did so expertly: "If you cut a loaf of bread in half, and then take one of the halves and cut that in half, and keep doing that, eventually you'll get down to the smallest bit possible. That's a particle." (p. 64).
	Centering this example on bread, which everyone is familiar with, makes even an intimidating concept like physics relatable. The example would also lend itself well to prop use during a presentation.
Fable or Parable	Coggins (2017) told of how Larry Cuban used the parable of the blind men and the elephant to introduce a lesson on policy:
	A group of blind men seek to learn about an elephant, but each one touches a different part. One feels the smooth, hard ivory tusk; another a pliable, wrinkly knee; a third man feels the heat and moisture at the end of the trunk; and yet another feels the big wall of the belly. When they describe what they feel, it is clear that they are having completely different experiences. There is no question that each of them is feeling what a real elephant feels like, but their own realities make it hard for them to understand the others' experience of the same elephant. I've never found a better analogy to explain education policy and the complexity of getting the different parts of the system to speak to one another (p. 22).
	The parable allows us to understand—in a way a mere statement like this would not achieve on its own—how people's own realities are concrete and difficult to augment.
Grouping	When most people present on how to improve data use, they focus solely on how to improve the data user (such as through training) or the climate surrounding users (such as through improved leadership). The tool used to view data is rarely addressed in some fields, and attendees could thus have a preconceived notion that the tool has little bearing on data use.
	To avoid this attitude (which could reduce audience attention to what I say about electronic data systems), I start one segment of my presentation by dividing the audience into two teams (an aisle down the middle makes this easy). I tell attendees to imagine their teams are going to race each other on the racetrack.
	I tell them, "You all take the same driving classes and thus receive the same training. You all have identical driving coaches and pit crews and thus have the same leadership and support. You start your engines. The gun fires and you start to drive. This team is driving a Lamborghini [slide shows gorgeous sports car], and this other team is driving my first car ever [slide shows 1973 Volkswagen Bus]. Who wins?"

(*Continued*)

Table 7.1 Continued

Magic/Hook	Example
	Laughter and shouts about the winning Lamborghini follow. "But they received the same great training," I say. "But they have the same leadership and support," I continue. The audience shouts that it doesn't matter. "So, you are saying the car makes a difference? In other words, the *tool* you use—regardless of how great your training or support is—makes a *massive* difference." Now I am ready to talk about needed improvements and components to the data systems people use to work with data, and my audience is ready to understand.
Humor	At the start of my AERA course on how to best share one's research, I stand behind the lectern and read (in monotone) an unattractive slide crammed with confusing research jargon. My audience starts giggling as they gradually catch on: I am demonstrating the bad speaking style seen too often in conference sessions. By the time I say, "Just kidding," attendees are amused, relieved I will not be teaching that way, and thinking about the impact of the course's topic.
Modeling	When sharing research on trauma, Kelly Knoche explained Dan Siegel's Hand Model of the Brain. Knoche could have simply held up her own hand in this model of how the brain stem (palm), limbic area (thumb, folded in), and cortex (fingers folding over thumb, operating as a higher part of the brain) function together, and what happens to these brain areas when we experience trauma (fingers flying back up). Knoche did use her own hand as a model, but she had all audience members raise their own hands and move their fingers as she did while following along with the explanation. This made the content more concrete. We remained seated, yet we were physically (and thus more mentally) engaged. Concepts are more understandable and memorable when they are concrete (such as based on easy-to-visualize images) (Heath & Heath, 2008).
Mystery	In studying the best ways to cover a course curriculum, Cialdini (2005) found the most frequent approach (describing phenomena) to be the least effective, asking students questions about the phenomena to be more effective, but generating mystery stories for students to solve (through an understanding of the phenomena) to be most effective because this spurs listeners to explain processes themselves. This approach can be successfully adapted for other presentations as well.
	For example, rather than begin a speech with study findings, or by a mere statement of the problem, you can introduce the problem as a mystery. What was happening that you could not initially understand? What solutions did you try that failed? Put the audience in your shoes to discover the solution "with" you, having their own guesses and theories along the way. This is an effective way to invest attendees in your topic while communicating its nature.

(*Continued*)

Table 7.1 Continued

Magic/Hook	Example
	Another way to use mystery is to embed lessons (related to your message) along the path to the solution. When I present to parents of gifted children, I need to convey lessons on nurturing their children's creativity, growth mindset, grit, determination, and more. I tell the story of Jack Andraka and his teenage journey to cure pancreatic cancer after the death of a loved one. As the audience experiences the mystery of a quest to cure cancer, I highlight aspects of Jack's journey that involved creativity, growth mindset, determination, and more and his parents' involvement in nurturing such qualities. The audience gets to experience how these traits advance Jack in unlocking various pieces of the pancreatic cancer puzzle. The audience remains hooked, anxious to learn how the mystery is solved, as they learn about nurturing their kids.
Personal Anecdote	Alda (2017) also described how the inventors of the world's thinnest glass needed a way to make their findings resonate with listeners. They needed a better entry point than the speakers would have jumping straight into the findings of their paper: *Direct Imaging of a Two-Dimensional Silica Glass on Graphene* (Huang et al., 2012).
	The nanoscientists learned that telling the story behind their discovery—which happened on accident when an air leak produced what they first mistook for muck—introduced a very human element that made people excited and want to know more (Alda, 2017). A personal anecdote can make content that is complicated and dry more interesting and accessible.
Props	Props can become gimmicky if they do not add to what you are saying, but when used effectively they help viewers remember and connect to your words. Heath and Heath (2008) tell of how UNICEF's director used to speak with rulers of developing countries about dehydration and the best method for saving youth from such deaths: Oral Rehydration Therapy (ORT) to replenish fluids and electrolytes. UNICEF's director would take a packet of salt and sugar (the ORT ingredients) from his pocket and say, "Do you know that this costs less than a cup of tea and it can save hundreds of thousands of children's lives in your country?" (p. 125). Consider how much more effective that statement was—paired with the simple prop—than mere words. If a prop will help you bring your presentation's content to life, consider how you might use it onstage.
Quiz	If you are giving a talk on Angela Duckworth's (2016) research on grit, why not start by giving the crowd the Grit Scale quiz (www.angeladuckworth.com/grit-scale) to assess their own grit? This would connect the topic to attendees' own lives. Throughout the rest of your talk, your listeners would be able to apply your recommendations to their own experiences, making the content more understandable and memorable.

(*Continued*)

Table 7.1 Continued

Magic/Hook	Example
Spontaneity	In a summit talk, Strayhorn (2016) stated his main thesis and three coordinating points, and then ran from the lectern, jumped atop a table, and explained how stakeholders need to work "across the aisle" to address higher education's Black male crisis. Strayhorn found his spontaneity to be an effective speaking tactic that kept the speech alive and injected energy.
Story	When I delivered a keynote with findings that many gifted learners are overlooked, I displayed a photo of a young Black girl named Gail. I detailed Gail's struggles in life (on welfare, abusive and neglectful home life, siblings lost to crime and violence) and in school (labeled a behavior problem, held back in first grade, struggling academically, told she was stupid).
	Then I displayed a photo of a professional Black woman delivering a speech on stage. The photo bore the name Gail Thompson, PhD. I shared that this woman became an esteemed professor, is a tireless advocate for students, writes books that help educators change students' lives, and has won more awards than I can list (when I delivered this same keynote in the Democratic Republic of the Congo, I also included slides of Dr. Thompson serving in the Peace Corps in the Congo).
	I then displayed the young and grown photos of Gail side-by-side and asked my audience, "How did *this* Gail grow up to be *this* Gail? Who made the difference in this child's life?" Many attendees called out, "A teacher!" I displayed a third photo of Gail's 6th-grade teacher. I tell the audience, "This teacher recognized that Gail ... was ..." With my arms extended to the audience, I let the crowd complete my sentence with "gifted!"
	The crowd had just seen how a gifted student can be overlooked, and also how a life (and the world) can be changed when a teacher recognizes and supports a student's giftedness. I then showed statistics reflecting these facts, which would not have resonated as strongly without Gail's story. When I went on to share strategies for engaging gifted students, the audience was invested in the need for such strategies to reach *all* gifted students.
	Stories disarm audiences, who are so caught up in the drama they lack the cognitive resources to resist what you are saying (Berger, 2013). Stories also make concepts more memorable (Heath & Heath, 2008). Just be sure your message is so essential to the story that it cannot be retold without carrying your message with it.

(*Continued*)

Table 7.1 Continued

Magic/Hook	Example
Surprising Statistic or Fascinating Fact	Oliver (2010) opened his TED Talk on diet by saying: Sadly, in the next 18 minutes when I do our chat, four Americans that are alive will be dead through the food that they eat. (0:37) This relatable statistic shocks viewers (emotion that encourages attention, care, and memory) and establishes the seriousness of the issue. Oliver then offers solutions the audience can use. See the "Guide to Slide Design" eResource for help visualizing data. Most attendees are easily overwhelmed by too many numbers, charts, or graphs. Statistics should be selected carefully based on what will best propel your message.
Video	Presenters sometimes show video clips to demonstrate a process they just introduced (like how archaeologists should clean their tools), show their topic in action (like body language similarities between humans and bonobo apes), or capture feedback from study participants. The key is to introduce a concept and show a quick clip, rather than letting a video take your place as the main presenter.
Visualization	A TED-Ed history video begins: Imagine setting sail from Hawaii in a canoe. Your target is a small island thousands of kilometers away in the middle of the Pacific Ocean. That's a body of water that covers more than 160 million square kilometers, *greater than all the landmasses on Earth combined*. For thousands of years, Polynesian navigators managed voyages like this without the help of modern navigational aids. (Tamayose & De Silva, 2017, 0:07) This visualization readies the audience for the information to come. When the narrators explain how Polynesian wayfinders worked, the audience has already been made keenly aware of their feat's magnitude and is eager to discover how it was accomplished.
Voices of Those Involved	Sharing the voices of those your study concerns (such as LGBT+ gang members or freedom fighters in Eritrea), as through soundbites, can drive home a message. Viewers can perceive presenters as having ulterior motives. They might think we primarily want our study to be well-received, or we want to sell books and more speaking engagements . . . and thus might exaggerate the merits of whatever we are recommending. Other stakeholders are perceived as trustworthy when they have nothing to gain by simply sharing their experience for someone else's presentation, and they are intimately involved in the topic. This gives these voices a different kind of credibility that helps an audience embrace what is being shared. If you display a clip of a minor, however, get his parent's written permission first.

Table 7.1 Continued

Magic/Hook	Example
Volunteers	Asking for volunteers to join you in an activity related to your topic can be powerful. Attendees tend to connect with what you are doing when they feel "one of their own" is actively involved. Volunteers also add an element of unpredictability that is exciting.
	Near the start of a session I attended on race and bias, the presenter, Kandice Sumner, conducted a Privilege Walk (search for "Privilege Walk" on YouTube to see one for yourself, noting versions vary). Sumner invited seven volunteers to line up at the front of the room. After ensuring participants were comfortable with what would transpire and establishing ground rules, like the need for attendees to remain silent and not judge participants, Sumner read a script for volunteers to follow. Directions included things like, "If you have a parent who graduated from college, take one step forward," and "If you speak English as a second language, take two steps backward."
	It was profound to watch the line of volunteers separate, with distance immediately and steadily growing between volunteers based on innate traits like skin color (and it arguably would have been even more stark if volunteers were not all academics enjoying financial stability, college- and graduate-level degrees, and other perks to which marginalized groups have less access). The exercise helped all attendees sense (albeit not to the extent of those experiencing bias in real life) how marginalized groups face more life obstacles than others. The room was silent and somber at the end of the exercise, forming the perfect moment for Sumner to facilitate discussion on race and bias.

Priming listeners to care about your topic can mean connecting them with your topic's impact on a single someone or something. Even though sharing big-picture statistics is valuable, remember what you learned in Chapter 4 about why charities mail us photos of individual children. Hearing one person's story is far more compelling, memorable, and action-inspiring than merely learning *of* the plight of a single person or group. A highly personal story draws the viewer in and makes him care.

Your own firsthand experiences can be especially powerful, as long as they are clearly tied to your message and your presentation's purpose, but telling stories you learned from others can also work well. Your colleagues, other stakeholders, and literature can offer stories and inspiration.

Consider Packaging

Consider concepts to package the lessons you give listeners. See the "Consider Packaging" section of Chapter 3 for details and inspiration.

Dream Up Magic (Emotion, Stories, and More)

After you have key audience "takeaways" in mind and have considered packaging, do not start outlining just yet. Once you outline your delivery, you end up with a clear game plan. It can then be hard to insert some magic into such a finished product. Spend time devising ways to include magic, as defined in Chapter 4. Recall what you learned there about the Deficit Model not working and the need to frame your message in ways that will overcome audience resistance or apathy.

Magic "wow" moments help audience members connect to your content and are typically the most memorable parts of your presentation. These moments help listeners care about your words and message, and they increase your presentation's impact. If you determine some of these magic moments up front, you can then produce an outline that incorporates them.

These memorable moments most commonly happen at the start of your speech, but they also occur at other points (like a demonstration of a concept). Like their written counterparts, magic elements of a presentation can take a variety of forms. See Table 7.1 for examples of these and more. Use the examples as inspiration for your own presentation.

You will notice in Table 7.1 that magic often takes the form of stories. Embedding stories throughout your speech is a great way to hold the audience's attention and make your message memorable. It is far easier for people to remember stories than facts because the human brain processes experiences we hear about in practically the same way it processes experiences that really happen to us (Gillett, 2014). Since your story will stick with people long after your speech, so will your message (as long as it is captured clearly by the story).

This is especially true if the stories make the audience feel emotion. Emotions make people more likely to care about, remember, tell others about, and act on information. Provoking arousal emotions like awe, amusement, excitement, anxiety, or anger make information particularly spread-worthy (Berger, 2013).

Most of the magic examples in Chapter 4 can also be adapted well for public speaking. You might also revisit the "Consider Packaging" section of Chapter 3 for inspiration; clever packaging of the lessons you present can certainly inject magic into your speech.

You will likely devise additional magic moments during and after outlining your presentation. Throughout the process, stay focused on your message and the best ways to meet audience needs, whether this means adding, removing, or changing the magic moments that will complement your delivery.

Plan to Address Inequity

The next chapter will cover recommendations like showing diversity in your slides and avoiding images that propagate stereotypes, but the words you speak should do something more. Unless you are giving a very short speech (like a TED Talk), there will be room in your presentation to address the equity aspects that impact your topic. Many topics intersect with problems where some populations are underrepresented or underserved, and addressing instances of disparity is part of covering a topic responsibly.

For example, I am often invited to present research concerning the best ways to challenge gifted students. The organizers and audience expect me to launch right into engagement strategies. However, I do not go there until I have addressed the fact that in the U.S., a Black student is half as likely to be labeled "gifted" by his school than a White student when he has *identical achievement scores*. In other words, Black students are just as frequently gifted as White students, yet their giftedness is frequently overlooked by their schools. I share similar statistics involving over-looked English-language learners, Hispanic students, and girls, and an even bleaker outlook for poor children. If I did not first address this disparity and share strategies for overcoming the inequity, then when I talked about engaging and challenging gifted students I would only be helping my audience engage and challenge *some* gifted students, without even knowing they were excluding many others.

In our mission to improve the world with our work, we have a moral respon-sibility to address the many times bias and disparity impact our fields. No matter your topic, I challenge you to find where equity intersects with it. If you do not, you will lose credibility with those in the audience aware of the inequity (who then have to watch you ignore an elephant in the room) and you will miss the chance to inform those in the audience unaware of the inequity. If you struggle in this endeavor, attend sessions related to gender, LGBT+, and racial/ethnic struggles at your next research conference; read related articles; and share your topic with friends whose demographics differ from yours.

Plan to Repeat Main Ideas and Actively Engage the Audience

Since repetition and activities will be reflected in your slides, these topics are covered in the "Guide to Slide Design" eResource (described later).

Create a Template

The first time you plan a speech, you will likely want to write your outline on a single page. However, in time you might want to outline directly with slides (like I do), using the "Slide Sorter" view in PowerPoint to move slides around, adding slides with a simple word or two to finish later, and so on. Either approach lets you play with a framework ahead of time before you delve into each slide's perfection.

If you do want to pull some slides together at this point as a template (such as creating a title slide and some basic section slides), go ahead. The "Guide to Slide Design" eResource will help you.

GUIDE TO SLIDE DESIGN

See the "eResources" section near the start of this book for details on accessing the "Guide to Slide Design". The guide will give you vital guidelines and resources for making slides that will engage and inform your audience.

Outline

See the "Specific Slide Types" section of the "Guide to Slide Design" eResource (described previously) to help plan which slides you will include. If you will speak for more than 15 minutes, it is a good idea to "chunk" your presentation into sub-topic segments, just like the parts and chapters that divide scholarly books.

As you outline, regularly reflect on your audience, message, and other concepts covered earlier in this chapter. When you finish outlining, skim this chapter again to be sure you hit all concepts. For example, does your outline reflect a presentation that will propel your message and meet the audience's needs? If your presentation description claimed attendees will walk away from your session knowing how to recognize arthritis in an ancient skeleton, does your plan provide attendees with the resources and knowledge they will need to accomplish that task? Adjust your outline as necessary, and deviate from it if you notice flaws while perfecting your actual slides and content.

Prepare Content

You may plan your content (examples, stories, bits of magic, etc.) in a number of ways, so pick what works best for you. Just as I outline directly with slides, I also plan my content directly in Microsoft PowerPoint (adding simple headings to slides as placeholders and using slides' "Notes" sections to record ideas on what to say). Some people like to write out all speaking notes in a single document before tackling slides. Others like to add phrases to their outline to remember ideas they plan to share. Do not worry about doing this perfectly, as you will have plenty of time to play, rearrange, and change your approach as you prepare your slides.

At this stage you will accomplish two main things:

- **Prepare compelling and effective slides**. There is a *lot* to know about this task. Read the next chapter, which covers this extensively.

158

- **Prepare an effective handout**. If you are scheduled to present in a "roundtable" format where slides are not used, handouts become especially crucial and can contain visuals you would normally display on slides.

  Your handouts should not be copies of your slides. If you follow the next chapter's recommendations, your slides will be image-heavy and text-sparse in order to complement (rather than replicate) your spoken words. Unless your handout pairs your slide images with written notes on what you said, they will be less helpful than handouts containing information attendees will likely want to reference later.

  Your handout can be a sheet or packet of paper—whatever length is necessary to provide all the web addresses and summaries you want your audience to have. I include any information I imagine my audience would write down during my presentation if I had not done this for them on the handout. If your presentation shares new research findings, visualize key data as an easy-to-interpret graph or infographic. Apply the same design savvy to your handouts about image, branding, and slides as you have learned in this book. Use headings and boxes as necessary to separate types of information and make things easy to find. These visual markers also help if you direct your audience to areas of the handout throughout your presentation.

  Consider physically distributing printed copies (such as a half-sheet that conserves paper), but definitely post your handout online for attendees to access electronically. This makes it easier for attendees to share your work. For example, I house a PDF of my handout beside where I mention the presentation on my website, and I also upload the handout to my session details on the event app when this function is available. In the interest of universal design, I add the following verbiage beside the download link (the "Click Here" link opens a contact form to reach me):

  - If you require another format, such as MS Word or RTF, to be compatible with assistive technologies for readers with impaired vision, please click here to request one.

SAMPLE HANDOUT

See the "eResources" section near the start of this book for details on accessing a handout I have used in the past. Note my handout looks nothing like a copy of slides.

If you follow this book's strategies, particularly from the guide presented here, your slides will be a collection of images, isolated words, and short phrases that will not make much sense without your explanation.

Your handout should package key information you shared in a way that is easy to digest.

As you work, reflect on what was already shared in this chapter. Most of all, do not forget to use magic (discussed earlier) to make your core message and key points accessible, informative, engaging, and memorable to attendees.

Practice

Once your slides are relatively complete you are ready to practice. Stand up, face a mirror (or videotape yourself to view afterwards, such as with your laptop's webcam), speak loudly, and time yourself.

Do not follow a script of pre-written sentences, which results in robotic, boring delivery. Rather, remember enough to recall the concept you are supposed to talk about with each new slide. Then just talk about each of those concepts, from your heart and with passion.

Pay attention to anything that feels "off" in your content, such as:

- Abrupt transitions
- Boring patches
- Timid speech (mitigated speech or excessive upspeak, which makes statements sound like questions)
- Concepts requiring better explanation or illustration
- Lack of magic (see Table 7.1) to make concepts come alive
- Lack of meaningful activities allowing audience to connect to materials
- Primary message getting lost
- Overkill (it is better to be selective about what you communicate than it is to force-feed audience brains)
- Slides not pulling their weight
- Leaving listeners without a way to act on a problem you shared

Adjust your slides as necessary and keep practicing. Read the rest of this chapter so you can practice applying the speaking strategies covered next.

WHILE SPEAKING ANYWHERE
Event Day

1. Before the day of the conference, learn what you should bring with you. A screen, projector, and microphone are usually provided for you. But note the following:
   - You are frequently expected to bring your own laptop and power cord.

- If you use a Mac, bring a "dongle" (adapter). This is sometimes needed for a Mac to connect to some projector hookups yet is rarely provided for you.
- If you will be introduced by someone prior to taking the stage (common for keynotes or panelists), bring a print-out of your bio to hand to this person, even if you have emailed it to event organizers ahead of time. I always bring a sheet with my bio written at different lengths (long, medium, and short versions) so the introducer is not forced to modify one he deems too long or short. See the bio eResource (from Chapter 2) for an example of such a sheet.

    Before this practice, I was frequently introduced incorrectly (to a surprising—and even comical—extent), imagined achievements were erroneously attributed to me, outdated information was provided, my most relevant and recent experience was omitted, and names of my affiliations were botched. The worst way I ever started a keynote occurred at a time when I only had one doctorate. Following an inaccurate intro, I felt a moral obligation to say, "Actually, I only have one PhD, not two" (to a chorus of disappointed sighs in the audience). Handing the introducer your bio saves you from this awkward experience.

Other items to ask about are the following:

- A clicker (to move through slides without having to touch your laptop); I always bring my own clicker because its familiarity makes me more comfortable.
- Handouts (how many should you bring, or will the organizers copy these for you?).

If you are new to presenting or tech-intimidated, you can ask for the name and cell number of whoever will be on hand to offer technical help setting up. If you cannot get it before the day of the event, ask again when checking in at the registration desk.

I always ask if a portable, wireless microphone (ideally a lapel mic—also called a lavalier or "lav"—that can be secured to my lapel) can be provided so that I can move around the room rather than be restricted to the lectern. A waistband, belt, or pocket makes it easier to attach a lapel mic's transmitter pack.

2. Arrive to your assigned presentation room at least 20 minutes early and set up your slides so they appear on the screen (click through several slides to be sure all is well). Use PowerPoint's "presenter view" so your laptop screen shows you the current slide you are on, but also gives you a peek at the next slide coming up.
3. Test your mic (lapel mics belong approximately 8 inches below your chin), and arrange your laptop and microphone so you will have as much

movement potential as possible. This way you can "work the room" and circulate as a good teacher does, rather than hide behind the lectern.

4. Set out your business cards, pen and paper or device (whatever makes it easiest for you to record important information, like a question you need to answer later), handouts, and any books you recommend. Author Gail Thompson taught me the importance of holding up books when you mention them. This is not about book sales; it is about connecting people with beneficial information.

5. Take a photo to use on social media. Sometimes I use TweetDeck to schedule such a tweet ahead of time, using my title slide as the image. A photo of your opening slide on the screen, with the podium to the side, can also serve as the image. About 15 minutes before your session begins, tweet this with your session details using the conference hashtag (#). For example:

> *What 2 practices drop a neighborhood's poverty rate by 90%? Join us 2:00 PM today #CPI2019 in "Frida Kahlo Ballroom" to talk solutions!*

This often brings in additional attendees who are watching the event's Twitter feed.

You can also post that photo after your session (covered later). If you take a photo of the audience minutes before you begin and announce you will Tweet the photo, some attendees will like to find their photo on social media after your session ends.

6. Power pose for one to two minutes: stand up straight, pull your shoulders back and down, and lift your chin slightly. If no one is around (like in an empty conference room or a bathroom stall), raise your arms in a victory V or plant your hands on your hips like a superhero, and widen your stance (basically open up your body).

Amy Cuddy (of Harvard Business School and viral TED Talk on body language), Wilmuth and Carney (2012) found that adopting an expansive (high-power) pose prior to delivering a speech resulted in reduced stress and significantly improved performance. Adjust your posture until you sense it embodies confidence. It can also help to visualize success—for example, the crowd applauding as you finish.

SCRAPPY TIP

If you feel nervous, tell yourself you are just excited. Brooks (2014) found that when people experiencing pre-performance anxiety told themselves "I am excited!" they consistently outperformed those who told themselves they were experiencing other emotions, like calm. The fact that nervousness and excitement are so similar (rapid heartbeat, stomach butterflies, etc.) makes this emotional reappraisal easy and successful, whereas you can not fool yourself into believing you are calm when you are not.

Simon Sinek (2014), whose TED Talks are the third most-watched of all time, uses this tip. Excitement gives speakers a big advantage, even over speakers who are calm. As politician consultant and Harvard University lecturer Marjorie Lee North (2017) notes, "Some nerves are good. The adrenaline rush that makes you sweat also makes you more alert and ready to give your best performance" (p. 1). Few people want an unexcited presenter. So, use that nervousness to your advantage and *get excited*!

7. Consider interacting with the audience before your start time. Walk among the seats or greet people as they arrive. Introduce yourself; find out attendees' names, where they are from, and what they do. Ask how they are enjoying the conference or event. People's cognitive systems use familiarity to judge if something is safe, which makes people prone to think they like someone simply because they have met the person (Markman, 2008); this will help your presentation be well-received. These interactions are also chances to establish commonality. People are more likely to agree with speakers they perceive as being similar to them (Alda, 2017).

Forgo pre-talk interaction, however, if it will throw you off your game. For example, if you have trouble quashing nervousness (for example, swapping it with excitement) and need to simply breathe deeply and visualize success before taking the stage, take that time for yourself.

8. Deliver your presentation using the strategies in this book. The next section will cover the presenting phase in depth.

When You Are Up (Speaking Strategies)

At a family reunion, the relatives might enjoy a game of touch football. If one of these family members is a professional football player, he will be acutely aware of the others' poor playing practices. But when Brother Lee runs in the wrong direction and Cousin Emmy catches the ball with her face, the pro player might just laugh or feel sympathy. After all, none of the other relatives should be expected to be football pros. It is not their professional field.

When I attend research conferences and events, I see a lot of communication blunders equivalent to the football mishaps of Cousin Emmy and Brother Lee. The difference here is that those speaking at these events *are* experts in their field. They should understand the fundamentals of their topics well enough to communicate core points easily. The audience is certainly expecting a good delivery of ideas. Yet scholars' lack of expertise in public speaking can prevent their field expertise from shining through. This makes the researcher look bad and means a missed opportunity for the audience to learn.

Regardless of the speaking venue, when you share your findings with others, *you are teaching*. It is important you use effective speaking and teaching strategies in order for your time with your audience to mean something. If you bore the crowd with a dry lecture, lose some attendees with jargon, fail to evoke emotion for the impact of findings, or deliver something forgettable, you waste or reduce your chance to impact lives.

In a seminal study at the University of Minnesota, Nichols and Stevens (1957) found the average person remembered only 50% of what he heard immediately after hearing it, regardless of how vigilantly he listened, and this retention dropped to as low as 33% within eight hours and to 25% after two months passed. Sullivan and Thompson (2013) also found it typical that after an oral presentation only 10 minutes long, only 50% of adult listeners could describe its content just moments after the talk, and only 25% of listeners could recall the subject matter 48 hours later. Aside from forgetting learned concepts, there is also the question of how much attendees will understand and learn in the first place.

Your job as a speaker is to sidestep these pitfalls as effectively as possible: to make your presentation riveting, clear, relevant, eye-opening, memorable, and packed full of potential to change your listeners in some way that will help them or others.

Nobody is perfect. I might inadvertently use "um" in my opening statement or fail to anticipate the number of questions (thus running short on time). But we should all *plan* to use effective speaking and teaching strategies when we present.

Subsequent chapters will cover a variety of speaking opportunities, and many of them offer a high level of comfort (such as speaking at online conferences). However, if you follow this chapter's guidelines and perfect your craft, you will likely catch the speaking bug and will deliver captivating presentations for some time to come. People will leave your presentations caring about your topic, understanding what you shared, and feeling ready to do something worthwhile with this new knowledge. Guidelines include:

- **Summon your inner teacher.** What you tell attendees does not matter; what attendees actually *learn* from you is what matters. If you just spray out information like a firehose without regard for how attendees connect with the concepts and add them securely to their mental repertoire, you will give a pointless presentation. Most of what we know about good teaching will work well with any presentation. For example:

- Just as it is great to meet students as they enter a classroom, it helps to meet and chat with attendees as they arrive, before your presentation begins.
- When teachers circulate throughout the classroom, it keeps students on task, helps hold their attention, and helps teacher/student connection. Circulating among your audience during appropriate times (like when the same slide will be in place for a while, or to make yourself easily accessible during an audience activity) is also helpful.
- A teacher's humor and gripping stories entertain students and keep them riveted in the classroom. Adult attendees are just as intrigued when a speaker leverages humor, storytelling, and other strategies to entertain.
- Students quickly tune out when they sense a teacher does not care. Things like a weak lesson, lackluster slides, or showing up late are telltale signs of an indifferent teacher. Your audience will feel disconnected if you do not care enough to plan an extraordinary session.
- A good teacher does not let a student or handful of students prevent others from finishing a lesson. If too many questions threaten to prevent you from delivering the content you promised to deliver, say, "This is the last question we will have time for, but I will be happy to answer any remaining questions immediately following this presentation," or, "So we are able to hear from all of you, please limit your questions to two sentences maximum."
- **Be very clear.** Your message from Chapter 3 needs to stand out clearly in your presentation. Whereas writing allows us to file our message down to a pitch or carefully selected statements, a live moment—complete with excitement or jitters—can cause key points to get buried in excess babble. Fortunately, in live moments we can leverage dramatic pauses, verbal emphasis, and strong gestures (like one hand chopping into the palm of the other with each new word) for the main words we want listeners to remember.

    In speeches we also have the assistance of slides. If you show a single slide displaying nothing but the words "YOU can stop the playpen-to-prison pipeline" during your stories on how children from key ethnic and racial groups were funneled into incarceration as adults, it is likely few attendees will forget the checklist you distributed of specific things they can do to end the racial homogeneity of our prison systems.

    The other hallmarks of clarity still pertain to speaking, just as they do for writing. Use packaging, straightforward sentences, substitutes for jargon (and if you absolutely must use a piece of jargon, explain it clearly), and establish context (when you say "facilities," what type of facilities do you mean?). When presenting for international audiences, clarify words that mean different things in different regions.

- **Do not focus on sounding smart.** Focus on helping all audience members understand your content, which means avoiding jargon and elaborate phrasing. When your sentences are difficult for the listener to process, they fight the listener's *cognitive ease*, which means he is less likely to trust you or believe what you are saying (Kahneman, 2011).

DEFINITION OF JARGON

Jargon describes terminology used by a specific group of people (such as terms and phrases professionals use when they "talk shop" that people outside their profession would not fully understand). These might be words used only by researchers, used only in your field, relating specifically to your topic, or used only by someone in your role.

Problems with Jargon

When you use jargon in a presentation:

- Some people do not understand the jargon, resulting in confusion.
- Some people partially understand the jargon but might have different interpretations as to its meaning.
- Some people understand the jargon but are not as comfortable using it as the speaker is.

In these cases, the speaker risks confusing or intimidating listeners. Intimidated listeners can experience an emotional filter that causes them to worry they do not understand what is being said. This fear can actually *prevent* listeners from understanding what is being said. Plus, no one likes feeling dumb or excluded.

When and How to Use Jargon

Jargon is helpful as a shorthand when communicating with a small number of people you know well enough to be sure they know this shorthand as you do. As soon as someone is in the room you do not know well—as is typically the case with public speaking—jargon has no place. If you *must* use jargon in a presentation, define it clearly and in an inviting way.

- **Do not overload your audience.** It is tempting to tell the audience every detail and every example concerning your topic. However, an audience is more likely to digest, maintain interest in, and remember what you say if you stick to the most important information (that which supports your message), allow time to pause, and do not overload your audience. Ira Flatow, host of NPR's *Science Friday*, gave this example of overload:

> I asked one scientist about why one alternative energy source is better than another, and he launched back into the history of civilization and how cavemen used fire. When we got to the discovery of oil in Pennsylvania, I stopped him.
>
> (American Association for the Advancement of Science, 2019, p. 8)

Some presentations allow for plenty of detail (like a half-day professional development class), while most (like a 15-minute television interview) force you to severely prioritize what you say so that what you *do* say gets across.

When stopping short of overload, you can always point attendees to resources for more information when they are ready. Handouts are great for this (whether online, for which you give the audience a web link, or printed, so attendees can take them home). If you use your time to get the audience to care about your topic and to understand its fundamental truths, they can use provided resources as a next step. If you want to personally walk your crowd through that next step, you can provide links to resource sheets, articles, or videos in which you personally provide more details and guidance.

SCRAPPY TIP

Establish and maintain commonality. People are more likely to accept the message of speakers they perceive as being similar to them (Alda, 2017). For example, Hayhoe (2018) found the most effective thing she has done when sharing climate science findings is to reveal that she is Christian, an audience often resistant to climate research.

If you are a researcher and author speaking to park rangers but spent your college summers as a park ranger volunteer, make that last fact clear. You can further a sense of unity with your speaking style. Imagine you are like your listeners and consider speaking to them that way.

Also, if people like you initially, they are more likely to like everything about you (such as what you have to share). This is known as the *halo effect*, where people tend to like (or dislike) everything about someone (Kahneman, 2011). Thus, establish commonality early.

- **Control your nonverbal signals.** Seminal research conducted at the University of California, Los Angeles (UCLA) (see Mehrabian & Ferris, 1967; Mehrabian & Wiener, 1967) revealed that 38% of communication comes from the tone of our voices and 55% comes from our body language, whereas only 7% of communication comes from the words we say. Though those findings are often too-liberally applied to all instances of information exchange, a series of subsequent works confirmed that much of a presenter's communication relates to how he delivers a message, outside of the message itself.

  I learned most of these tips working with the fabulous speaking coach Danny Slomoff:
  - Maintain good posture and do not make angles with your body, such as tilting your hips to one side. Poor posture looks weak. Slomoff said, "While you stand straight, your chest has to be relaxed. A stiff chest makes you rigid. A soft relaxed chest conveys confidence."
  - Use gestures that describe your sentences to the audience, rather than unrelated gestures like fidgeting or hand-wringing. Slomoff said, "Descriptive gestures are always perceived as projecting presence."
  - Establish eye contact with one audience member at a time (giving each a sentence) rather than sweeping your gaze over the audience. Vary who these people are. Slomoff said, "Great communicators don't talk to floors, walls, or ceilings. To project presence, they go through the eyes to their listener's mind. They make mind contact."
  - Match your expression to your words. Slomoff said, "Presence requires emotional congruence. That means whatever you compose you want to match your facial expression and tone to your words. You can't have a blank expression on your face while saying 'I am so excited to be here.' You can't have a smile when you're giving strong feedback."

    The people-pleaser in me makes me want to smile when I am on stage, but this is inappropriate when I am talking about people dying (something I do as I introduce how data impacts lives). At other moments, however, a smile puts the audience at ease and promotes trust. Just be sure your demeanor matches what you are talking about.
- **Do not read your slides.** Sweller's (1988) work on cognitive load theory established that when someone reads text on a slide and hears it (from the presenter) at the same time, this overloads the brain and reduces cognition. This finding was reiterated by researchers like Mayer (2014). Hopefully you kept your slides text-sparse anyway, as recommended earlier in this chapter.
- **Move.** Covering more territory is a sign of power, keeps your audience alert (following movement is an innate component to our survival), and allows you to move closer to different attendees at different times to

further draw them in. Work the stage. If it will not mess up a film crew, hop down from the stage and get out into the audience, as well. Use strong gestures, and physically point to places you want your audience to look.

- **Embrace emotions.** I open my speeches on gifted research by telling of a student who endured great hardships (in and out of school) and almost slipped through the cracks but was empowered by a teacher who recognized her giftedness. As I reach the point in this story where the child becomes a professor, I cannot hold back my tears or keep my voice from cracking. I am too moved by this story, as is my audience.

  Do not be afraid to let your feelings show. As long as your mood fits your message, your feelings can help carry your audience with you and embrace the weight of your message. If your audience feels emotion during your talk, as well, your words will be more memorable. You might make them laugh or you might make them cry, but either way you will make them remember.

- **Use an appropriate and consistent style.** Do you want to sound like you are speaking to the reader in a familiar, casual way? Do you want to be humorous or formal? The answer to questions like these is a very personal one. Use a style that will fit your nature and your purpose.

- **Alter and control your voice.** Monotone tells the audience to tune out. Even if every sentence is said passionately, this continuity gets stale and makes it harder for listeners to navigate your meaning. Speak your sentences the way the content requires. Speak slower than you might impulsively speak, and pause after you want a particular sentence to sink in. Listen to TED Talks or podcasts and note how the speaker's voice works for or against your engagement.

- **Speak confidently.** Tina Fey (2011) wrote

  > Speak in statements instead of apologetic questions. No one wants to go to a doctor who says, 'I'm going to be your surgeon? I'm here to talk to you about your procedure? I was first in my class at Johns Hopkins?
  >
  > (p. 77)

  Your attendees will quickly lose confidence in what you are saying if they suspect *you* do not have confidence in what you are saying.

  Search www.TED.com for Julian Treasure's TED Talk titled "How to Speak so That People Want to Listen." Starting halfway through, Treasure delivers examples of how you can manipulate your pace, pitch, and more to speak powerfully.

- **Remain flexible.** Despite your best plans, you might discover that the first of a set of audience exercises goes poorly, or your humor might fall flat. To improve the situation, you can do your next planned exercises in a different way or omit the jokes for that particular crowd. Change things up

169

in ways that will not cause your presentation to fall apart (for example, you can skip some slides, but you cannot redesign individual slides on the fly).

Remember Martin Luther King's "I Have a Dream" speech? That famous "I have a dream" line was not even written into what King had planned; rather, 11 minutes into the speech, a gospel singer named Mahalia Jackson shouted, "Tell 'em about the dream, Martin!" (Grant, 2016, p. 100), compelling King to spontaneously add the entire "I have a dream" section of his speech. Unlike King, you probably have an audience smaller than 250,000 in person and millions watching from home, and the stakes might not be of the magnitude of the Civil Rights Movement. Surely you can wing it, too, to modify your presentation as necessary based on how your audience is responding.

RESOURCE TIP

Consider joining Toastmasters (www.toastmasters. org), which helps members improve speaking and leadership skills.

- **Actively engage the audience.** Though you already planned for this in the "Before Speaking Anywhere" section of this chapter, remain aware of this need during your presentation. This will allow you to spot opportunities to engage and to intervene if your audience's energy drops (such as saying, "Raise your hand if . . ." to wake up attendees).
- **Recap.** See the "Specific Slide Types" section of the "Guide to Slide Design" eResource for tips on this type of repetition.
- **Thank your audience.** Those present gave their time and attention to you (precious commodities these days). A simple, "Thank you for participating here today, and for all you do for our field," communicates gratitude and lets your audience know the session has ended.

In the movie "The Guilt Trip," Seth Rogen's character presents a cleaning solution to an audience of buyers in a way one might expect: sharing facts and listing the solution's attributes. Rogen then realizes attendees are checking their cell phones, sending emails, or otherwise tuned out. Rather than continuing to plod through his list of scientific facts and selling points, Rogen shifts gears. He asks the moderator about her home life and cleaning needs. Rogen then notes how safe his product is for her family, pours his cleaning product into a glass, and drinks the entire glass of cleaning solution. Even though the scene is fictional, the reasons why Rogen ultimately caused the audience to invest in his solution are real.

170

Rogen's enhanced approach involved learning the audience's needs, remaining flexible, connecting with the audience, matching his message to the audience, and other strategies from this chapter (such as using a prop and surprising the audience). When you apply this chapter's tips as best suited to your own message, you can—like Rogen's character—win over the crowd, get listeners to care about what you are saying, and spur them to action.

Fielding Questions

Question asking is typically a sign that listeners are engaged. To further the impact of your presentation, note the following:

- Somewhere near the beginning of your presentation, establish **whether attendees should ask questions throughout your session** or save them for a "Q&A" period at the end. Some presenters provide notecards for the audience to submit questions, which can be reviewed during a bathroom break or by a colleague (who can condense wording and combine similar questions) and answered later. Whatever your approach, be sure your audience knows about it.
- If time is limited, **ask attendees to limit each question** to one sentence if you have any of these circumstances, which can lead to a long-winded Q&A:
  - Fifty or more attendees (large audiences mean more potential questions),
  - Attendees known for their inquisitiveness (for example, Mensans love to question, and young children often raise their hands simply to get involved),
  - Attendees who love to hear themselves talk (some high-level leaders fit this mold), or
  - Your stance is highly controversial (for example, if you present "Pollution Is Beneficial," expect many folks to challenge what you have said).
- **Do not make a questioner look bad.** Attendees deserve respect for their time and investment, and questioners deserve added appreciation for their vulnerability and contribution to dialogue. Try to be grateful for the question ("Thank you for bringing that up, as it is a common question," or, "I think others are probably wondering that, too"). Even the worst questions can be approached in a positive fashion. See Table 7.2 for examples.
- **If you do not know an answer, do not try to fake it.** You would risk giving your audience misinformation, and that could prove harmful. Rather, it is perfectly acceptable to say:
  - "I do not specialize in that [related] topic, so I would not feel right about answering that question, but if you were to contact [organizations], I am sure they could give you that information."

171

Table 7.2 Ways to Respond to Unideal Questions

Question Type	Response Examples
The question concerns something you will address later (this is especially common in long training sessions).	• "I love that you are wondering about that, because we will cover it extensively after the bathroom break." • "That provides a perfect transition into this next section of the training . . ."
The question is misguided.	• "I have been reading that lately, too, since a lot of sources are saying that. However, the true situation . . ." • "I can see why you would think that, because common sense tells us that [support of question]. However, due to . . ."
The question is defeatist or insulting.	• "I know firsthand how frustrating that situation is. It can be tempting to think our efforts are futile, but research shows us that mentality makes matters worse because . . ." • "I am sorry you feel I am anti-[role]. I served in [role] for 16 years, and I believe [role] to be our most influential stakeholders. When I say [role] are misinformed, I do not mean this as an attack on [role]. Rather . . ."
The question is confusing.	• "I want to be sure I am understanding you so I can give you the best answer. Are you saying . . ." • "I can think of two ways to interpret that question, and both of them can be helpful for the audience, so I will answer in terms of both [A] and [B]."

- "I had never thought about that direction. I will do some research to find a definitive answer and will post it on my website [provided to audience] by the week's end."
- "I would need to review those examples in depth to give you an accurate answer. If you please email me [provided to audience] or talk to me after this session, we can arrange for that."
- **When you are presenting online**, there is typically a chat field where attendees can ask questions throughout your presentation. Some presenters are able to monitor this feed as they speak, and to immediately integrate answers as they present. I have tried this but find it difficult to do. There is unexplained silence as I read the questions, I lose my train of thought, and the answers are out of place with my current comments. Thus, I tell attendees early on to use the field, but that I will answer questions there at the end of the presentation.

For online conferences, there is usually at least one other person contributing to the session, either as a co-presenter or a facilitator. The latter is often a tech-savvy volunteer who logs on early with you, makes sure your audio and visuals work, and remains virtually present to support you. I ask this person to monitor the chat field for me. Advantages include:

- If a question is one that everyone is likely having and their understanding hinges on me answering it immediately (such as a clarifying question), this person can interrupt me with that single question.
- If this person is also an expert on my topic, she can answer many of the questions.
- This person can assemble all unanswered questions, combining similar questions and condensing wording as necessary, to ask them audibly at the end of the session. This also gives the questions a voice all attendees can hear.

AFTER SPEAKING ANYWHERE

Congratulations, you braved the stage and shared important information. As you enjoy the presentation afterglow, complete just a few more tasks to make a positive difference for future sharing.

Tweet, Post, and More

I post the photo I took on social media (Item #5 in the earlier "Event Day" section), using the event's hashtag, and sharing something positive about the event. For example, "Loved working with the brilliant, enthusiastic researchers at #CERA19! #ProfLife." Chapter 11 has additional tips to make the most of your appearance.

Consider Feedback

Now it is time to reflect on how things went. Some judge whether or not they did a good job by asking:

- Did I avoid freezing up and embarrassing myself?
- Did I come across as competent?
- Did I get through everything I planned to say?

These are OK considerations for your first time on stage. However, there are more refined markers of success you should strive to consider if you want to assess and perfect your delivery. Reflect on your presentation and ask:

- Was my audience telling me non-verbally that they were following my message (nodding their heads, leaning in, maintaining eye contact and looking

173

at places I pointed, using facial expressions that matched what I was saying) rather than disengaged (using electronic devices for purposes unrelated to the presentation, looking confused, having off-topic conversations, etc.)?

- During activities, did attendees understand what to do? Did they seem engaged and energized?
- Did attendees ask questions that indicated an interest in applying what they were learning (rather than questions indicating frustrated confusion, or no questions at all)?
- After the presentation, did I get a vigorous (rather than cursory) applause?
- Did some attendees approach me afterwards to express their gratitude, share how the topic relates to their work, or ask deeper questions?

If a feedback form, conference app, or online form was used to collect attendee comments, ask conference organizers if they can send you input related to your session. Consider feedback with an open mind and use it to improve your next presentation.

Even if some input is harsh, do not judge yourself too harshly: you got up and shared information that can make a difference. When you consider feedback, know that every presentation you give will likely be better than the one before, so keep at it.

Others' Sessions

Anytime you are at a conference, attend other people's sessions. You can learn what these presenters are sharing, but you can also learn from *how* they are sharing. Take note of

- What they do that does not work (resolve to not do this in your future presentations) and
- What they do that does work (consider incorporating similar elements into your future presentations).

You can learn something from every presentation you attend to help you better deliver your message in the future.

Courtesy for Organizers

Always thank event organizers. This step is especially important if you were invited to speak or were one of the event's main speakers.

Event organizers work hard and juggle much to make an event come together. Just as you appreciate an audience member thanking you for your session, it is courteous to thank event organizers for pulling together a great event and for giving you the chance to share your message.

I aim to thank organizers in person as I leave, but only if they are easily available (an organizer quarreling with the caterer will hardly appreciate being pulled away for some small talk). I also send an email afterwards in which I thank anyone who played a role in arranging for me to speak or assisted me at the event.

REFERENCES

Alda, A. (2017). *If I understood you, would I have this look on my face?: My adventures in the art and science of relating and communicating.* New York, NY: Random House.

American Association for the Advancement of Science. (2019). *Tips from science journalists.* Retrieved from www.aaas.org/programs/center-public-engagement-science-and-technology/tips-science-journalists

Berger, J. (2013). *Contagious: Why things catch on.* New York, NY: Simon & Schuster.

Brooks, A. W. (2014, June). Get excited: Reappraising pre-performance anxiety as excitement. *Journal of Experimental Psychology: General, 143*(3), 1144–1158.

Cialdini, R. B. (2005). What's the best secret device for engaging student interest? The answer is in the title. *Journal of Social and Clinical Psychology, 24*(1), 22–29.

Coggins, C. (2017). *How to be heard: 10 lessons teachers need to advocate for their students and profession.* San Francisco, CA: Jossey-Bass.

Cuddy, A. J. C., Wilmuth, C. A., & Carney, D. R. (2012, September). *The benefit of power posing before a high-stakes social evaluation.* Harvard Business School Working Paper, No. 13–027.

Duckworth, A. (2016). *Grit: The power of passion and perseverance.* New York, NY: Simon & Schuster.

Eng, N. (2017). *Teaching college: The ultimate guide to lecturing, presenting, and engaging students.* New York, NY: Author.

Fey, T. (2011). *Bossypants.* New York, NY: Reagan Arthur Books.

Gillett, R. (2014, September 18). Why we're more likely to remember content with images and video (infographic). *Fast Company.* Retrieved from www.fastcompany.com/3035856/why-were-more-likely-to-remember-content-with-images-and-video-infogr

Grant, A. (2016). *Originals: How non-conformists move the world.* New York, NY: Penguin Books.

Hayhoe, K. (2018, June). When facts are not enough. *Science, 360*(6392), 943. doi:10.1126/science.aau2565

Heath, C., & Heath, D. (2008). *Made to stick: Why some ideas survive and others die.* New York, NY: Random House.

Huang, P. Y., Kurasch, S., Srivastava, A., Skakalova, V., Kotakoski, J., Krasheninnikov, A. V., . . . Kaiser, U. (2012). Direct imaging of a two-dimensional silica glass on graphene. *Nano Letters, 12*(2), 1081–1086. doi:10.1021/nl204423x

175

Kahneman, D. (2011). *Thinking, fast and slow*. New York, NY: Farrar, Straus and Giroux.

Markman, A. (2008, November 20). To know me is to like me I: Mere exposure. *Psychology Today*. Retrieved from www.psychologytoday.com/blog/ulterior-motives/2008 11/know-me-is-me-i-mere-exposure

Mayer, R. E. (2014). Cognitive theory of multimedia learning. In R. E. Mayer (Ed.), *Cambridge handbooks in psychology. The Cambridge handbook of multimedia learning* (pp. 43–71). Cambridge, NY: Cambridge University Press.

Mehrabian, A., & Ferris, S. R. (1967). Inference of attitudes from nonverbal communication in two channels. *Journal of Consulting Psychology, 31*(3), 248–258.

Mehrabian, A., & Wiener, M. (1967). Decoding of inconsistent communications. *Journal of Personality and Social Psychology, 6*, 109–114.

Nichols, R. G., & Stevens, L. A. (1957, September). Listening to people. *Harvard Business Review*. Retrieved from https://hbr.org/1957/09/listening-to-people

North, M. L. (2017). 10 tips for improving your public speaking skills. *Harvard University Blog*. Retrieved from www.extension.harvard.edu/professional-development/blog/10-tips-improving-your-public-speaking-skills

Oliver, J. (2010). *Teach every child about food*. [TED Talk video]. Retrieved from www.ted.com/talks/jamie_oliver#t-1293954

Rossen, J. (2017, May 18). The most famous anti-drug ad turns 30. Any questions? *Mental Floss*. Retrieved from www.mentalfloss.com/article/500800/most-famous-anti-drug-ad-turns-30-any-questions

Strayhorn, T. L. (2016). Big ideas in academic public speaking. In M. Gasman (Ed.), *Academics going public: How to write and speak beyond academe* (pp. 39–53). New York, NY: Routledge, Taylor & Francis.

Sullivan, B., & Thompson, H. (2013). Now hear this! Most people stink at listening [excerpt]. *Scientific American*. Retrieved from www.scientificamerican.com/article/plateau-effect-digital-gadget-distraction-attention

Sweller, J. (1988). Cognitive load during problem solving: Effects on learning. *Cognitive Science, 12*, 257–285.

Tamayose, A., & De Silva, S. (2017). *How did Polynesian wayfinders navigate the Pacific Ocean?* [TED-Ed video]. Retrieved from https://ed.ted.com/lessons/how-did-polynesian-wayfinders-navigate-the-pacific-ocean-alan-tamayose-and-shantell-de-silva#review

Chapter 8

Speaking at Conferences and Other Events

Think of something you did in the past that scared you—riding a roller coaster, skydiving, giving birth, asking someone out on a date—but that you ended up being glad you did. There has to be something that added a valuable, proud memory to your life that would be missing if you had not pushed through that terrified feeling.

Bad public speaking can leave you feeling awful afterwards . . . but apply the strategies in this book to do an incredible job, and the thrill of having done it will leave you feeling proud, joyous, and wanting to brave the stage again. Even if you are visibly nervous the whole way through, a well-laid plan with well-crafted content (covered in the previous two chapters) will still impress your audience. You do not have to be perfect: just plan well, take that chance on stage, and celebrate afterwards.

Your involvement is especially needed if you are female. A survey of 60,000 event speakers spanning industries, 23 countries, and the past five years revealed that 69% of event speakers are men (Kumar, 2018).

HOW THIS CHAPTER WORKS

(You Need Chapter 7)

Chapter 7 provided you with the fundamental guidelines that apply to all speaking opportunities described in this book. The speaking guidelines provided in this chapter are supplemental and are meant to be considered *with* the guidelines in Chapter 7.

LIST OF CONFERENCES (INCLUDING SYMPOSIUMS, CONGRESSES, ONLINE CONFERENCES, RESEARCH MEETINGS, AND OTHER EVENTS)

LIST OF CONFERENCES

This book lists hundreds of speaking opportunities (including symposiums, congresses, online conferences, research meetings, and other events) for you in an electronic file that makes it easy to find and pursue speaking engagements. You can sort the file by event type or location or month, visit each website with a simple click, and add additional events that are specific to your research area and work. The list contains details like submission link, deadlines, conference type, location, event date, and manipulation-friendly fields you can use to track your submissions. This file also includes TED Talks covered in the next chapter (since Talks are events that are also broadcast). See the "eResources" section near the start of this book for details on accessing and using this "List of Conferences".

CONFERENCE SESSIONS

There are so many research conferences that you could attend one per day if you were so inclined. Use the "List of Conferences" eResource (described earlier) for examples. Also visit websites within your field for listings, such as *Nature*'s Science Events Directory (www.nature.com/natureevents/science). New events arise regularly, and there are many specialized conferences you might find on your own that match your specialties.

To save on travel costs, you can Google your local convention center and skim its calendar for upcoming events related to your research topics. You can also contact your local universities and other organizations (or search their webpages) to learn of events in your area. If money is an issue, find out (before applying to present) if conference organizers let presenters attend for free (not all do) or if travel grants are offered (common for large research associations).

 ## SCRAPPY TIP

Some conferences require you to submit an unpublished paper when applying to speak. This paper is then peer reviewed and is often automatically published in the conference proceedings if you are accepted as a speaker. The Society for Information Technology & Teacher Education (SITE) International Conference is one example (you can even request to make this presentation online). This provides early career researchers with a peer reviewed publishing credit to add to their CVs, which can make a lack of journal publications less jarring.

Volunteer to be a session chair or discussant, a position in which you get to introduce presenters and often to sum up presentations at the end (adding your own impressions or pointing out recurring themes) and ask questions of presentation panel members. This is a great option if you are not ready to give your own presentation or if you did not get accepted to present but still want to participate.

Acceptance

For many presentations (such as for conference sessions), you will submit an application to speak. Submission requirements vary; you might have to submit a simple description, a formal abstract, or even a complete paper. Less-common requests include links to previous speeches or a presentation outline.

TIME-SAVING TIP

When you apply to speak somewhere (entering session description and other information on an online form), always save the information you enter on a Word document on your computer, as well. I have a single "Conferences" folder on my computer that contains a separate folder (within it) for each conference to which I apply (example: "SXSW2019"). This way I can quickly find and then copy/paste my information to reuse it in the future. Also, since composition takes time, an online form can "time out" during the entry process (losing your information) before you finish your submission.

One or more people will review your application to determine if you can present. To increase your odds of acceptance:

- **Check to see if the event offers acceptance tips**, and ensure your entry adheres to those tips. For example, the Neural Information Processing

Systems conference offers guidelines for writing an effective NeuralIPS paper to present at its conference (https://nips.cc/Conferences/2015/PaperInformation/EvaluationCriteria), and the Association for Public Policy Analysis and Management offers a recorded webinar on how to craft a presentation submission that will get accepted for its research conference (www.appam.org/events/fall-research-conference/2018-fall-research-conference-proposal-submission). Other organizations post sample proposals that were accepted.

- **Avoid long titles**. Aim for brevity, rich with meaning and appeal.
- **Avoid confusing titles**. If only viewing your title, people should be able to guess what your presentation will cover.
- **Avoid dry titles and descriptions**. Planners and reviewers want to offer sessions that people will be excited to attend. An intriguing title will also mean more attendees, which means more people you can inform.

SCRAPPY TIP

For huge conferences like the American Educational Research Association Annual Meeting (with more than 2,500 sessions) that alphabetically list the sessions for each time slot, start your title with "A." This will put your session at the top of the list where most people will see it. Otherwise, some attendees will see another session first that interests them and never read the rest of the long list to discover your session.

- **Determine what the conference acceptance criteria is.** Sometimes the rubric that peer reviewers use to score entries is shared with applicants. Before, during, and after you prepare your entry, consider how your description will meet all criteria.
- **If submitting a paper entry, note guidelines about sections**, like, "Submissions will be reviewed on the following elements: purpose, theoretical framework, modes of inquiry, [etc.]," use those exact words (like "Purpose") as the subheadings in your paper. This way the judges, who could include students or others new to paper terminology, will experience no confusion over whether or not you addressed a particular element they score.
- **If submitting an abstract**, write with reviewers *and* attendees in mind. The abstracts of accepted work will likely appear in the event program, so they must ultimately hook conference-goers into attending your session.

- **If asked to submit learning outcomes**, your goals should reflect a session that engages attendees and arms them for action. Thus your goals should be light on passive-audience outcomes (like "Attendees will understand . . ." and "Attendees will comprehend . . ."), and heavy on action-orientated outcomes (like "Participants will implement . . ." and "Participants will use provided resources to . . ."). Also make objectives positive (like "retain study participants") rather than negative ("stop participants from leaving").
- **Determine what the conference theme is** (if there is one). Be sure your session's title and description both relate to this theme (this differs from reiterating the theme). If there is no theme, instead reflect the hosting organization's mission and values.
- **Determine the appropriate strand for your presentation** (if the event categorizes presentations by strand). Strands are usually topics or target audiences stipulated in the conference program to help attendees who want to stick to a particular presentation type.
- **Determine the best presentation format**. A typical conference session might require you have a recent study to present, whereas a workshop or panel might offer more flexibility.
- **Be sure your session will appeal to at least one of the conference's key audiences.** Often this is an audience you specify from a menu of options. Write your submission with this audience in mind.
- **If you have an accomplishment that is related to the session** and appropriate to include, see if you can mention it in the session's description without sounding egotistical. For example, if you work at a particularly prestigious university you might write, "The presenter will share content from the class he teaches on this topic at Harvard University." If you delivered a TED Talk, you might try, "The presenter will include segments from his TED Talk."
- **Write with enough clarity** that even people unfamiliar with your topic (as planners or reviewers might be) can easily understand your message and its appeal.
- **Do not be intimidated by research conference submission processes.** If you have not completed a doctoral degree and have not completed an official study, you can still typically present at a research conference. Well-written literature reviews and interpretations of another's data make quality research papers and conference presentations. Rich data sources include the Civil Rights Data Collection (https://ocrdata.ed.gov), Pew Research Center (www.pewresearch.org), National Center Education Statistics (www.nces.ed.gov), Statistics at DfE (www.gov.uk/government/organisations/department-for-education/about/statistics), and Gallup (www.gallup.com).

181

When applications to speak involve submitting an original research paper, these papers are often housed somewhere the public can access online. Reference these papers to get a feel for the type of work that is accepted.

SCRAPPY TIP

Many conferences use peer review, in which volunteers apply specific criteria to score applications and determine who gets to speak. Around the time the conference is announced, the conference website or emails will call for people to apply to volunteer. Volunteers are often in short supply, whereas it is desirable to have many volunteers (meaning less work for each volunteer and increased fairness of determinations). It is thus relatively easy for professionals to be approved to serve on review panels.

Serving on a review panel will give you an inside peek into the review process, what organizers are looking for, common flaws in submissions, and more. This inside scoop can help you prepare a submission that is selected for this conference in the future, but also for others. Plus, early career researchers can include service as an expert reviewer as an honor on sparse CVs.

Sometimes only one or two people determine your submission's score and acceptance. Thus the selection process can be capricious (one year, reviewers might dislike your entry, whereas the next year, they love it). Keep this in mind if you are not accepted, and try again (at other venues, and for this same event in the future).

ONLINE CONFERENCES

Online conferences are great for all presenters, but if you are a beginning speaker I especially encourage you to present in an online conference. Open this book's "List of Conferences" eResource (described earlier), sort the file by its "Location" column to find conferences listed as "Online," and augment the list with any additional events that suit your message (a Google search will render more conferences specific to your field).

Because of the internet and conferencing technology (which event organizers will help you use), online conferences:

- Allow you to speak from the comfort of your own home. No one can see you (as long as you keep your webcam display turned off, which is expected), so you can even be in your pajamas. The audience only sees your PowerPoint slides and hears your voice.
- Are easy to do well at because you can have your notes in front of you the whole time with no one knowing, since no one can see you. It is also less intimidating to speak in front of an audience you cannot see.
- Often have international audiences, which means you can select from a range of time slots and widen your net of influence.
- Typically have a moderator present who helps you with any technology questions and field questions the audience submits.
- Give you a speaking credit to list on your CV without the expense of travel.
- Are often recorded, which means you will have a link to the recording you can submit if other conference organizers require video evidence of your prior speaking (as TED Talk submissions require).

Once you have some online conferences under your belt, you will find it much easier to present the same material before a live audience.

SCRAPPY TIP

Find the CVs of professionals you admire (on their websites or www.LinkedIn.com) and see which conferences they have spoken at, which awards they have won, and where they have published. Then apply to the opportunities that match your own expertise.

POSTER PRESENTATIONS

If you have just completed your dissertation or study, a common way to share your findings is with a poster. These are typically presented in a large room displaying many people's posters over the course of a conference. There is often a designated time when presenters must be present for interaction with visitors.

Poster's Nature

A good research poster grabs viewers from 10 feet away and draws them in to learn more about your study. The sections are similar to that of a dissertation: your information (title, name, email address, and affiliation), abstract, introduction, purpose and hypotheses, methods, results with visualized data, conclusion, and references. However, rather than dense write-ups, these sections should use visuals and succinct summaries viewers can scan and digest quickly.

Use bullets, callout boxes, images . . . whatever it takes to make key points stand out, because most viewers will not read your whole poster to find those points. You might favor Mike Morrison's design (www.youtube.com/watch?v=1RwJbhkCA58) where QR codes lead to study details. Include plenty of empty space to cushion text and sections; this will help content appear digestible and inviting. Use a pleasing color scheme (Google "modern color schemes") rather than dull or chaotic coloring.

Pick a layout that best suits the communication of your particular ideas (even if it deviates from the sections and order I provided in the previous paragraph). For example, if your study is best shared with a photo of a brain in the middle and 7 textboxes shooting out from that image in a circular array, then use that arrangement. Unique posters can still communicate all of the standard poster components, and chances are they will be more appealing and memorable.

Most research posters land somewhere between 36 to 48 inches (91 cm–122 cm) on their shorter sides and 72 to 96 inches (183 cm–244 cm) on their longer sides. Headings should be around 40–100-point font (with headings larger than subheadings, but both within this range), and body text should never be smaller than 18-point font. Use fonts like Arial or Helvetica that are more streamlined than Times New Roman.

Google "poster presentation" to reveal many free templates and examples after which you can model your poster. Some of these make all text look the same (which renders the words forgettable for many viewers), but you can enhance these posters with design tricks (mentioned earlier) that make key points stand out.

Poster's Display

Some venues provide tacks and bulletin boards to hang posters, but others offer easels on which to prop stiff posters. I opted for a poster I could roll up and then post, but inside the tube I used to carry the poster, I kept four thin slats of wood and large bull clips so I could fashion a hard frame in cases when it had to be propped. This allowed a single poster to function in either display environment. Check with conference organizers ahead of time on what will be provided, but note you might show your poster at other venues in the future that will have different setups.

Tack your business card next to your poster (people can take a photo of your information when you are busy talking to others) and have the actual dissertation on hand, as well as other literature of interest to visitors. You might even match your attire to your poster's color scheme, which Keegan and Bannister (2003) found made more visitors approach a poster.

CONFERENCE KEYNOTES

Use this book's "List of Conferences" eResource, adding more field-specific events you know about, to find conferences for which you could give an appropriate keynote or plenary (the terms are used interchangeably so often that I will simply use the term "keynote" here). Whenever you believe the conference organizers will begin planning for the next conference (perhaps three months after an annual conference's last conference, and often before a call for regular session presenters is announced), email the conference organizers and officials. You can often find their email addresses on the conference or organization's webpage or on emails relating to the previous year's conference.

SCRAPPY TIP

Search social media sites (Twitter especially) and the internet for calls for keynote speakers. I search phrases like "call for keynote" and "suggest keynote speaker". I often add "-if –my -me" to these Twitter searches to exclude tweets in which people are proposing themselves as speakers (there are many, and they typically include those words). Be sure you are on pertinent conferences' emailing lists to be aware if they put out a call for keynotes.

Do not dismiss giving your first keynote presentation at a venue that will not reach many in your target audiences. Once you are able to say (and add to your CV) that you are a keynote speaker, this opens the door to countless future keynote speaking opportunities where you can reach tens of thousands of appropriate listeners. Since you have valuable knowledge to share, any keynote speaking venue that launches this journey will be worth it.

Even if you suspect the keynote has already been selected, it does not hurt to approach conference organizers. Once I was told the keynote had already been booked, but I was offered $3,000 (plus paid travel and hotel) to be one of the conference's "Featured Speakers." Although this did not give me the whole conference's audience, it still gave me hundreds of listeners with whom to share my work (and funds for future travel to reach more audiences). Even small audiences add up to a bigger influence than you will have if you never reach out to conference teams.

185

Another response I received, from another conference's organizer, essentially read, "We already have a tentative keynote speaker lined up. However, if that should change, I will enlist your help." This can position you to step in at the last minute (as I have done in the past), or to be considered as keynote for the organizers' future events (as has also worked for me).

See the "Sample Email" textbox (note that underlined words are hyperlinks, which the reader can click for more information online). Compose a similar email in which you suggest yourself as an event's next keynote speaker. Some key points to make include:

- Your experience with the keynote topic
- Your experience speaking and (if applicable) giving keynotes
- Why your topic is of importance to the conference audience (timely, impactful, etc.)
- How your topic works well with the conference theme (if there is one; otherwise, relate your topic to the hosting organization's mission and values)

SAMPLE EMAIL I SENT A CONFERENCE PRESIDENT TO BOOK A KEYNOTE

Dear [First Name],

I would love to deliver the opening keynote/plenary at [Conference] 2019 on *Moving from Data to Action* or similar topic for these reasons:

- I have completed multiple **research** studies on this topic, and most of my **books** are on this topic.
- I am a **skilled public speaker** who has given a TED Talk, speaks extensively and regularly, and regularly teaches other academics how to best give a killer keynote. In fact, my most recent books cover how researchers can rock public speaking.
- I have given very successful, engaging (e.g., with audience participation) **keynotes** on this topic to a wide range of educators and other audiences.
- This keynote topic is a clear complement to the 2019 **conference theme** of "Data Visualization."

My bio, press/media kit, and former speeches offer more details. Thank you for your consideration.

Best wishes,
Dr. Jenny Grant Rankin

Sometimes conference organizers put out an open call for keynote speakers, and you will want to heed those calls. For example, ASCD periodically posts a "Suggest a Keynote for an ASCD Conference" form on its website.

SCRAPPY TIP

Sometimes event organizers come under fire for the absence of diversity in their keynote lineup. For example, CES is the largest technology convention in the world (and one many involved in research attend). In 2017, CES was called out by Gender Avenger (www.gender-avenger.com) for featuring zero women in its extensive keynote lineups for both 2017 and (as announced for) 2018 (Captain, 2017). Within a month of that criticism, CES added five women to its nineteen keynote speaker lineup for 2018.

If an event only has one keynote speaker and that speaker is a White man, no one should criticize the choice. However, if the event has six keynote speakers who are all White, or if the event has hosted only male keynotes since its first annual conference 20 years ago, this raises diversity red flags (and the same goes if the keynotes were always women or always from another single racial or ethnic group).

When event organizers are called out, you can help. Email organizers immediately to suggest yourself or a respected colleague (if either would break the homogeneity) as keynote speaker. Even if organizers deem it too late to change the upcoming lineup, they can save your information to offer a more inclusive keynote offering the subsequent year. Once in that position, use your voice. Let your unique wisdom shine and share your unique perspective.

Targeting smaller conferences first will increase your odds of acceptance. Consider events hosted by local universities or citizen groups, which love to open with a respected keynote. Once you have done a keynote at a smaller venue, your odds of being accepted at a larger event increase.

Tell professional acquaintances of your desire to book keynotes. My first keynote (which opened the door to more keynotes) happened because the scheduled keynote speaker got sick. Because he knew I would be interested and qualified, he asked me if I could take his place. I agreed and quickly sent him my short bio, CV, and sample slides from a previous presentation to ensure he could easily convince event organizers to give me a chance. He was then able to arrange for me to take his place at the last minute.

As soon as you have given one keynote presentation, add "keynote speaker" to your description on social media sites, your business card, and anywhere else that feels appropriate. If your keynote was filmed, obtain a link to the recording, which you can place on your website and provide when seeking other opportunities.

SCRAPPY TIP

Byron (2017) suggested that upon finishing a presentation you ask your audience about other venues at which you should speak, and ask that audience members tell those venues about you, too. You can ask attendees who approach you after your talk rather than ask the whole audience from the podium.

BOOKING AGENCIES

If you want to jump wholeheartedly into the speaking circuit, you might want to join a list of keynote speakers, which some organizations maintain to facilitate booking. When conference organizers, event planners, large corporations, or government branches want to book a keynote speaker or hire a consultant, they often turn to these one-stop shops for likely candidates.

Maintainers of such lists come in many forms. See Table 8.1 for some examples. If you are a person of color, female, or transgender, note the organizations in Table 8.1 that promote speaker diversity.

SCRAPPY TIP

If there is a particular event at which you aspire to give the keynote, linger after a current keynote presentation and politely ask the presenter (privately) how she landed the job. Then pursue the same path.

Table 8.1 Types of Speaker Booking Agencies

Type	Example
Agent	Coleman (https://experts.colemanrg.com), Executive Speakers Bureau (www.executivespeakers.com), Geniecast (https://geniecast.com), Royce Carlton (www.roycecarlton.com), and Washington Speakers Bureau (www.wsb.com)
Database	Chartwell Speakers Database (www.chartwellspeakers.com), Free Speaker Bureau (www.freespeakerbureau.com), and SpeakerHub (www.speakerhub.com)
Promoter of Speaker Diversity	500 Queer Scientists (www.500queerscientists.com), Experts of Color Network (https://insightcced.org/tools-metrics/experts-of-color-network), Request a Woman in STEMM (https://request500womenscientists.org), Women Present (www.womenpresent.com), Women Talk Design (https://womentalkdesign.com; also for other underrepresented genders, like transgender), and Women Who Keynote (https://womenwhokeynote.com).
Publisher	ASCD Resource Speakers (www.ascd.org/about-ascd/Affiliates/Affiliate-Community/Resources-$-Forms/Resource-Speakers.aspx) and Routledge Consultants (www.routledge.com/posts/education-consultants)

Experts who dislike searching and applying for individual speaking opportunities find booking agencies favorable (they do not have to go to the prospects; the prospects come to them). Meanwhile, if there are key events at which it would be beneficial to share your work, you can continue to apply to individual conferences while also sitting on one of these booking lists.

If you pursue a booking agency, you will apply through the entity's submission process. If accepted, you will typically get to choose which speaking gigs you undertake and can turn down any that do not fit your goals.

IF YOU PREFER TO START SLOW

As covered earlier, I highly recommend online conferences as a great place to begin presenting. However, if you do not feel ready to present in front of a large audience or one of your peers, consider some of these less-intimidating options for your early foray into speaking:

- Present your work to colleagues or the general public at your place of work.
- Local service organizations and clubs (like Lions Club, Chamber of Commerce, and Rotary clubs) need content for their meetings, and it would help them if you offered to speak there; www.meetup.com and www.eventbrite.com also list meetings by area (Byron, 2017), and some could suit your topic.

- Events that are not field-specific can still pertain to your specialty. For example, a neuroscientist speaking on what happens in our brains could join the gathering of an IQ-based society like Mensa, and an urban poverty researcher would be an appropriate fit for a symposium of business professionals wanting to improve the focus of their community outreach efforts.

  Reach out to these venues and ask if they would like you to speak at any meetings or events. Even when these engagements lack prestige within our field, this approach will let you practice before live audiences before you present at a research event.

- Community centers have a huge impact on lives. For example, Denzel Washington is one of thousands who credits the Boys & Girls Club as being a prime reason he stayed on a positive trajectory while his friends did not (Boys & Girls Clubs of America, 2018). You can offer to speak (at no cost) to a community center's staff or members. For example, I sometimes teach this book's content (modified to focus on sharing one's voice with the world) to foster youth and troubled teens.

- See if a local school would welcome a student-friendly demonstration from an expert like you. You could talk about your career or show a real-world application of a concept the teacher is covering.

PLAN A CONFERENCE

If an important facet of the field would benefit from an event but none is offered already, consider planning a conference of your own. When I used to plan the Illuminate Education User Conferences, I found it was a lot of work but well worth the effort.

If you can get a school or university to host outside of class hours, the expense can easily be covered by registration fees. Also consider an online venue (for inspiration, attend conferences categorized as "Online" in this book's "List of Conferences" eResource). Speak with organizations who might want to get involved (they can also promote the event to members) and like-minded colleagues to form a conference committee.

PUT PARTS TOGETHER

Chapter 7 provided guidance to present well. This chapter provided added tips, as well as multiple opportunities to share your findings at conferences and other occasions. Select an event (use the "List of Conferences" eResource for suggestions) to which you will apply to present. Then complete Exercise 8.1 to plan your submission and presentation. Reference sections in this chapter and the previous two chapters as you complete the exercise.

EXERCISE 8.1: EVENT SPEAKING PLAN

1. At what type of presentation will you be presenting?
   - In-Person Conference Session
   - Online Conference Session
   - Poster Presentation
   - Conference Keynote
   - TED Talk (covered in the next chapter)
   - Other (Describe)

2. At which event will you apply to speak?

3. Read the event's submission guidelines. What is on the rubric that reviewers use to determine acceptance, what is the required description word count, and so on?

4. Note any details that will influence what you present (such as event theme, presentation strand, and presentation type).

5. Who is your audience? This can be one main audience or a few key groups.

6. What is your key purpose (what does your audience need from you)?

7. What primary message will run through the entire presentation?

8. With what new understanding will your audience leave your presentation?

9. What will your audience be able to do after your presentation?

10. Describe what your style will be (humorous, casual, formal, etc.).

11. What will your presentation's title be?

12. What is your session's description? Multiple descriptions might be required (such as a short description for the conference app, list of objectives, and abstract for the program).

13. What magic will you use to make concepts resonate? Remember Table 7.1.

14. Create a PowerPoint template and use it to outline your presentation (or outline separately from the template). Then add and improve slides, gradually turning your template into a set of polished slides.

15. Practice your presentation, and proof and revise your slides and content as necessary. Ensure your speech matches what you promised in your submission, as well as criteria described in this chapter and the previous two chapters (actively engages the audience, communicates your core message, does not overload your reader, etc.).

REFERENCES

Boys & Girls Clubs of America. (2018) *Alumni hall of fame*. Retrieved from www.bgca. org/about-us/alumni-hall-of-fame/denzel-washington

Byron, L. (2017). 17 ways to find speaking opportunities. *Famous in Your Field*. Retrieved from http://famousinyourfield.com/17-ways-to-find-speaking-opportunities

Captain, S. (2017, December 4). CES slammed for not including any female keynote speakers this year. *Fast Company*. Retrieved from www.fastcompany.com/40503227/ces-slammed-for-not-including-any-female-keynote-speakers-this-year

Keegan, D. A., & Bannister, S. L. (2003). Effect of color coordination of attire with poster presentation on poster popularity. *Canadian Medical Association Journal*, *169*(12), 1291–1292.

Kumar, S. (2018, November 1). Gender diversity & inclusion in events report. *Bizzabo*. Retrieved from https://blog.bizzabo.com/event-gender-diversity-study

Chapter 9

Speaking on Air and Recordings

Steven Goldfarb is part of a team of scientists that works on the particle collider at the European Organization for Nuclear Research, known as CERN, and discovered the Higgs boson. Upon naming the Higgs boson "Particle of the Year," *TIME* magazine declared, "Forget Person of the Year—the discovery this summer by the Large Hadron Collider of the Higgs boson particle was one of science's greatest achievements" (TIME staff, 2012, p. 1).

So, Goldfarb could consider the news of his discovery as shared and stick to discussing particle physics with his colleagues at CERN and in scientific journals. Surely many a researcher of physics or any other topic would have no qualms about sticking to familiar circles after such recognition for a discovery. But Goldfarb is an exception from whom we can learn.

Goldfarb and I became friends in 2015, when we gave TED Talks at TEDxTUM in Munich. "That is incredible, to see a physicist of such acclaim doing something to share his ideas and findings with the general public," I thought then. I did not know at the time what an understatement that was.

When I returned home to California, I turned on *60 Minutes* and saw Goldfarb on the screen, talking to Leslie Stahl about the Higgs discovery . . . again, taking the time to share his findings with a new and varied audience. Throughout that week I noticed Goldfarb's ample use of social media to share more. The following week I was perusing TED-Ed lessons (where often-complicated concepts are explained in engaging ways) and stumbled across one featuring Goldfarb: he and another member of his team at CERN provided voices for an animated short in which they explained the Higgs boson to kids.

And that is not all. Last year Goldfarb enthusiastically co-taught the PostDoc Masterclass at University of Cambridge with me. I spent the first half of an evening teaching Life Science doctoral students how to best share their research findings with the world, and then Goldfarb joined us from Geneva via video conferencing software, took us on a virtual tour of CERN, and answered questions about particle physics and his team's findings.

It should come as no surprise that Goldfarb chairs the International Particle Physics Outreach Group and is a fellow of the American Physical Society Forum for Outreach and Engaging the Public. What might surprise you, though, is how impactful his sharing of very technical findings is on mainstream audiences from a wide range of backgrounds.

We researchers have a well-known tendency to communicate in silos. We talk about things like *confirmatory analyses* with folks who know what terms like that mean, whether they share our workspace, role, or field. When we step outside these silos, like broadcasting can help us do, we can reach countless people both within and outside of our silos. The impact of this act can be huge.

Consider that episode of *60 Minutes* I mentioned, in which Goldfarb and correspondent Stahl discussed an online webcast that announced and described the Higgs discovery. Stahl (2015) said, "Goldfarb told us that he was amazed at how many people went online to watch the meeting at which the discovery was announced." Then Goldfarb said, "You know, one billion people by the end of that week had seen video from that webcast. So, a significant portion of our planet was interested enough to watch something which was a very technical seminar."

One *billion* people in one week. If you are tempted to dismiss the idea that people outside your field can understand and find value in the very specialized information you have to share, remember that your knowledge is likely no more complicated than particle physics. Plus, many TED Talks, video blogs, news media, radio shows, podcasts, webcasts, television shows, and videos reach those working within your field, too.

Speak on air and in recordings to reach all types of audiences. Believe in people's potential to do good things with your findings. You never know how people's connection to your ideas is going to spark an idea that can change the world. Step onto the live or recorded stage to share your ideas, and see what happens.

HOW THIS CHAPTER WORKS

(You Need Chapter 7)

Chapter 7 provided you with the fundamental guidelines that apply to all speaking opportunities described in this book. The speaking guidelines provided in this chapter are supplemental and are meant to be considered *with* the guidelines in Chapter 7.

SCRAPPY FAST TRACK

If you want to skyrocket to appearances on huge-audience media (like you have never been interviewed but are anxious to be heard on NPR), I recommend you use the information in this chapter (including its eResource to find opportunities) to take this route:

Step 1. Apply to broadcasts specific to your field, if such programs exist. Field-specific broadcasts offer better acceptance odds and reach the primary audience for your work. The facilitator or interviewer is likely to be familiar with your topic, which usually means insightful questions and dialogue. This experience can also help you land and perform well for larger audiences.

Step 2. Perfect your speaking skills (covered in Chapter 7) and pursue the wide range of opportunities covered in this book. For example, awards, books, and fellowships do not involve radio but will enhance your CV and make you more guest-worthy to those deciding whether or not to feature you in a broadcast. Also work on your branding (covered in Chapter 2) so the specific expertise you offer is clear, and maintain a press page (covered in Chapter 3).

Step 3. Apply to appear on NPR and other big producers covered in this chapter. If you are familiar with NPR and the other organizations' huge audiences, you might be taken aback by the notion you should apply before you are an icon in your industry. In this book I encourage you to be scrappy and aim high. Being featured on NPR – something that carries much clout – will likely open countless doors for you. Those opened doors mean more chances for others to learn your findings. See the "National Public Radio (NPR)" section of this chapter to see how many ways such a privilege can be made possible.

195

> **Step 4.** Make your NPR (or similar) experience obvious to anyone visiting your social media sites, reading your email signature, visiting your website, or reading your CV. This will lead to even more opportunities to share your message.

LIST OF BROADCASTING OPPORTUNITIES (PODCASTS, RADIO, TELEVISION, VIDEOS, AND WEBCASTS)

LIST OF BROADCASTING OPPORTUNITIES

This book lists more than one hundred broadcasting opportunities (such as podcasts, radio, television, videos, and webcasts) for you in an electronic file that makes it easy to find and pursue opportunities. You can sort the file by broadcast type, visit each website with a simple click, and add additional broadcasts that are specific to your research area and work. The list contains details like type, website link, and manipulation-friendly fields you can use to track your submissions. Note TED Talks are included on the "List of Conferences" eResource, covered in the previous chapter, since Talks are organized like conference keynotes (and submission processes are like that of conferences). See the "eResources" section near the start of this book for details on accessing and using this "List of Broadcasting Opportunities".

TED TALKS

If you are not familiar with TED Talks, you will want to visit www.ted.com and watch a few. Carol Dweck, Bill Gates, Stephen Hawking, Arianna Huffington, Gayle King, and more have all done TED Talks. These are live presentations of 18 minutes or less that usually center on a unique, world-changing idea. The speeches are recorded and distributed widely for avid fans (typically a worldwide intellectual audience that spans ages, backgrounds, and fields).

Doing a TED Talk, which is considered prestigious, will open countless doors for you. I believe I never would have been selected as lecturer of the PostDoc Masterclass at the University of Cambridge if I had not done my Talk at TEDxTUM. Also, TED will expose a large audience to your work. My TED Talk reached over 500 viewers when I delivered it on stage, then thousands of viewers within its first month online on TED's website, and then thousands more over time. Some TED Talks have been viewed tens of millions of times.

Researchers contribute to life-changing innovations, merge inspiration from varied fields, and can have important and large-scale impact. If you are a researcher, it is likely you can share something unique and valuable with a larger community. TED is looking for such speakers to inspire viewers with original, powerful ideas.

You can see some TED opportunities listed in this book's "List of Conferences" eResource (described earlier). Sort the file alphabetically by "Conference" to find TED speaking prospects. You can be selected to give a TED Talk in any of the following ways:

- Get invited (like if you are famous).
- Apply (or have someone nominate you) to speak at TED or TEDGlobal (https://speaker-nominations.ted.com) or a less-regular TED event like TEDFest (www.ted.com/about/conferences).
- Apply (or have someone nominate you) to speak at a TEDx event (www. ted.com/tedx/events). Many Talks began at TEDx events before becoming TED Talks on the TED website. If a TEDx listing you pick has an event website, you can often find a submission form there (timelines vary, but organizers tend to select speakers 3–10 months before the event). Note that TEDxYouth events are only for children and teens, universities often limit speakers to their faculty and students, and city-specific talks typically limit speakers to residents.
- Apply to bring TED Institute (www.ted.com/about/programs-initiatives/ ted-institute) to your organization. This will involve working with TED to identify internal idea-makers, polish ideas, and prepare TED Talks.
- Apply (or have someone nominate you) for the TED Prize (www.ted. com/participate/ted-prize/nominate) to execute your world-changing idea. The deadline is usually in March.
- Apply to become a TED Fellow (www.ted.com/participate/ted-fellows-program), which puts you in the pipeline to give a TED Talk. The deadline is usually in September.
- If you can live in New York City's Soho for four months, consider TED Residency (www.ted.com/about/programs-initiatives/ted-residency), which also puts you in the TED Talk pipeline.
- Apply (or have someone nominate you) to develop an animated TED-Ed lesson (http://ed.ted.com/nominate_an_educator).

Acceptance

These qualities will help you pass the competitive screening process to give a TED Talk:

- Have a finding or idea worth spreading (unique, interesting, inspiring, and impactful).

- Base your claims on sound science and do not inflate the implications of findings. Talks related to health or science, in particular, must be backed by peer-reviewed research.
- Avoid the following topics, of which organizers are cautioned to be wary: alchemy, energy fields, free energy, perpetual motion, reiki healing, time travel, the neuroscience of something, and misused language concerning quantum physics (Snippe, 2019).
- Pick a TEDx event with a location, focus, and theme that match your message and circumstances. For example, my TED Talk took place at the Technical University of Munich ("the MIT of Europe"), which matched my research topics of design, data, and technology, not to mention my focus on education and students. The event's theme was "Facets," and my research involved a facet of data use that is often overlooked. Conversely, I was also selected to give a TED Talk at a local university's TEDx event but was dropped after higher-ups ruled speakers could only be from their own university.
- If picked to audition, be as prepared and passionate as if you were giving an actual, polished TED Talk.
- Keep your slides highly visual and as word-free as possible. If you ultimately give a TED Talk, many of your slides will get cut in the editing stage when a camera angle focuses on your face rather than what is projected, so your words should be able to stand on their own.
- Make your concept clear enough to summarize in one sentence (your elevator pitch).
- Watch a lot of TED Talks and consider what has already been done.

Other ways to get involved with TED include:

- Organize a TEDx event (www.ted.com/participate/organize-a-local-tedx-event). You can informally plan a simple "viewing party" where you and colleagues view a lineup of Talks you select for attendees. Alternatively, you can apply to host a full-fledged TEDx event for which you are trained to select, coach, and host speakers whose talks could end up on the TED website. In either case, you can curate Talks that further your message or relate to your research area.
- Create your own TED-Ed lesson (http://ed.ted.com/videos) that integrates an existing Talk. For example, my Talk became a data visualization lesson for students.
- Facilitate a TEDxYouth event (www.ted.com/participate/organize-a-local-tedx-event/before-you-start/event-types/youth-event) or apply to offer TED-Ed Clubs (http://ed.ted.com/clubs) for students aged 8 to 18. Efforts can center on a topic related to your studies.

NEWS MEDIA AND TELEVISION

News shows, in which stories revolve around current events and issues, are always looking for important topics to cover. But coverage will be more beneficial if research-based evidence and perspectives such as yours are included in the dialogue.

News coverage influences how policymakers and the public think about issues and helps to frame which of these issues are deemed important (Coe & Kuttner, 2018). Other coverage on air and film is meant specifically for stakeholders in specific fields. Establishing a presence through these media can help you inform professional and public dialogue concerning your area of research to ultimately inform related decisions. For example, how climate change is framed in news stories impacts how the public thinks and talks about climate change, and public opinion impacts how politicians make decisions that impact the environment.

Despite the importance of the media "getting it right" when covering topics, experts are not always consulted for stories. For example, when Media Matters analyzed education coverage on cable news programs (CNN, Fox News, and MSNBC) during a 10-month timespan, only 9% (16) of the 185 guests discussing education policy were actual educators or had advanced degrees in education (Tone, Power, & Torres, 2014). Voices from researchers like you could be missing from coverage that shapes the public's view and influences policies related to your area of study.

Media outlets also cover research topics in different ways, so you might push for airtime on networks currently disregarding your findings. Consider this book's opening example of climate change. In a study of climate change coverage on Fox News, CNN, and MSNBC, Feldman, Maibach, Roser-Renouf, and Leiserowitz (2012) found that Fox—as compared to CNN and MSNBC—interviewed a greater ratio of climate change doubters to believers and took a more dismissive tone toward climate change. Hmielowski, Feldman, Myers, Leiserowitz, and Maibach (2014) then analyzed survey data on thousands of Americans and found that people were more skeptical of climate change the more they consumed conservative media like Fox, that conservative media consumption decreased trust in scientists as well as certainty that global warming is occurring, and that non-conservative media consumption increased trust in scientists and this increased certainty that global warming is occurring. Thus a researcher with findings in support of climate change would find it important to change conservative media discourse on this topic.

Timing

Inserting yourself into news coverage involves widening your networks and establishing yourself as a credible expert so you are ready when chances to share your research open. Badgett (2016) describes how Stephanie Coontz's work on

American families was relegated to academic audiences until Coontz published a book in 1992 to counteract the public's misconceptions. That same year, Vice President Dan Quayle happened to criticize the fictional TV character Murphy Brown for being a single mother. This alignment of current events with Coontz's sharing of research catapulted Coontz into the media as the topic's go-to expert.

Consider how your message might squeeze into current media coverage on which your study has bearing. Your wisdom could counter myths about a publicized topic or fill an information void.

Delivering Your Pitch

Unless reporters seek you out for a story, getting airtime involves a pitch. See "Chapter 3: Preparation" for help writing your media pitch, including a sample.

You or your organization's outreach team can send producers your pitch, couching your expertise within a story you imagine interesting viewers or relating to current hot topics. Aim to offer something new, such as a new finding or a new perspective on an existing topic.

Networks differ in how stories should be pitched to them, so search show and network webpages for details. For example, CBS' *60 Minutes* receives concise story suggestions via email (60m@cbsnews.com) or mail (Story Editor, *60 Minutes*, CBS News, 524 West 57th Street, New York, NY 10019), and the correspondents and producers find stories rather than someone dictating journalistic direction from above them. NBC's *Today Show* and CNN's programming, however, have forms (www.today.com/news/send-us-your-uplifting-inspiring-story-our-everyone-has-story-t39496) through which viewers suggest features they would like a show to cover.

Use this book's "List of Broadcasting Opportunities" eResource, adding field-specific shows you know about, to find television venues to which you (or others on your team) can pitch your expertise in contributing to a segment. Searching network websites and social media can render additional opportunities, which you can save to the "List of Broadcasting Opportunities" file once you have saved it to your own computer.

For example, an "Advanced Search" on Twitter allowed me to specify tweets only made by @PBS that featured the phrase "looking for." This immediately produced a tweet by PBS (2012) reading, "PBS is looking for people to feature in on-air spots." A web search revealed a PBS LearningMedia (2017) post announcing, "We're looking for educators who love what they do, and who have found creative and thoughtful ways to integrate technology and digital media" (p. 1), with details to become a PBS Digital Innovator and share one's ideas in national settings. Though they ended up not needing me, I was on standby for a PBS documentary all because of Twitter.

If you are passionate about being featured on a particular network or show but are not getting a response from its staff, get scrappy to pitch your idea through additional avenues. For example, consider CNN. There is a form for you to submit ideas, but CNN reporters can also be reached via Facebook (like Anderson Cooper at www.facebook.com/AC360 and John King at www.facebook.com/JohnKingCNN) or Twitter (like Nancy Grace at @NancyGrace and Abby Phillip at @AbbyDPhillip). Pitching to a specific individual often renders you more success than pitching a social media account devoted to an entire station. You can also use CNN's feedback form (www.cnn.com/feedback), an individual CNN show's feedback form, a general CNN email address (cnn.feedback@cnn.com or community@cnn.com), or the email signup form in case pitching opportunities are shared there (www.cnn.com/login.html).

You should never harass a station or person by pursuing contact avenues repeatedly, but you can contact a venue in new ways over time in case it might interest a new recipient when it failed to strike a chord with the last. Though I have never tried this approach with CNN, it worked for me with NPR.

SCRAPPY TIP

Regularly interacting with your favorite reporters within social media, a strategy pushed elsewhere in this book, can also prompt reporters to reach out to you. For example, reporter Michael Koenigs (2013) tweeted to a single Twitter user: "we're looking for an expert for an upcoming segment for ABC News. Please reach me at . . ." (p. 1).

Reporters often invite people to send them news stories via Twitter. Put "send me news stories" or "DMs open" in Twitter's search field, then select the "People" option to filter results by people using those words in their profile, and you will see plenty of reporters (from BBC News, in particular) asking you to pitch them stories. Changing your search to "send news stories", "looking for news stories", and other variations will render additional reporters.

Local networks, news shows, and talk shows are worth contacting whenever their nature suits your message. Their proximity makes it easier for them to film you in your classroom, office, lab, or outreach environment, and your work in their viewers' neighborhood makes you more relevant to their audience. Local stations allow you to reach your area's residents, such as prompting participants to sign up for your study or encouraging community members to apply your recommendations.

Since "scrappy me" likes to aim high, I suggest submitting your suggestion to local stations *and* larger networks, wherever your story fits. The same message can be written once and then modified in small ways to suit each network. Thus, after you have written the message once for one venue, it costs you negligible work to also reach out to others. Visit Chapter 3 for tips that prompt news stations to *find you* to solicit your opinion and soundbites.

The next few sections in this chapter cover some broadcasting venues that cover research-related topics and more.

NATIONAL PUBLIC RADIO (NPR)

NPR is a non-profit syndicator of programs to individual public radio stations around the U.S. Public radio stations can apply to become members of NPR, but not every show on such a station is produced by NPR. People view NPR as prestigious and being heard on NPR can open many sharing-opportunity doors for you.

My journey to get on NPR was a scrappy one. "Academics don't end up on NPR or the *PBS NewsHour*, at the White House, or in front of lawmakers by accident or blind luck. Making a difference by engaging in the public conversation or debate about the issues that your work addresses. . . [is] a matter of being effective and strategic" (Badgett, 2016, p. 8). I tried many avenues, such as interacting with journalists on social media, responding to NPR's Facebook posts calling for input, emailing producers individually, and submitting copies of my books.

SCRAPPY TIP

Want stations like NPR to track *you* down? See the "Be Press-Accessible: Registered Source" section of Chapter 3 for details. You will learn how to join databases that journalists use to find sources to contact for knowledge, insight, and soundbites.

Some approaches *almost* paid off (an NPR staffer and I would email for a bit or talk on the phone, but a production never came to fruition), but it took me many creative tries to finally get featured on NPR. Note even when I was not ultimately heard on a show, I still had the benefit of sharing my perspective with reporters, which might have shaped their coverage. Also note none of my approaches was pushy. For example, I did not harass any NPR reporter with repeated requests, as that would be inappropriate. Rather, I thought outside of the box, searched for new ways in when I had a quick moment, and tried one approach after another over time.

TECH TIP

Richard Reddick (2016), a professor who has appeared on NPR and the Associated Press, suggests asking for a digital copy of interviews and other audiovisual media opportunities, since "many news organizations keep these media for a short time only on their sites. With archival media sites like YouTube and SoundCloud, these appearances can be kept and referenced to well after the original airdate" (p. 62).

BRITISH BROADCASTING CORPORATION (BBC)

BBC dominates broadcasting in the U.K., with a strong presence on TV, radio, and other formats. For example, BBC Radio (just one of BBC's arms) reaches 34.85 million listeners per week (BBC, 2017).

BBC is like NPR in that there are multiple ways to request an appearance. Visit www.bbc.com as a starting point to visit show sites, use contact options, find reporters, and more.

Also, BBC reporters make extensive use of social media, and many BBC reporters put "send me news stories" in their Twitter profiles or use #journorequest or #journorequests in tweets, which means you can set up a free JournoRequests (www.journorequests.com) account to get such requests emailed to you (see Chapter 3 for details). Pursue these invitations with your pitch if BBC is a good fit for your message.

OTHER RADIO AND PODCASTS

Other broadcasts are also worth pursuing. Open this book's "List of Broadcasting Opportunities" eResource (described earlier) and note the assortment of broadcast types, as characterized in the "Category" column. Those categorized as "Radio" can be heard live (as they occur) on the air, whereas shows categorized as "Podcast" are recorded so listeners can download and listen to them anytime, though it is common for a show to function in both formats.

Some of these stations are devoted entirely to a single field. Google your area of expertise beside the word "podcast" or "radio" to find broadcasts suited to your work. Approaching field-specific programs first can offer better acceptance odds and allow your work to reach the most appropriate audience.

Note opportunities labeled as "Radio Org" in the eResource's "Category" column. These producers of broadcasted content reach massive audiences. For example, American Public Media reaches 20 million listeners per week

(American Public Media, 2019), and Radiotopia (just one Public Radio Exchange podcast collection) garners more than 17 million downloads per month (PRX, 2017). Getting featured on one of these organizations' shows can bless your work with great exposure, particularly if your research holds mainstream relevance (such as how much "screen time" our brains can productively handle). Like online conferences (covered in the previous chapter) and webinars (covered later in this chapter), radio interviews can often be held from your own home, where you "phone in" to participate with an interviewer who is physically elsewhere.

Although some opportunities offer clear "Contact" or "Pitch Page" links (like https://airmedia.org/resources/the-pitch-page) on their websites, not every station offers an obvious path to being featured. You might thus need to get scrappy in your approach. Sometimes this means finding the host or producer of an airing and Googling the person to find her contact information. When you reach out, provide your succinct pitch, related literature (such as a study you just published), and a link to your press page (covered in this book's final chapter) so what you offer listeners is clear.

Of course, you can also create your own podcast, like the TED podcast *WorkLife with Adam Grant*, with a free audio editing tool like Audacity (www.audacityteam.org). An estimated 112 million people have listened to podcasts, 24% have listened to a podcast in the last month, and 86% of listeners finish most or all of the podcasts they hear (Edison Research, 2017). Google "create your own podcast" and you will find lots of information on how this can be achieved. NPR maintains a call for new podcasts (www.nprstorylab.submittable.com/submit) and anyone can submit their podcast for consideration to join NPR's lineup.

SCRAPPY TIP

Look for radio show or station booths at conferences you attend. Many shows pre-record a series of shows (or broadcast directly from) events, as there they can easily interview one expert after another. They are often on the lookout for people to interview, or have gaps in their schedule where they could easily accommodate another scholar.

Do not be shy: Politely inquire as to whether the program would like to interview you. Be ready with your quick pitch or message, plus an accomplishment or two ("I devised a way to preserve underwater artifacts, and *Forbes* magazine named me Researcher of the Year"). Even if there is no time at the event, your interview could be scheduled for another date.

Preparation

Because the audience cannot see you when you are on radio, you can have notes in front of you. Having your message, pitch, and talking points from Chapter 3 helps you stay on topic and prevents you from overlooking key information (you can check off talking points as you share them). I find it most helpful to keep statistics and names I plan to cite nearby. If there is anything you want to share but might not be able to remember entirely, have those details in front of you.

Well before an interview, I ask if I can have a copy of the questions I will be asked. These are sometimes provided (sometimes the host even asks me to write possible questions). I draft answers ahead of time (in abbreviated, bullet form) to be sure I do not miss anything on the air. If callers will be asking questions, I consider what those questions might be (especially questions that skeptics might ask) and plan answers to those, as well. I have usually written such answers in an article or correspondence before, so assembling answers is easy. Just be sure you speak naturally and in the moment, covering the answers' key points but not reading them.

SCRAPPY TIP

If your interview is recorded (rather than live) and will be professionally edited, you can ask to restate something if you botched an answer (like if you rambled). Just use the option sparingly.

WEBCASTS AND OTHER WEBINARS

Webcasts such as webinars run more like online conference presentations than they do like this chapter's other broadcasts. For example, you might upload PowerPoint slides and use your computer's or phone's audio and mic to narrate progression through your slides with or without the audience seeing your face. Organizations (like in the next chapter's "List of Organizations" eResource) often run webinars as one form of ongoing professional development for their followers.

When you learn of a webinar being offered through a group that suits your research area, ask its announcer how you can get involved in the future. Those who offer webinars are eager for expert content and you can expect the reception to be warm. In fact, as scrappy as I am, I have never contacted anyone about giving a webinar because they have always reached out to me first. Surely a webinar provider will not be able to resist your pitch, talking points, and willingness to give your time so its followers can benefit.

DOCUMENTARY

Filmed documentaries, aired in theaters and on television, have the power to shift a nation. For example, the research-based documentary *Waiting for "Superman"* caused a surge of charter school support and teachers' union opposition in the U.S. when it was released in 2010. You can agree to be featured in someone else's documentary, or (if you have the time, resources, and skills) partner with others to film your own (see www.desktop-documentaries.com for guidance).

VIDEOS AND VIDEO BLOGGING (VLOGGING)

Blog posts do not always have to be written. You can set up a free video channel on YouTube (www.youtube.com) or Vimeo (https://vimeo.com) to post videos you create. This is especially appealing to those who hate to write or who find it faster to just say what they are thinking.

If you want to post videos regularly you can make your channel a video blog (vlog), or you can merely upload a single video for each new study. Although YouTube gets more traffic, Vimeo contains no adult content and is thus less likely to be blocked by institutions' internet firewalls. Create a channel on both platforms and post your videos to each.

Options can be as simple as filming yourself with your laptop's webcam or using free Movie Maker (for PC) or iMovie (for Mac) to turn PowerPoint slides into a presentation you narrate. These videos need not be lengthy or polished to be effective. In a study involving 110 undergraduate student participants and the review of 270 peer-reviewed articles, Carmichael, Reid, and Karpicke (2018) found that shorter videos increased engagement (with 6 minutes per video or segment established as the optimum time period), and a conversational style was found to be more beneficial than a more formal speaking approach. And Berger (2013) found "most [videos] that go viral are blurred and out of focus, shot by an amateur on an inexpensive camera or cell phone" (p. 6).

If you would like to produce something more elaborate and you are based at a university (or other site that has these), you might find help with filming, lighting, audio, or editing from

- Production class students or teachers,
- Technology Department team, or
- Campus audio/visual labs or the Communications Department.

VIDEO LIBRARIES

Video allows you to show and demonstrate skills in a way written formats cannot capture. Carmichael et al. (2018) found video to be superior to written materials when it came to visually demonstrating "how-to" processes and helping the audience develop practical skills.

When I filmed my first 15-minute video for the SAGE Video Collection, I was hooked. This library of videos, which features academics speaking about specific research topics, reaches an international audience of university educators, researchers, and students. I was paid for my time, I got to plug my related books, and the filming took place in conjunction with a conference I was attending, so I incurred no travel costs. I kept in contact with organizers and quickly signed up to film more.

Open this book's "List of Broadcasting Opportunities" eResource (described earlier). Find opportunities categorized as "Video" and add field-specific venues that you know about to your own copy of the eResource. Reach out to those collections that seem a good fit for your areas of study.

PUT PARTS TOGETHER

Chapter 3 and Chapter 7 provided guidance to share your research well. This chapter provided added tips, as well as multiple chances to share your knowledge on the air or in recordings. Select a broadcast (use the "List of Broadcasting Opportunities" eResource for suggestions) you will approach with the desire to present. Once accepted, complete Exercise 9.1 to plan your talking points. Reference sections in previous Chapters 3, 7, and 10 as necessary as you complete the exercise.

EXERCISE 9.1: BROADCASTING SPEAKING PLAN

1. On what type of broadcast will you be speaking? Use Exercise 8.1, instead, for a TED Talk.
   - Podcast
   - Radio Show
   - Television Show
   - Video
   - Webcast
   - Other

2. For which broadcast will you speak?

3. What are the broadcast parameters (host name, show length, video conferencing site to log in ahead of time, etc.)?

4. Who is your audience? This can be one main audience or a few key groups.

5. What is your key purpose in joining this broadcast?

6. What primary message will you communicate in this broadcast?

7. What will your talking points be, listed by importance? Use Exercise 3.3 as a starting point but adjust to suit this venue and audience. Alternatively, if you were provided with interview questions ahead of time, write the questions with your answers.

8. What magic will you use to make concepts resonate? Remember Chapter 7 and Table 7.1.

9. Plan any supplementary materials as required (slides, list of online resources, images for pre-broadcast advertising, etc.).

REFERENCES

American Public Media. (2019). We're everywhere you listen. *American Public Media.* Retrieved from www.americanpublicmedia.org/about.

Badgett, M. V. L. (2016). *The public professor: How to use your research to change the world.* New York, NY: NYU Press.

BBC. (2017). *Record BBC Radio 6 music listeners and increased BBC digital radio audiences.* Retrieved from www.bbc.co.uk/mediacentre/latestnews/2017/rajar-q3

Berger, J. (2013). *Contagious: Why things catch on.* New York, NY: Simon & Schuster.

Carmichael, M., Reid, A., & Karpicke, J. (2018, February). *Assessing the impact of educational video on student engagement, critical thinking, and learning: The current state of play.* SAGE Publishing. Retrieved from https://us.sagepub.com/sites/default/files/hevideolearning.pdf

Coe, K., & Kuttner, P. J. (2018, January 11). Education coverage in television news: A typology and analysis of 35 years of topics. *AERA Open, 4*(1). Retrieved from https://doi.org/10.1177/2332858417751694

Edison Research. (2017). *The podcast consumer 2017 report.* Retrieved from www.edison-research.com/the-podcast-consumer-2017

Feldman, L., Maibach, E. W., Roser-Renouf, C., & Leiserowitz, A. (2012). Climate on cable: The nature and impact of global warming coverage on Fox News, CNN, and MSNBC. *The International Journal of Press/Politics, 17*(1), 3–31. doi:10.1177/1940161211425410

Hmielowski, J. D., Feldman, L., Myers, T. A., Leiserowitz, A., & Maibach, E. (2014). An attack on science? Media use, trust in scientists, and perceptions of global warming. *Public Understanding of Science, 23*(7), 866–883. doi:10.1177/0963662513480091

Koenigs, M. [@mcckoenigs]. (2013, July 9). *@MoneyConfidante we're looking for an expert for an upcoming segment for ABC News. Please reach me at* [omitted]. *thanks!* [Twitter moment]. Retrieved from https://twitter.com/mcckoenigs

PBS. [@pbs]. (2012, October 31). PBS is looking for people to feature in on-air spots. Has PBS helped you explore new ideas or worlds? *Visit www.pbs.org.* [Twitter moment]. Retrieved from https://twitter.com/pbs

PBS LearningMedia. (2017, January 12). Networking—Kentucky Educational Television. *PBS LearningMedia.* Retrieved from blogs.ket.org/networking/?tag= pbs-learningmedia

PRX. (2017). About PRX. *PRX.* Retrieved from www.prx.org/about-us/what-is-prx

Reddick, R. J. (2016). Using social media to promote scholarship. In M. Gasman (Ed.), *Academics going public: How to write and speak beyond academe* (pp. 55–70). New York, NY: Routledge, Taylor & Francis.

Snippe, E. (2019, August 15). TED: The banned talks and what we can learn from them. *SpeakerHub.* Retrieved from https://speakerhub.com/skillcamp/ ted-banned-talks-and-what-we-can-learn-them

Stahl, L. (Writer). (2015, November 8). The collider [Television series episode]. In A. Court, K. Sharman, & S. Fitzpatrick (Producers), *60 minutes.* Meyrin, Canton of Geneva, Switzerland: CBS News.

TIME Staff. (2012, December 19). The Higgs boson: Particle of the year. *TIME Magazine.* Retrieved from http://poy.time.com/2012/12/19/the-higgs-boson-particle-of-the-year

Tone, H., Power, L., & Torres, L. (2014, November 20). Report: Only 9 percent of guests discussing education on evening cable news were educators. *Media Matters.* Retrieved from www.mediamatters.org/research/2014/11/20/report-only-9-percent-of-guests-discussing-educ/201659

Part IV

More Options

Chapter 10

Connecting

I got to volunteer in the Democratic Republic of the Congo (DRC) at a school called Africa New Day (Un Jour Nouveau, or UJN). The DRC is the rape capital of the world (Wilén & Ingelaere, 2017) and violence and crime are commonplace, so you can imagine it is difficult to run a school for impoverished kids who walk miles for an education. UJN teachers could keep their eyes solely on teaching, but how could their students learn on long-empty stomachs? When they have been traumatized? When they worry for their moms and siblings who have been violated? When they have no clothes or shoes to wear to class?

Just about every world problem is influenced by so many variables that we cannot make a difference if we view our work through tunnel vision. The UJN change makers recognize this, so they further their goals by connecting with others. They collaborate with business leaders, the community, soldiers, peacekeepers, foreigners, and more to provide what is needed for the whole child: food, safety, shelter, counseling, a job for a mother, career training for an older sibling, self-defense lessons, side businesses and donations that make outreach programs sustainable, and a steady stream of volunteers to work with teachers and students. This approach pays off: I saw children beaming and thriving despite personal stories that would bring you to your knees.

Sharing research is about more than how great your findings are; it is about the impact that sharing those findings can have. Like UJN, you might have a mission of helping a group of people, community, environment, or our world. Like UJN, your contributions will expand and multiply when you connect with others. Tunnel vision—just looking forward and not interacting with those around you on your journey—will shortchange you and those you hope to help.

Connecting with new people exposes you to ideas and resources you would not otherwise find and gives you more avenues to spread your own knowledge. Many connections lead to friendships in which you regularly lead one another to new opportunities for information distribution.

Yet when I hear the term *network*, my natural response is to cringe. And I am not even an introvert. This is because my initial understanding of networking was that it meant having awkward, forced conversations with strangers in which everyone is only trying to get something from one another.

It was not until I actually engaged with strangers within my field that I found relationships taking form without ever trying to do the dreaded act of "networking." I was not "after" anything—I was just swapping ideas with the goal of helping those whose lives my field touches. I learned what effective networking really is: it is about connecting with others over shared passion.

I favor Brené Brown's definition of connection (see text box). If you approach others with a synergistic spirit in mind, your connections will be more authentic, more enjoyable, and more likely to benefit our planet.

DEFINITION OF NETWORKING	DEFINITION OF CONNECTION
Merriam-Webster (2017, p. 1) defines *networking* as:	Brené Brown (2010, p. 19) defines *connection* as:
"The exchange of information or services among individuals, groups, or institutions; specifically: the cultivation of productive relationships for employment or business"	"The energy that exists between people when they feel seen, heard, and valued; when they can give and receive without judgment; and when they derive sustenance and strength from the relationship."

TO MAKE CONNECTING EASIER (EVEN IF YOU HATE IT)

This section's strategies encourage connections without a "forced" feeling.

Connecting at Events

- **Visit discussion tables** or other arrangements made at some conferences to facilitate interaction. You can always sit quietly and listen, so the risk for a shy person need not be high. Though once you have gotten comfortable, your interest in the issue being discussed could prompt you to participate.
- **Set goals low enough to reach.** Curtin (2016) suggests aiming to make just one new connection at an event, as this takes the pressure off, provides a clear metric, and makes later follow up with contacts more manageable.
- **Get someone you know to attend with you.** A friendly security blanket can put you at ease, and a more-assertive friend can initiate conversations of which you can then be part, even if you are shy.

- **Volunteer for a conference you are attending**, such as working the information booth or chairing a panel. This positions you for engagement with participants and presenters, even if you would not normally initiate conversation on your own.

Connecting Anywhere (Online, by Phone, at Events, Etc.)

- **Give something**. Ask for someone's email address to send him a resource related to a shared area of interest. This could lead to further dialogue. My motivation when I give and help is simply that I like to give and help (for those who've read Malcolm Gladwell's *The Tipping Point*: I am one of those overeager Mavens), but those who do not naturally volunteer resources to others can be convinced by research to do so. According to the *norm of reciprocity* founded on the research of Kunz and Woolcott (1976), people are motivated to do things for you when you do things for them (Smith, 2017; Tannenbaum, 2015).
- **Put out a call for participation or invite feedback.** This is how I met Margie Johnson, who has become a dear friend and frequent collaborator. She lives in Tennessee and I live in California. We met nonetheless (first over the phone) when I was conducting a study and released a call for participation. Margie called me because the study related to work she was doing. We connected well over the phone and were soon presenting together at conferences. Margie connected me with state-level government officials who then applied my research, adding to my credibility (for those who've read Gladwell's *The Tipping Point*: Margie is a Connector). When I landed the chance to lecture at the University of Cambridge, I arranged for Margie to co-teach the first class with me. When you find someone whose ideas and character you respect, it is natural to want to help her succeed. It does not feel forced and it is not insincere; it is simply enjoying a friend who shares your passion and enjoying the chance to help good ideas spread.

> ## SCRAPPY TIP
>
> If you are unable to attend a particular conference, you can still take part in its twitter conversations, where speakers' key points are shared and then discussed. Search Twitter for the conference's designated hashtag (this is often the organization abbreviation and conference year, like #ASPO2019), follow along, and contribute your knowledge.

- **Join social media dialogue during events.** This is a great way to connect at the conference and also afterwards (through new social media both followers and followed). Research conferences often announce a

215

designated hashtag (such as #ACRC2019) for the event, otherwise you can search likely hashtags and find the one most people are using. Add this hashtag to any tweets and other social media messages you post in relation to what you are learning or doing at the conference.

Alderton, Brunsell, and Bariexca (2011) found that use of Twitter for backchannel conversations during conferences supported networking; for example, one participant stated that while using Twitter at conferences, "I have met and collaborated with other educators from around the country to share ideas and best practices. These kinds of exchanges strengthened my experiences . . . socially and professionally" (p. 7).

TWITTER CHAT DEFINITION

A *Twitter chat* is a conversation between users of the social media tool Twitter, who are brought together by the use of a unique hashtag in their tweets and follow the stream of posts using this hashtag in order to view and participate in a single discussion. For example, the National Institute of Mental Health uses the hashtag #NIMHchats for its Twitter chats, so anyone participating adds #NIMHchats to their Tweets to contribute to a single conversation. These discussions are often formally organized and recurring, such as at the same time and on the same day of every week.

- **Join social media dialogue anytime.** Posting comments and work that interests you, and reading the same from others, lets you connect with people across geographic boundaries. Chances are it will not feel like networking; it will just feel like enjoying a shared passion with others, which is what this chapter is all about.

  You can also participate through planned social media discussions. Every week there are hundreds of scheduled chats on Twitter related to different fields and topic. If you visit www.tweetreports.com/twitter-chat-schedule, you should find many to choose from. This allows you to converse from the comfort of your own home with people who share your interests.

GOOD CONNECTING HABITS

The previous section gave you low-risk ways to put yourself out there, even if you hate networking. But once you are *in* the throes of connecting, there are additional guidelines to encourage success:

- **Carry business cards with you.** If your employer does not provide them, order or make your own.

MONEY-SAVING TIP

Sites like www.VistaPrint.com often run promotions where you can order professional-looking business cards for free.

If you hear a presenter or conference attendee mention something that correlates with your work, you can approach him afterwards, state what you appreciated hearing, and hand him your business card while adding that you would love to talk more. Writing a note on the back of the card can help this person remember what you said.

If he gives you a business card as well, note on the back of it what sparked the connection. Then send this person an email or call within the week initiating a conversation. If you give this person something, such as a link to a related article, this can help you feel less awkward about reaching out.

- **Write notes on the backs of business cards you receive.** Even if you think, "I will never forget this person!" when he hands you a business card, figuring out later who is who in a stack of collected cards can be daunting.

  Whenever I get a business card from someone, I write a note on the back related to our connection. For example, "working on a book like my 4th" or "has brother at BBC Radio who might want to interview me." These notes are a huge help when I follow up with people later.

- **Determine if an expert you admire will be making an appearance you can attend.** Just as I recommend you list your upcoming presentations and media appearances on your website, you will find that other researchers often do the same. If you admire someone's work, look for her upcoming engagements. If you can attend one of these, reach out to the expert in the way described next.

- **Reach out to speakers prior to events.** When a conference's program is released in advance, you will spot sessions devoted to your area of expertise. You will see great speakers with whom to connect, but they could be drowning in a crowd of other interested attendees if you wait to approach them at the conclusion of their talks.

  Send a speaker a message by email or social media well before an event if you want to connect there. Succinctly explain how your ideas might correlate and politely ask if the speaker would have some time for you over the course of the conference (such as grabbing a cup of coffee or sitting at the same table during the conference lunch buffet). Posting a positive social media message (such as tagging the speaker while expressing excitement

217

about his last book or upcoming keynote) around the same time can help your invitation stand out.

I receive emails like this regularly (one just popped up in my inbox as I wrote the previous paragraph), and I have yet to turn anyone down. Like you, most speakers are seeking to have a positive impact on the world. Swapping ideas with other scholars is yet another way to do this.

SCRAPPY TIP

The first time I taught a course on this book's topic at the American Educational Research Association (AERA) Annual Meeting, I mentioned I was working on the book *Sharing Your Education Expertise with the World: Make Research Resonate and Widen Your Impact*. After class, Norman Eng (2017) handed me a free copy of his book, which relates to presenting. I read the book on the plane and promptly gave it a 5-star review on Amazon, recommended it to colleagues, and cited it several times in that book.

Handing a speaker a paper, article, or other resource you wrote (paired with a mention of why you believe he would find the work helpful) can increase the odds that he will read it, benefit from it, and share it with others.

- **Follow up.** Sandberg (2013) told of meeting a social media expert at a conference who shared impressive ideas and, over time, reached out to Sandberg with some interesting information but never asked to get together or infringe on Sandberg's time. When Sandberg later left the Starbucks board of directors, she suggested this woman as a replacement. This conference contact was then invited to join the Starbucks board of directors at only 29 years old.

No matter your field or role, when you follow up with the people you meet in helpful (not overbearing) ways, this can lead to collaboration. It can also open you up to new opportunities to share your discoveries.

GUIDE TO A DIFFERENT MENTOR

This guide is not about the mentor who helps you get better at your job. Rather, this guide is about the mentor who helps you share your discoveries with the world, such as through landing opportunities to reach a wider audience. This guide will help you find, keep, and make the most of such a mentor. See the "eResources" section near the start of this book for details on accessing the "Guide to a Different Mentor".

GOOD CONNECTING MINDSET

Approach connection-making with the right state of mind:

- **Be in it for those your research impacts** (such as the terminally ill, victims, children, immigrants, wildlife . . . whomever your findings have a chance to help). One of the reasons people cringe at the thought of networking is that we have seen so many superficial, what-can-you-do-for-me networkers.

  When your core motivation is helping others, and you are making connections in order to help even more, this intention shines through. In these cases, you are connecting with others over ideas and altruistic plans. You are just as excited to offer a way to help someone else share findings (you say things like, "Let me introduce you to a reporter interested in that same topic!") as you are to advance your own ideas. Some people are still suspicious of the well-intentioned, but most people will recognize your goodwill as they get to know you.

- **Conscientiously strive for diversity.** Being around people who are different from us provokes thought, makes us more industrious, exposes us to added information and perspectives, and even makes us more creative (Phillips, 2014). Even if your intention when connecting with others is to share rather than to receive, you and your work will benefit substantially if you open yourself to learning from a wide range of fellow experts.

  Do not miss that I wrote *if you open yourself to learning from*. It is vital that no member of a group is added for the sake of a gesture. Rather, every member will have a unique viewpoint and knowledgebase from which you can and should learn. As Leslie Odom, Jr. (2018) wrote, "If you have a person from an underrepresented group on your team and you aren't tapping them for their unique and varied perspectives and contributions, it may be tokenism. And if it's tokenism, it's always a missed opportunity" (p. 93).

  Researchers cannot be fully aware of equity issues intersecting their fields if they do not hear from diverse voices. You cannot gain a lifetime of understanding from what you hear secondhand, but each person's experience is only their own anyway; the goal is to learn from as many different people as we can to get as mindful as we can about the wide array of circumstances in our world. Aiming for interaction with people of all backgrounds, races, ethnicities, genders, creeds, ages, and sexual orientations exposes us to a wider range of perspectives and—with that—ideas and opportunities that can help us better serve our fields.

- **Be approachable.** If someone initiates discussion with you online, do you give a curt answer? As you await the start of a conference session or enjoy the lunchtime buffet, are you hunched over your cellphone or salad? I hope not.

  Whether you interact with someone in person or not, give thoughtful responses and ask questions that invite discussion. When you attend events, sit up, display open body language, and smile to people who pass by or join you. These habits communicate you are open to talking, which is required if you are going to exchange ideas that can aid your research and its impact on the world.

- **Be positive.** In academia, people connect in hopes of finding, sharing, and expanding upon solutions. If you are discussing a topic you know a lot about—imagine it is the pursuit of democracy in countries with authoritarian regimes—and all you do is rant, you are not offering anything to your discussion partner. Even if you do not have an easy solution, surely your research has informed you enough to propose *possible* ideas and questions worth investigating, or you can mention other people or groups who can offer support.

  In other words, you can still highlight problems while offering helpful ideas. Discussing problems is important, but pair these discussions with words that move dialogue toward improvements.

CLOSE TO HOME (SPECIAL-INTEREST GROUPS AND MORE)

This book covers some far-reaching types of opportunities, both geographically and in terms of their wow factor. However, it is also worth considering what you can do *within* your workplace and circles to share your expertise. Although such possibilities are endless, a few include:

- Step up for a leadership role (committee head, new job, professional association leadership, etc.).
- Form or join a special interest group (SIG) or other gathering (like a Lean In circle, http://leanincircles.org).
- Collaborate with coworkers on a new endeavor.
- Arrange to conduct training sessions for your colleagues.

Brainstorm on what other options are possible within your sector, and pursue those that interest you. Many opportunities (writing, speaking, and more) take place online, making them "close to home," as well.

LIST OF ORGANIZATIONS (JOINING AND SUBSCRIBING OPPORTUNITIES)

LIST OF ORGANIZATIONS

This book lists hundreds of organizations for you in an electronic file that makes it easy to find and pursue groups to join or to subscribe to its e-newsletter. You can sort the file by type, visit each website with a simple click, and add additional organizations that are specific to your research area and work. The list contains details and manipulation-friendly fields you can use to track your subscriptions and memberships. See the "eResources" section near the start of this book for details on accessing and using this "List of Organizations".

ORGANIZATIONS

Organizations offer pathways to meet and interact with professionals who share your research interests. View this book's "List of Organizations" eResources (described earlier) for a list of organizations relating to education (a field all other fields touch), as well as their websites. Consider joining any relevant organization (including those not on this list, as there are likely numerous groups within your field) and setting up a member profile page. A "Guide to Hunting and Harvesting" eResource (introduced in this book's final chapter) covers many benefits you can get from organizations.

Blaze Your Own Trail

If you find a necessary organization to be nonexistent, consider founding it yourself. Another option is to start a new Special Interest Group (SIG) within an organization that offers them if you find your specific passion is not addressed by an existing SIG. Starting a new SIG is usually a petition process in which you must establish that other current members of the organization want the SIG to exist. Search the organization's website or speak with its representatives for application specifics.

CALLS FOR INPUT

Government bodies, companies, research institutions, organizations, and more put out a "call for input" when they want experts or other stakeholders to contribute feedback. This often relates to a problem they seek to solve.

Calls for input are chances for you to contribute to decisions and affect policies in quick, convenient ways. Some calls allow you to include your contact information and can lead to more extensive, follow-up involvement in an endeavor.

Keep an eye out for calls for input from your professional affiliations. Various factions of the U.K. Parliament, U.S. White House, and other governing bodies announce calls for input, as do research associations. On such entities' websites, search for "call for input" (using the search field and placing the phrase in quotes) to produce a list of upcoming calls. Searching "call for knowledge" and "call for findings" is also worthwhile.

The "List of Serving Opportunities" eResource, covered later in this chapter, contains specific calls for input with the details needed to pursue them. Some calls are one-time occurrences, but those issuing the calls often post different calls in the future. Note some government administrations issue requests for feedback more frequently than others, so if you do not see many calls during one leader's term, it is worth checking again after the torch has been passed.

News publications also issue calls for input to collect quotes and leads for stories. You can search your favorite news sites or e-newsletter feeds for terms like "to hear from you," usually preceded by "We'd like," "We want," "[This publication] would like," "Looking for," and so on. For example, a *Forbes* journalist issued this call with her contact information: "I am looking to hear from neuroscientists with a behavioral, social and cultural focus for an interview feature. The selected source will need to be available for an interview on 03/17 or 03/18" (Montañez, 2019, p. 21) (do not try to follow up with her now, as calls expire soon after they are posted). Also keep an eye on a publication's social media, where such invitations are commonly released.

POLICYMAKING

Policy scholars have not settled on a single, agreed-upon definition of what constitutes "policy" (Cairney, 2011), but we can think of "policy" as meaning any established decision (such as by a governmental body) made so that future matters will run in a favorable way. Policies improve when they reflect evidence-based thinking, which means researchers have much to add to policy discussions.

If you are intimidated by the prospect of addressing politicians and other policymakers, note that even Elmo (a Muppet from the show *Sesame Street*) testified before U.S. Congress, resulting in $225,000 in federal funding allotted to research on music and the brain (Ward & Suk, 2018). All researchers (meaning you) offer a unique perspective to inform decisions that impact our world.

Where Decisions Are Made

To impact policy decisions, first determine where they are made for your particular field. For example, only 6% of U.S. federal spending (as opposed to 49% of state spending) goes to education, and "very little decision making happens in Washington D.C. . . . most of the power to set direction in education resides at the state and local levels" (Coggins, 2017, p. xvi). Thus an education researcher would focus most on influencing policy at state and local levels.

Getting face time with politicians is easier than many people guess. Just picking up the phone can land you an appointment with a member of a state assembly in the U.S. (it did for me here in California), a member of the House of Lords in the U.K., and more. I found it very easy to have one-on-one conversations with state assemblypersons, state and federal department representatives, city councilpersons, ambassadors, and other people in government positions. In fact, I even provided congressional testimonies (to inform legislation) prompted by a Facebook post. Likewise, getting discussion time with members of organizations devoted to my areas of research (even founders and CEOs) was remarkably simple. These people generally want to know new findings related to their missions, so remember that you have something to offer them.

Opportunities to Impact Policy

There are many ways to impact policy. First, consider current public dialogue and debate on your area of study and determine where you fit in and what you have to offer. If such public discourse is missing entirely, consider what aspects of your topic are most important to bring to policymakers' and the general public's attention first.

Next, consider these approaches to inform those whose votes or decisions shape reform:

- Read the previous "Calls for Input" section, which covers one of the ways political bodies collect feedback to inform policy.
- Reach members of the U.S. Congress via www.house.gov/representatives/find or www.govtrack.us. Reach U.K. Members of Parliament, Lords, and officers at www.parliament.uk/mps-lords-and-offices. Find individual departments' webpages on those sites or elsewhere (like www.energy.gov). Call offices and make appointments to meet about specific issues and current policies.

  Congressional staff (mainly in the majority party's interests) determines who gives in-person testimonies before U.S. Congress by speaking with insider networks, advocacy organizations, and other experts for names of likely witnesses (Badgett, 2016). By that point, members generally have their minds made up on an issue and simply seek to prove their points. Thus, there is much value in speaking with politicians early and informally to influence their stances before legislation is being enacted.

- Visit other governing bodies' websites for opportunities to contribute.

- Unlike congressional hearings, state and city level hearings often are open to the public. Call ahead of time to determine what the signup process is, then show up and share your professional opinion on a related topic.
- Internships listed in the "List of Serving Opportunities" eResource (covered later in this chapter) are another way in which you can work closely with policymakers (such as at The White House or House of Commons).
- Watch state or regional entities' websites (like www.wildlife.ca.gov) for invitations to provide feedback on new initiatives. It can also help to determine who is on state or regional advisory teams, then reach out to members to offer your expertise. Also build relationships with regional and state officials within a division that matches your research area.
- Think tanks, federal research programs, and other players in the research arena are go-to sources of input for government policymakers. *The Guardian* maintains a list of U.K. think tanks at www.theguardian.com/politics/2013/sep/30/list-thinktanks-uk. For the U.S., Comprehensive Centers are listed at www2.ed.gov/about/contacts/gen/othersites/compcenters.html, and Regional Educational Laboratories are listed at https://ies.ed.gov/ncee/edlabs. Google searches and use of this book's "List of Organizations" eResources will direct you to more. You can email a program in your area to learn how you might get involved (organizations are regularly looking to forge partnerships) or look for calls for participation in their publications and at national conferences.
- Some events are devoted entirely to merging research with policy. For example, the Association for Public Policy Analysis and Management (www.appam.org) hosts a fall conference involving research from 15 different fields of study.
- Partner with an organization that helps empower and position researchers to participate in evidence-informed policymaking. International Centre for Policy Advocacy (www.icpolicyadvocacy.org) and Center for Science Diplomacy (www.aaas.org/programs/center-science-diplomacy) are examples. Some of the programs listed as "Fellowships/Programs" in this book's "List of Serving Opportunities" eResource also help researchers influence policy.
- Connect with a knowledge broker. This role can be found at organizations like the Economic and Social Research Council Genomics Policy and Research Forum in Edinburgh.
- When you are aware of a new policy in the works or a policy revision, write an op-ed with research-backed suggestions. Chapter 5 contained a "Newspaper" section and introduced this book's "List of

Writing Opportunities" eResource, containing a wealth of places to submit commentaries.

- University news and public relations offices often maintain a list of faculty experts to share with media and policymakers. If you work at a university, get on such a list.
- Write a letter to top officials. When President Bill Clinton won his presidential election, Teresa Ghilarducci wrote him a congratulatory note that offered her help and some ideas on pension reform; the letter was passed around among Clinton's insiders and led to Ghilarducci being invited to serve on important boards (Badgett, 2016). You can use the same verbiage in letters you send elsewhere, so it costs you negligible added time to reach high with your correspondence.

Chances to influence policy are often based on long-term relationships, so any entry point with decision-makers can lead to increased involvement over time.

SCRAPPY TIP

Twitter is the social media platform favored by policymakers (Badgett, 2016). Join dialogue with influencers there.

Approach

When speaking with policymakers, avoid long-winded or negative rants. Policymakers are busy people looking for solutions. Your ideas should be presented and backed up succinctly, just as you learned to do with your pitch and talking points in Chapter 3.

Be open to listening and entertaining compromises, as policymakers face constraints that determine what can and cannot be done. When speaking with legislators, researchers should plan to help them balance budgets, spend tax dollars in a way voters would find wise, identify prospective funds (such as grants), and ensure an equitable distribution of resources across the system, knowing that 49% of state budget dollars are spent on education, 25% on health care, 11% on public safety, and 15% on other causes) (Coggins, 2017). Decision-makers will not listen to you because they want to help you; rather, they will listen to you because they want *you* to help *them*, and they will continue to listen if you provide that help in a timely, accommodating way.

> ## BRIEFING PAPERS AND EXECUTIVE SUMMARIES
>
> A briefing paper (for which you write a brief summary, outline facts, and suggest action) can help whomever you speak with to understand your points and respond as you recommend.
>
> If you provide policymakers with a research report, some might request an executive summary. An executive summary states the problem the report addresses; your purpose in writing the report; and your findings, conclusions, and recommendations. It is like a report abstract (covered in Chapter 7), except it is meant for non-academic audiences. Also unlike an abstract, an executive summary is typically a full page and sometimes spans up to 10 pages if it summarizes a long report.

Timing

Policymaking experts suggest waiting for a "policy window" to open, which means a time when your area of expertise becomes a hot topic in the media. "As the window opens, new ideas and voices will find it easier to get into the mix" (Badgett, 2016, p. 41). This is great advice and worth following; this is often how someone goes from quietly working on his research to suddenly testifying before Congress and being quoted in major papers as the go-to expert.

However, do not sit back and *only* wait for a policy window. By the time politicians are debating a topic for the cameras, they typically have already consulted experts and have already made up their minds on an issue (and politicians get bad press for changing their minds, so by then they are reticent to change their public stances). While you are on the lookout for a window to open, speak with policymakers, establish yourself as an expert, widen your network of those who know you know your topic. That way you can make some progress while you await the opening of a policy window, and you will be ready to stick your head through that window when it opens.

SERVING

An internship at the White House is something to crow about. A National Aeronautics and Space Administration Fellowship Activity provides independent researchers with world-class guidance—hardly a trifling feat. Other countries offer equally impressive programs. An eResource guide is available for readers interested in ways to learn while serving the field through internships, fellowships, boards, panels, or other compelling ways.

LIST AND GUIDE TO SERVING OPPORTUNITIES

GUIDE TO SERVING

This book directs you to many opportunities to share your research with the world, but there are more that involve learning while also serving the field in compelling ways. This involves pursuing calls for input, calls for participation, fellowships, programs, internships, panels, boards, or opportunities to be a judge or reviewer. See the "eResources" section near the start of this book for details on accessing the "Guide to Serving".

LIST OF SERVING OPPORTUNITIES

This book lists more than one hundred serving opportunities (such as calls for input, calls for participation, fellowships, programs, internships, panels, boards, and opportunities to be a judge or reviewer) for you in an electronic file that makes it easy to find and pursue opportunities to serve your field. You can sort the file by category or deadline, visit each website with a simple click, and add additional opportunities that are specific to your research area and work. The list contains details like opportunity category and manipulation-friendly fields you can use to track your submissions. See the "eResources" section near the start of this book for details on accessing and using this "List of Serving Opportunities".

HONORS

Some researchers have mixed feelings about applying for awards or other honors. They worry it means they are conceited, or they feel guilty devoting time to the endeavor. However, since awards can make a CV more impressive, and since a more impressive CV opens doors for you and allows you to share your findings on a larger scale, earning accolades ultimately can help you help more people or other benefactors. Often awards are tied to specific works (such as a paper you wrote or a program you developed) and increase the work's credibility and circulation and thus its impact. An eResource guide and list of hundreds of awards are available for readers ready to earn honors that can expose their work to larger audiences.

LIST AND GUIDE TO AWARDS AND OTHER HONORS

GUIDE TO AWARDS

This book directs you to many opportunities to share your research with the world, but there are more ways to gain exposure for your work, such as pursuing book awards, other awards, contests, competitions, dissertation awards, grants, and other options. See the "eResources" section near the start of this book for details on accessing the "Guide to Awards".

LIST OF AWARDS

This book lists hundreds of honors (such as awards, book awards, contests, competitions, dissertation awards, and grants, as well as award lists containing additional awards) for you in an electronic file that makes it easy to find and pursue honors. You can sort the file by submission deadline, visit each website with a simple click, and add additional honors that are specific to your research area and work. The list contains details like deadline to apply, submission link, award type, and manipulation-friendly fields you can use to track your submissions. See the "eResources" section near the start of this book for details on accessing and using this "List of Awards"

Part of using your connecting powers for good is championing others who have important insight to share about your field. As you connect with others, find ways to introduce colleagues to like minds, point colleagues in the direction of new opportunities, and share tips and venues you have found to be effective in spreading your own work. These endeavors will allow you to draw even more benefit from whatever area you study.

REFERENCES

Alderton, E., Brunsell, E., & Bariexca, D. (2011, September). The end of isolation. *Journal of Online Learning and Teaching*, 7(3), 1–14.

Badgett, M. V. L. (2016). *The public professor: How to use your research to change the world.* New York, NY: NYU Press.

Brown, B. (2010). *The gifts of imperfection.* Center City, MN: Hazelden Publishing.

Cairney, P. (2011). *Understanding public policy: Theories and issues*. Basingstoke, UK: Palgrave Macmillan.

Coggins, C. (2017). *How to be heard: 10 lessons teachers need to advocate for their students and profession*. San Francisco, CA: Jossey-Bass.

Curtin, M. (2016, May 23). A networking trick you'll like even if you hate networking. *Inc.* Retrieved from www.inc.com/melanie-curtin/a-surprisingly-effective-networking-trick-for-introverts.html

Eng, N. (2017). *Teaching college: The ultimate guide to lecturing, presenting, and engaging students*. New York, NY: Author.

Kunz, P. R., & Woolcott, M. (1976). Season's greetings: From my status to yours. *Social Science Research, 5*, 269–278.

Merriam-Webster. (2017). *Dictionary: Network*. Retrieved from www.merriam-5. Ships

Montañez, R. [haro@helpareporter.com]. (2019, March 12). *[HARO] Tuesday evening edition*. [email].

Odom, L. (2018). *Failing up: How to take risks, aim higher, and never stop learning*. New York, NY: Feiwel and Friends.

Phillips, K. W. (2014, October). How diversity makes us smarter. *Scientific American*. Retrieved from www.scientificamerican.com/article/how-diversity-makes-us-smarter

Sandberg, S. (2013). *Lean in: Women, work, and the will to lead*. New York, NY: Alfred A. Knopf.

Smith, R. (2017, February 25). Exploiting the norm of reciprocity on Bourbon Street. *Psychology Today*. Retrieved from www.psychologytoday.com/blog/joy-and-pain/201702/exploiting-the-norm-reciprocity-bourbon-street

Tannenbaum, M. (2015, January 2). PsySociety: I'll show you my holiday card if you show me yours. *Scientific American*. Retrieved from https://blogs.scientificamerican.com/psysociety/i-8217-ll-show-you-my-holiday-card-if-you-show-me-yours

Ward, A., & Suk, A. (2018, February 28). The surprising stories of Sesame Street. *Scatterbrained @ Mental Floss*. Podcast Retrieved from http://mentalfloss.com/article/533609/surprising-stories-sesame-street

Wilén, N., & Ingelaere, B. (2017, August 31). War-torn Congo has been called the "rape capital of the world." *The Washington Post*. Retrieved from www.washingtonpost.com/news/monkey-cage/wp/2017/08/28/what-do-rebels-think-about-sexual-violence-in-congo-we-asked-them/?utm_term=.5e93d0c0c701

Chapter 11

Multiply Your Impact

If you have gone to the trouble of writing a piece, delivering a speech, getting interviewed by the media, or sharing your research some other way, you can make this effort far more impactful by increasing the audience that consumes it. This chapter will help you maximize each of your endeavors by promoting and spreading it further. This is not about self-promotion or hubris; this is about ensuring your wisdom reaches as many people as possible—and thus helps as many people or other benefactors as possible.

Of course, if you are not careful, your efforts to *spread* your research could cut into your time spent furthering your research. As you follow this chapter's strategies, remain conscientious about striking a healthy balance between your work in the field and sharing that work with others. You do not have to do everything in this chapter; just do what you can accomplish without sacrificing your professional practice.

SCRAPPY FAST TRACK

If you want to catapult the reach of your findings on a tight time frame (like if you have done limited branding and have limited social media presence but want much exposure for your discovery), I recommend you use the information in this chapter and Chapter 2 to take this route:

Step 1. At very least, establish your pitch and a professional website (even if it is just your workplace profile page) where journalists can find your bio and press information (including contact information). Chapters 2 and 3 will help you with this.

Step 2. If you have published a book or work at a university, your publisher or university likely has a PR Department. Engage with its team members to plan efforts to promote your work. Try to get a list of journalists they feel will be most interested in your work and approach them about interviewing you, doing a feature on your findings, or quoting you. If a journalist in the public eye shares your work, it will instantly reach far more people than you are likely to reach on your own.

Step 3. Add yourself to the journalist databases discussed in Chapter 3. Also use this book's strategies to engage with three to five targeted journalists regularly (but not overbearingly). Share your work with them as you produce articles and other outreach pieces recommended in this book.

Step 4. Regularly be on the lookout for reporters to interact with them in person. Stein (2016), Executive Director of Communications at University of Pennsylvania, suggested looking in the working pressroom of a major academic conference for journalists who are there looking for news. "Ask them about what they are finding interesting about the conference and establish a relationship. If a reporter calls you at any point, keep their contact information! ... This is perhaps one of the most useful and rarely used communication strategies" (p. 108).

Step 5. Do not stop aiming for other "vast reach" opportunities covered in this book, like doing a TED Talk or getting interviewed on *PBS NewsHour*. Opportunities like those will gain your work much exposure.

PROMOTE OTHERS

When I first attended a research conference with Gail Thompson, we constantly ran into people who knew her (she is very accomplished and prolific). Dr. Thompson would excitedly introduce me like this, "You have to meet

Dr. Jenny Rankin, who has taught at Cambridge. Do you know *five* of her books were published just this year? You might have seen her TED Talk." Each person exchanged business cards with me and was surely more interested in what I said than they would have been if Thompson had not given me such a generous endorsement. Thompson's example inspired me to pump up the passion with which I introduce people I respect.

If you are female, people of any gender are likely to be overly critical of your promotion efforts. Women often avoid touting their accomplishments because of society's discouragement of this trait in women; for example, a woman can lower her chances of getting hired if she explains her qualifications or accomplishments in a job interview (Sandberg, 2013). But Sandberg described how a group of women at Merrill Lynch circumvented this stigma and rose to the executive level by bragging about *one another's* accomplishments at meetings. Now that they are leaders in their institution, they are in stronger position to make it a place where women can speak about their own successes without repercussions. Promoting colleagues' efforts can be equally powerful in the research arena. We can find many ways to support one another when we look for the chances.

I have met the opposite of Dr. Thompson: people who fear praising others will somehow hurt their own chances to shine. Examples include speaking in a presentation as if a group study were that person's sole project; giving weak excuses to not mention some people's sessions in a SIG email meant to detail all member presentations at an upcoming conference; or publicly posting, "How did *you* get that?" when a colleague posts an accomplishment on social media. The worst offender I have personally encountered in our field (having made all these slights and more) is a woman, so groups commonly facing bias can also be the ones guilty of slamming doors on others.

I encourage us all to try to compensate for these disparagers by lifting one another up. As you promote your work, liberally promote others' quality work, too. If your greatest goal is furthering your field or its impact, championing anyone whose information can help the world is worthwhile.

PROMOTE YOUR WORK

Make it easy for people to promote you. For example, anytime you are giving a keynote and will be introduced or have written an article for which a publication will include a byline, provide the bio and byline to your contact person even if you are not asked for it. Otherwise that person might find information on you online from an outdated site or might write one that does not mention the achievements you most like to promote. This is not about arrogance; rather, the better you look, the more likely people are to listen to and learn from you, increasing your studies' benefit to others.

Throughout your promotion efforts, avoid the following pitfalls:

- Being excessively humble (if you are a woman who struggles with this, read Sandberg's book *Lean In* for inspiration).
- Only being interested in promotion (not in meeting people, discussing or learning about your topic, etc.).
- Being pushy or disregarding others' needs (this includes not catering your presentations to your audience).
- Taking sole or misleadingly-large credit for a group effort (remember the "Honesty and Integrity" section guidelines in Chapter 1).
- Appearing arrogant or promoting yourself rather than your research.

Though this book recommends confidence, you do not want to be pushy. When we sense people are trying to persuade us, such as influencing us through unbridled confidence, we raise our mental shields against them (Grant, 2016). Let your confidence stem from knowing you have something valuable to share and that you have crafted a compelling way to present it. That kind of preparation and sureness will prevent an overly- aggressive delivery.

Grant (2016) found you can even point out problems with your idea that you are still trying to solve; this establishes you as trustworthy and also shifts the audience away from self-defense and into problem-solving mode. Suddenly your idea becomes their idea, too, which is favorable.

EXPOSURE FOR YOUR ANYTHING

When you have an upcoming speaking engagement, or your program will be highlighted on the news, or you published another article or paper, your knowledge-sharing will have greater impact if more people know about it. Do each of the following, depending on your resources:

Search Engine Optimization

Search Engine Optimization (SEO) is the process of making a website or webpage appear earlier and more frequently in the results rendered when people use an online search engine like Google. This encompasses your website, books, papers, and more available online. To increase your works' visibility:

- Consider which words and phrases potential readers would search for, and embed these keywords within each paper abstract, chapter description, image caption, table caption, and webpage.
- When possible, use synonyms rather than repeat keywords. Using the same keywords on your different webpages will cause the pages to compete with one another for visibility, and Google will actually decrease your visibility

if you copy the same content on multiple webpages within your same website. Avoiding repetition of keywords will also increase the discoverability of your chapters and papers.

- However, repetition between a paper's title and abstract, or between an article's title and body, is recommended. "Include crucial keywords in the abstract and reiterate the key words or phrases from the title within the abstract itself. It is best to focus on a maximum of three or four different keyword phrases in an abstract rather than try to get across too many points" (Cacean & Harzing, 2019, p. 7).
- Place keywords near the beginning of your abstract (Routledge, 2017). When search engines encounter each abstract, they will determine whether or not to recommend your work based on whether you used the keywords the searcher used and whether these words appeared near the start of your abstract.
- For images (like figures) that contain keywords, use vector graphics (meaning files ending in. ai,. drw,. eps, or. svg, such as those created in Adobe Illustrator or CorelDraw). Words in image-based graphics (meaning files ending in. bmp,. gif,. jpeg, or. png) cannot be read by search engines, whereas words in vector graphics can be indexed and thus increase your piece's visibility in search engines (Cacean & Harzing, 2019).
- Increasing the number of webpages linking to your work—called backlinks—increases your page's search engine ranking. Ways to create backlinks include sharing a link to a paper on social media or submitting your blog to directories like www.blogscholar.com and www.blogarama.com (you can find hundreds more by searching online and might look into an RSS feeds generator like www.rssground.com for this task).

Social Media

Announce your new endeavor on each of your social media accounts (see Chapter 2 for help). This shares the work with your networks and also creates more backlinks (to raise the work's search engine ranking).

For some accounts, like Facebook and LinkedIn, there are also groups and pages on which you can announce your work. For example, when I publish something new related to giftedness, I commonly share it on Mensa's private "Exceptionally & Profoundly Gifted SIG" Facebook group page (which has 190 members). I also visit the Mensa group pages on LinkedIn that I follow and post it as a new conversation on those pages (which reach 25,000 followers).

In Twitter, "pin" your tweet so it remains at the top of your profile. For example, I will pin a tweet of my latest book to the top of my Twitter profile for about a month so that my additional tweets and retweets do not push the book tweet down during that time.

Note the area of your Twitter screen where trending topics (in the form of #hashtags) are shown. If your work relates to one of these, use it in your tweets. This will dramatically increase the number of users who see your post.

If an organization facilitated your endeavor (the magazine your article is in, the publisher of your book, the association hosting the conference you will keynote, etc.), check if that organization has a social media account. Include a tag or reference to that account (such as a Twitter handle) in your post so they can see your marketing efforts, "like" the posts, and repost them with their expansive networks. Knowing you are actively hustling on behalf of your work can also keep you in promoters' minds when new opportunities arise. For example, a radio station asks your publisher for an expert to interview, and your publisher's staff thinks of you for the task, knowing you will likely accept.

Twitter Chat

Offer to moderate (or get interviewed during) a field-related Twitter chat (see Chapter 10 if you are unfamiliar with Twitter chats). Being the moderator is like being the invited guest on a radio show; your involvement will be promoted and visitors will be eager to interact with you. When I moderated an Edutopia (@ Edutopia) Twitter chat on teacher burnout, over 4,600 people participated in the 1-hour chat. That meant thousands of people with whom I could interact and impact with my research.

Some chats even ask for moderator suggestions, such as @nbclearn (NBC Learn, 2015). You can volunteer by tweeting your willingness with the hashtag of the chat you wish to moderate or reach out to the chat's organizer (private message him on Twitter or track down his email address).

Uniform Resource Locators (URLs)

Sharing URLs—meaning web addresses rather than only hard copies—of your latest papers, interviews, and more makes sharing your work easier for others. At presentations, be sure everyone has the URL to your paper or related handouts. Write a URL to your latest work on the backs of your business cards (this is easy if you print the title and URL on labels and add those to the cards). Important URLs should also appear in your automated email signature.

Author Pages

Update your author pages (covered in the next "Exposure for Your Books" section) with the new item if you do not already have a link there to direct people to where new presentations, publications, and more are listed on your webpage. I include a link whenever possible so that I only have to keep one location (my website) up-to-date.

Helpers (Like Marketing and PR Teams)

If you have written a book, your publishing house likely has a marketing team or PR contact you are invited to consult. Find out who these people are and introduce yourself. Ask if you can have a phone conversation to talk about ways you can promote your research (not just your book, but your other endeavors, too). I have learned a wealth of strategies this way and also landed additional opportunities (like my PR contact delivering my article straight to her magazine editor contact, resulting in a speedy publication).

Regularly notify your publisher's marketing team and editor of anything newsworthy you are doing (like a symposium where you will be speaking or a new paper you wrote). They will typically use their newsletters, social media, correspondence with reporters and other authors, and other outlets to help you spread the word. For example, this book's publisher operates over 60 different social media accounts devoted to different subjects and audiences (Routledge, Taylor & Francis Group, 2017), so when I notify Routledge of something I am doing, they post for the audiences that might be interested.

If you work at a university, you might also have access to a marketing team or PR contact there. Meet with this person for valuable promotion tips and prospects. Also utilize your university's interdisciplinary center and RIMs to share your work across disciplines. University websites and department notice boards can also feature your latest work.

Share this book with your marketing and PR contacts as well. Teaming up can help you tackle the book's recommendations in an efficient way and avoid unnecessarily duplicating efforts.

Also notify your mentors, students, and colleagues (former and current) as appropriate. Use Exercise 11.1 to maintain a list of people to reach out to when you have a new piece of work to promote, such as a study, publication, or appearance. Depending on the size of your list, you might use a free www.MailChimp.com account to manage these communications.

EXERCISE 11.1: IDENTIFYING HELPERS

1. Write a list of people (and their contact information) you should reach out to every time you have a new piece of work to share with the world. Be sure to consider these sources:
   - Publisher (such as editor, marketing team, PR contacts)
   - University (like a marketing team, PR contacts, interdisciplinary center, RIMs, college websites, Public Information Office, department notice boards)
   - Your mentors, colleagues, and students

2. On this list, note any reminders that will save you time (for example, maybe a PR contact will write press releases for you, saving you from doing the bulk of that job yourself).

Press Release

Journalists rate press releases as the top content they wish to receive (73%), even above invitations to events (60%) and original research reports (57%), and this preference has persisted for years (Cision, 2019b). Issue a press release for your work, customized to the news outlet if possible. If you work at a university, it likely has a press office, PR staff, or communications team that will write and issue press releases for you, yet you will still need to provide information to the writers and will want to proof the piece before release. Many journals in which your papers appear are also open to issuing press releases with your assistance.

Google "press release" and your field to peruse samples. If you are writing your own, apply the following guidelines.

Just like other modes of writing, in a press release you will want to hook the reader and use a tantalizing headline (such as, "97% of Marriages Share a Communication Flaw"). Your first sentence (and typically your title) should convey whatever is most newsworthy about your announcement (such as a study's main finding). From there, briefly introduce key information (who, what, why, where, when) of descending importance, add details and findings, offer a couple of quotes from experts involved in the project, and conclude with a short summary.

Present the event or findings in a jargon-free way that is of public interest. In fact, aim for a press release that could be printed by a newspaper without any

DEFINITION OF PRESS RELEASE

A **press release**—also called a media release, news release, or press statement—is a document sent directly to journalists and news editors of all media (magazines, newspapers, radio, television, etc.) to announce something newsworthy. Press releases are commonly issued for completed research studies and planned events, but other occasions qualify if they would be of high interest to those reading news outlets.

A press release is unbiased, whereas a pitch (covered in earlier chapters) tries to persuade a reporter to run with a particular story idea. A press release and pitch may be sent together or alone, depending on what you deem most appropriate for your ideas and which each journalist prefers.

major changes. Be very concise: you are trying to grab journalists' interest, and they can always ask you to elaborate when they contact you.

Include a brief bio of each expert involved, as well as contact information journalists can use for more information and quotes. Reporters also like receiving a low-resolution headshot, an infographic or other public-friendly image, or a link to a video or other item the reporter can opt to embed in the story (Stein, 2016).

Email your press release to journalists. Do not miss the Associated Press (AP), which has journalists devoted to different fields. Many news outlets get their news from AP; in fact, more than 50% of the world's population sees AP's content every day (Associated Press, 2018). There is a "submit press release" option on the contact form at www.ap.org/contact-us.

See the "Craft Your Media Pitch" section of Chapter 3 for help including a pitch in the body of your email. Also share your press release through social media and place it in research repositories, covered later in the "Exposure for Your Other Writing" section.

Virtual Signatures

Adjust your virtual signatures (automatic email signature, online forum signatures, etc.) to feature a link you are particularly passionate about sharing (like to Oprah Winfrey interviewing you) below your name. You can also add these links to your bios (appearing at the end of your articles, in your social media profile, etc.).

Resume and CV

Immediately update your resume (including online resumes, such as at https://chroniclevitae.com), CV, and website with the new publication, event, or honor. I do this immediately upon acceptance so that I am never behind or overwhelmed by a growing mountain of additions. The only exceptions are my resumes in job hunt repositories, which (in the interest of saving time) I will only update if I hunt for a new job.

Discussions of Your Work

Visit the comments section, which often appears under an article or appearance you post online, and converse cordially with those who comment there. This is a great chance to share elaborations or online resources to help readers implement your ideas.

Academia.edu has a "reason for downloading" message center you can treat in the same way. This, many blog software tools, and other writing venues will automatically notify you when someone posts a response to your work.

"At times, other experts and commenters of note (public figures, other academics) will join the discussion—providing another opportunity to link to their thoughts (and even connect to them via social media networks such as Facebook, LinkedIn, and Twitter)" (Reddick, 2016, p. 62). You can use the comments section to further inform and engage readers in ways that help them consider your findings and implement evidence-based recommendations.

Some websites track who is interested in your work. Elsevier's Mendeley Stats displays who cited each journal article, who tweeted it, and more. Elsevier publisher Jennifer Franklin suggested authors use this information to make connections with their readers.

Discussions of Others' Work

You likely read a lot of online content about your study topics. There is often an option at the bottom of the webpage to comment on online articles. Use those fields to share your thoughts. Sometimes mentioning one of your articles or studies here is appropriate. Just be sure the work you mention is highly relevant, and that your post adds to the discussion rather than sidetracks the author's message. Posting a link to content on your website can also boost your site's search engine ranking through establishing backlinks from related sites.

On the same note, when you engage in Twitter chats, forum conversations, or other online discussions, mention one of your resources when it will help readers (like "For a reference sheet on Dabrowsky's overexcitabilities, visit www . . ."). Since much online content is "forever up," it is fun to see how comments you made years ago still bring new people to your website and resources you offer the field (if your website's analytics tool reveals how people were brought to your site).

Reference Sites

Recall the "Reference Sites" section of Chapter 5 and consider whether your piece should be referenced on articles within Wikipedia, answers within Quora, or other reference sites. As long as your references conform to site policies (such as furthering conversations versus furthering self-interests), you can introduce visitors to your study so it can affect more lives.

Alerts

Set up Google Alerts (www.google.com/alerts) and Talkwalker Alerts (www.talkwalker.com/alerts) to send you an email anytime your name, book title, paper title, or specialized research concept is mentioned on the internet. Another approach to this is to Google your name or work every now and then. Either approach will connect you with other people and organizations who are following your research, doing similar work, and so on.

Also search for your name and any recent endeavor (such as an archaeological dig you led, a keynote you have been scheduled to give, etc.) on social media platforms. Interact with those who are posting about it.

Social Bookmarking Sites

You can spread your (and others') online content with social bookmarking tools like Digg (http://digg.com), Newsvine (www.newsvine.com), Reddit (www.reddit.com), Scoop.it! (www.scoop.it), and Tumblr (www.tumblr.com). Posting links to your content on social bookmarking sites builds quality backlinks to that content, which contributes to SEO (covered earlier in this chapter) and increases works' visibility.

Handouts

At presentations, add web addresses to key resources (your book, a study summary sheet you made, etc.) to your presentation handout and mention these during your presentation. If your presentation shares new research findings, visualize key data as an easy-to-interpret graph or infographic. See Chapter 7 for guidance creating handouts.

Newsletters and Listservs

Any time you can get mention of a publication or an appearance into a newsletter or e-newsletter, you expose a whole new list of subscribers to your work. Sometimes these are listservs, on which you have permission (such as through membership) to submit an update to a particular email address, and software then sends your updates to all group members.

Consider every organization of which you are a member, every publishing house for which you are an author, and every institution for which you work. Many of these have newsletters or e-newsletters in which industry news is shared. Reach out to the organization or its news editor to request that your latest publication or appearance be added. Reach out to them as soon as the terms of the accomplishment are solidified so they have time to place the listing in their newsletters.

Member Updates

Note which organizations you have joined communicate news specifically about members. For example, the National Communication Association publication *NCA Insight & Out* has a recurring "Member News" segment. Divisions and SIGs within larger organizations often mention (in emails or newsletters) members' new work.

These groups will often display directions for submitting your own updates to be shared with all members. Notify the appropriate people in these groups whenever you have a new endeavor from which they could benefit. Provide a title, one-sentence synopsis of the work, and a link to where the piece (or information on it) can be found online. Your wording should match the way such announcements are sent to members so it can simply be pasted into an email or publication without being reworked.

SCRAPPY TIP

Reaching out to journalists (such as with a press release) before 10:00 AM will allow you to catch them before they begin writing their stories for the day (Stein, 2016).

Spokesperson

Empower others to carry your message for you. People will resist your message when it doesn't align with their current beliefs, for example:

- Heroin users hearing they can visit a local police station to exchange dirty needles for clean ones, when they deem their past experiences with police as unhelpful.
- Parents hearing that spanking kids is ineffective, whereas these parents were raised being spanked and believe they turned out well.

You can bypass disbelief if listeners receive your message from someone they view as sharing their belief systems. For example, anti-littering ads in which Native Americans and wildlife decry environmental damage do not deter littering, because those who throw trash do not care about the environment or those they hurt within it. Conversely, Texas solved its massive littering problem only after airing ads in which Dallas Cowboys athletes [and country musicians], whom the typical litterer admired, pick up and crush a littered can while saying, "Don't mess with Texas" (Heath & Heath, 2008). Littering in Texas finally plummeted, and that 1980s ad campaign was so successful that its catchphrase is well-known even today.

The spokesperson strategy is powerful, as long as the right message is communicated. Berger (2013) wrote of a "Just Say No" anti-drug commercial that showed a teenager going about her day and being offered different drugs by different people, which she declined—yet the ads *increased* drug use. The commercials sent the message that lots of teens (all those trying to tempt the ad's star) are doing drugs. Berger (2013) also writes of how Koreen Johannessen tried to combat the binge drinking that 44% of students do. Stunts like putting a coffin on campus with stats on drinking deaths didn't work. However, when Johannessen ran a student newspaper ad citing student feedback, which revealed 69% of students have no more than four drinks when they party (below the binge-drinking practice), heavy drinking dropped by nearly 30%. Johannessen essentially used students as the messengers, but also ensured the right message came across through them.

Consider how you could empower appropriate messengers to deliver your message to others. For example, rather than sharing a message meant to help the U.S.'s Dreamers (those who began living in the U.S. illegally as children), you might collaborate with a single or few Dreamers to deliver the message. Rather than stand as a lone conservative sharing your message with a liberal audience (or other way around), you might forge a bipartisan team that supports your message and then deliver that message together.

More

The next two sections ("Exposure for Your Books" and "Exposure for Your Other Writing") include suggestions relative to promoting written pieces. However, you might apply some of those sections' tips to promoting other works (your speech, your interview, etc.), too.

EXPOSURE FOR YOUR BOOKS

It would be a shame if the influence of your book or book chapter was limited by meager readership. Even though your publisher will likely promote your book in a variety of ways, do not rely on that alone. Rather, apply the following tips, along with the previous section's tips, to join in your book's promotion.

Social Media

In addition to the social media announcements covered in this chapter's "Exposure for Your Everything" section, tweet a link to your book and a compelling statement or question (like, "Is the quest to colonize Mars doomed to fail?") directly to high-profile reporters. They might want to cite or profile you and your book in an upcoming article.

Author Pages

As soon as any book or book chapter you authored has been published, you will want it attributed to you on an "author page" you set up with each popular book site. Setting up these pages does not involve siding against independent bookstores; buyers peruse megastores' book reviews even when they ultimately purchase elsewhere.

Set up and manage an author page with each of the following (note that many booksellers do not have an author page feature; hence their absence from this list):

- **Amazon** (https://authorcentral.amazon.com)
- **Barnes & Noble** (https://help.barnesandnoble.com/app/answers/ detail/a_id/3611/kw/author; submit author bio and book affiliations to titles@bn.com)
- **Goodreads** (www.goodreads.com/author/program)

Do not count on new publications being automatically associated with your author pages. Often they are not, or they are associated with a duplicate name that does not sync with your author page, or another mistake is made. This is especially true of books for which you wrote a single chapter (which should be attributed to you as one of multiple contributing authors). Check your author page after each publication and follow the site's guidelines to ensure new books are attributed to you properly.

Your publisher will likely give you an author page as well. Maintain this page in the same way as your other author pages.

The aforementioned sites usually allow you to post news like upcoming speaking engagements. I find a way to post a link to my website's presentation page in these cases, so readers get an up-to-date account of speaking engagements without me having to list them on multiple webpages.

TIME-SAVING TIP

As you set up multiple author pages, multiple profile pages for different organizations, etc., you will find it hard to keep these up-to-date with new career developments. For this reason, whenever possible, I post a link to a single webpage where I keep all of my latest developments. For example, if there is an "Event" field on a profile page, I post a link to the page of my website where I post all my upcoming appearances. If there is a "Publications" field, I post a link to the page where I list each new publication. If there is merely a bio field, I provide a general bio and end it with "See www.JennyRankin.com/bio for complete bio and CV." This way I only have to keep one area current, without having to maintain every profile page individually.

Bookseller Promotions

Some book sellers facilitate authors' promotion of their books, such as through book giveaways, conversing with readers, or hosting online discussions about your books. Explore sites to know your options.

Helpers (Like Marketing & PR Teams)

Reach out to helpers you identified in Exercise 11.1 in whatever way they can be of service. For example, researcher Victor Wang notes:

> As soon as a book is about to hit the press (if not sooner), I start to send flyers to colleagues and associates via listservs . . . so they can recommend publications to their librarian for addition to the library. By the time the librarian makes the decision to acquire your book and then order it through a distributor, it takes as long as 3–6 months.
>
> (IG Global, 2016, p. 3)

Whenever I have a newsworthy item (such as an article I published or an upcoming speaking engagement) related to my book's topic, I email my publisher's assigned marketing contact and copy my editor with a brief, tweetable mention about it. They often ensure this news is added to their newsletters, social media channels, and more, which helps promote the book. This practice also keeps you on the team's minds when future opportunities crop up, like when a journalist asks for an expert to quote.

Experts Mentioned

I go through the reference list of every book I write. When the book is published, I contact authors cited (I usually find either a Twitter handle or a university email address) and let the author know I cited her work. Often, I will hear back from these experts, who sometimes purchase the book or mention it in social media or elsewhere.

Reading Lists

Reach out to groups that maintain reading lists related to your book's topic. You can often find these lists by exploring organizations' websites. For example, the American Academy of Pediatrics (www.aap.org) posts a suggested reading list. Use a contact page or other avenue to suggest your book be featured (include a few sentences summarizing the book and reflecting its value to the group's efforts).

Also look for such lists in relation to events that make field news. For example, following the 2017 tragedy in Charlottesville, the Collaborative for Academic, Social, and Emotional Learning (CASEL) posted a list of resources for promoting respectful climates and helping children recover from the tragedy (www.casel. org/safe-and-respectful-environment-for-learning). There was even an invitation on the webpage to suggest additional resources for the list, and CASEL promoted the list in its newsletter.

Book Reviews

Submit your book to be reviewed. The average consumer reads 10 online reviews before she decides whether or not to buy something, and 88% of consumers trust reviews as much as recommendations from people they know (Bernazzani, 2019). Book reviews are evidence that others are reading your book, which (in itself) contributes to sales through social proof, a phenomenon in which people seek to copy the behavior of others.

Nonfiction book reviews we are familiar with—such as *The New York Times* and *Kirkus Reviews*—typically only review general-interest books. Thus it would only be worth submitting your book to these if it is one non-researchers would enjoy. However, specialized sites and publications review books that cover their topics. For example, when I wrote the book *Engaging & Challenging Gifted Students*, it was reviewed by the *Twice-Exceptional (2e) Newsletter*, *Mensa Bulletin Magazine*, and *Mensa World Journal*. These were different publication types (a newsletter, magazine, and journal), yet they all featured book reviews and were all devoted to that book's topic (giftedness).

To submit your book for numerous review columns, visit the websites and print materials of journals (like *The Journal of Politics* at www.journals.uchicago.edu/journals/jop/book-reviews), magazines (like *Science* at https://blogs.sciencemag.org/books/about-the-editor), and other publications and organizations devoted to your specific topic. "For books by new or relatively unknown authors, negative reviews increased sales by 45 percent" (Berger, 2013, pp. 80–81), so do not worry about the outcome.

When a book review comes out, add a snippet of it to the editorial reviews for every format (paperback, hardcover, etc.) of your book on sites like Amazon, Barnes & Noble, and Goodreads. Let your editor and publisher's marketing or PR team know as well, and post links to the review on social media. I also let the review's author know I am doing this, which lends me the author's blessing and possible feedback on which snippet to use.

You will also want the kind of informal reviews people post online, such as on bookseller sites. "A five-star review on Amazon.com leads to approximately twenty more books sold than a one-star review" (Berger, 2013, p. 8).

If I know a colleague has read my book, I email her the link and directions to add a review for the book to prominent online sellers. See the "Sample Email" textbox (note that the underlined words are hyperlinks the reader can follow to the precise webpage where she can add reviews, which have unnecessary URL extensions like "/ref=. . ." removed) and compose a similar email. Colleagues are busy, so making it easy for them to post reviews will increase the odds they will do so. According to Amazon bestselling author Norman Eng, "The more reviews you get, the more Amazon's algorithms will notice and promote your book. Most books published by academics have less than 10 reviews, but 20 is better. With 50, you're going to get noticed."

SAMPLE EMAIL I SEND COLLEAGUES WHO READ MY BOOK

Hi [Colleague's Name],

Thank you very much for reading my book; I hope you enjoyed it. If you want to post a short review of the book online, here are links for you to do so on Amazon, Barnes & Noble, and GoodReads. Thank you so much for your time and feedback!

Have a great day,
[Your Name]

Book Awards

Submit your book to win awards. This is not about chasing accolades; rather, winning awards brings added credibility and attention to your book, and this means more readers who can use your findings for good. See the awards that read "Book Award" in the "Category" column in this book's "List of Awards" eResource, as well as any book awards specific to your particular research area. Note many book awards require entry months before the book is published (via drafts or galley proofs).

Blog

Around your book's publication date, write a blog post about it for your website (and any other places for which you regularly write). If you have synced your site with a tool like www.MailChimp.com, this post will automatically be emailed to everyone who subscribed to your blog via your site's signup form.

Articles

Approach publications (such as those on this book's "List of Writing Opportunities" eResource) about writing an article that focuses on one of your book's chapters (with some teaser text, depending on what your publisher allows) or key points.

Reference Lists

Cite your book in your articles and other works as appropriate. This can alert one piece's readers to your other relevant works.

Conferences

Notify your editor and publisher's marketing team when you commit to attending a conference. Your publisher might have a booth (as many do), and this could impact how your book is displayed. Your publisher might also schedule you for a "meet and greet" or book signing at the booth or arrange for other opportunities like a radio interview. No matter what, visit the booth and give those working it the chance to take your photo with your book, editor, or readers, as they will post this on social media.

If you ask in advance, most publishers will send you fliers (about your book), which you can distribute to your session's attendees. These sometimes have discount codes on them, which the audience appreciates.

Bring your books to all your related speaking engagements. My mentor, the prolific author Gail Thompson, taught me the value of holding up my books at such events and having copies handy for interested attendees to peruse after the talks.

If you are a conference's keynote or featured speaker, inquire as to whether you could do a book signing or "meet and greet" at the event right after you present. Some authors sell their own copies at events (check with event organizers and your publisher before you do).

Email List

If you are working on a book that has not yet been released, pass around a "Please Notify Me When Your Next Book Comes Out" signup sheet (collecting email addresses) at each of your related speaking engagements. You can then send these folks an email when your book is released, including a link to a related blog post and a link to where they can purchase a copy. I house all these email addresses in my free MailChimp (www.mailchimp.com) account, which makes it easy to send polished emails to growing lists of people.

Interviews

A new book is interview-worthy. See the "List of Broadcasting Opportunities" eResource described in Chapter 9 and reach out to likely interviewers. Let them know you have a new book and include an extremely succinct account of what the book is about and why it is an important read and information about your professional background.

Timing

Although a natural time to promote your book is just after its publication, also pursue interviews when major developments in your field take place (Routledge, 2017) and write pieces that tie your book topic to recent events. Recall in Chapter 4 how 2017's unusually numerous and severe natural disasters prompted me to write an article on how gifted students are affected by trauma in unique ways. That article promoted a book I had previously written about gifted students.

Contacts

When you make a strong connection with someone in a high-profile position (like thee president of an association) related to your book's topic, mention how your books relate to her work. Ask your publisher (via your editor or marketing contact) if it can send a copy of your book to this person. Follow up with the reader if there are particular sections she should not miss.

Give a free copy of your book to other key people. Sometimes your publisher is willing to do this for you (at no cost to you) if you provide compelling rationale. If not, you can send people some of the extra free copies you get from your publisher, or buy copies using an author discount. As I mentioned in Chapter 10, Norman Eng gave me a copy of his book after attending a class I taught at a research conference; as a result, his book is cited throughout a previous book and this one, too. If you are confident your book is good, giving a copy away can help the receiver while likely leading to more book sales.

Audiobooks

Consider creating an audiobook. When author Valerie Geller produced an audio edition of her book, an option that is free if you join www.audible.com, her book gained further marketing power (Routledge, 2017).

Research Repositories

Add a flier for your book (publishers will typically provide this to you if asked, or you can make one yourself) and add it to research repositories. These are covered in the "Exposure for Your Other Writing" section (presented next).

Author Identification

Associate each new book with all your author identification accounts. These are covered in the next section.

EXPOSURE FOR YOUR OTHER WRITING

In addition to ideas provided in this chapter's "Exposure for Your Everything" section, additional tips follow that are specific to non-book written work.

Research Repositories

You can add your publications (papers, articles, etc.) to sites known as research libraries, databases, registries, or lists. There is extensive cross-over between these, citation analytics, ASNSs, and other tools. See the text box to find appropriate venues for your publications. You might begin with:

- Academia (www.academia.edu) is accessed by over 53 million members (Academia, 2017a), and papers uploaded to the site have been read by 850 million people around the world (Academia, 2017b). Papers received a 69% increase in citations over the course of five years when they were uploaded to Academia (Niyazov et al., 2016).
- ResearchGate (www.researchgate.net) allows you to share and collaborate on research at any stage in its completion. ResearchGate has more than 13 million users (ResearchGate, 2017), and approximately 6,000 new members sign up each day (Mangan, 2012).
- SSRN (www.elsevier.com/solutions/ssrn) of Elsevier—which includes Education Research Network (EduRN)—has more than 2.2 million users and 6 million citations (Elsevier, 2018).

Such repositories lend your work greater exposure and increase its likelihood of having an impact. However, you may only share your work in this way if doing so will not violate any agreements you have made. Honor each repository's and publication's specific policies, which typically support the following:

- If you wrote a paper published in a journal, and you signed away your right to reprint or share the paper outside of the journal, you cannot upload this paper to a research repository. You can, however, check to see if the publisher will allow you to upload the paper's abstract with citation details and a link to the paper's original location. This way the paper can still receive added exposure through the site.
- If you wrote a published book, and you signed away your right to reprint or share the book's content, you can upload a flier announcing the book to a research repository, but you cannot upload the book itself.
- If you wrote an article for a publication that left you with rights to share the article as you want, you can upload the article to a research repository. In this case make it clear (in the document) where the article was first published.

Even if you do not retain the right to share your publication, many journals automatically share their papers with repositories for you (as is the case for over 1,000 journals indexed in ERIC). Whenever you have the right to upload your work to a research repository, or when you can upload a flier or abstract directing people to the work, I recommend considering the repositories listed in the textbox (some of which also serve as ASNSs).

RESEARCH REPOSITORIES AND RELATED TOOLS

- Academia (www.academia.edu)
- AERA Online Paper Repository (www.aera.net/publications/online-paper-repository)
- AfricArxiv (https://osf.io/preprints/africarxiv)
- ARNIE Docs (www.arniedocs.info)
- Banco de Dissertações e Teses da CAPES (catalogodeteses.capes.gov.br)
- Bepress (www.bepress.com)
- COnnecting REpositories (CORE) (https://core.ac.uk)
- EdTech Docs (www.edtechdocs.info)
- EBSCO Academic Databases (www.ebsco.com/who-we-serve/academic-libraries)
- ERIC (https://eric.ed.gov)
- Figshare (www.figshare.com)
- Guardian Higher Education Network (www.theguardian.com/higher-education-network)
- Humanities Commons (https://hcommons.org)
- Open Science Framework (https://osf.io)
- Publons (www.publons.com)
- Reddit Journal of Science (www.reddit.com/r/science)
- ResearchGate (www.researchgate.net)
- Research Papers in Economics (RePEc) (http://repec.org)
- SSRN (www.elsevier.com/solutions/ssrn)
- Web of Science (www.webofknowledge.com)
- What Works Clearinghouse (https://ies.ed.gov)
- Zenodo (https://zenodo.org)

For some repositories, you set up a free account and then upload your own work or select work you authored. For others (such as ERIC), you must submit your work for consideration, and the work appears in the repository only after it is approved.

Many of these sites offer analytics, so you can track who is viewing which papers. These statistics can be used when you need to provide evidence of your online presence and exposure (such as for a book proposal or a potential job).

There is some controversy concerning these types of sites. Critics question into whose hands scholars are putting their work and whether these networks will eventually start charging money for their use. Others worry about having their work or ideas stolen and published by others, particularly when in-progress research is shared.

My stance is one in favor of using such networks for published work (when publishers allow for sharing via these venues or via an uploaded book flier or abstract with link to a published study) and removing my work should I disagree with future policy changes. I do not use these sites for works in progress, but you might feel comfortable doing so. See Espinoza Vasquez and Caicedo Bastidas (2015); Jeng, DesAutels, He, and Li (2017); and Jordan (2014) for help determining how you want to use these tools.

Author Identification

Register for accounts in Google Scholar (https://scholar.google.com), Kudos (www.growkudos.com), Microsoft Academic (https://academic.microsoft.com), ORCID (www.orcid.org), ScienceOpen (www.scienceopen.com), and SCOPUS (www.scopus.com). If English is not the primary language spoken in your country, search for similar sites specific to your location, such as India's Shodhganga (https://shodhganga.inflibnet.ac.in).

To save time, link publications to your account in Google Scholar or SCOPUS first, then import that information into ORCID to automatically link the same publications to your ORCID profile, then import your ORCID profile to your other accounts (Kudos, ScienceOpen, etc.). Tie each of these three accounts to each new scholarly publication you produce. This increases online discoveries of your work.

Social Media

During the first week your new piece is published, include hashtags and account handles to alert pertinent groups to your work. For example, adding "#TellEWA" to a compelling tweet about a new written piece alerts the Education Writers Association (EWA), which uses such tweets to select "EWA Story of the Week" content, which it shares with its thousands of journalist readers.

Every day or two within the first two weeks of your publication, search for the title of your article or paper on Twitter (or whatever automatically populates tweets when readers click the Twitter "share" icon that accompanies your piece), LinkedIn, and other sites. This will show people who have shared your work but did not know your handle or account name in order to copy you on the share.

"Like" all of the shares you find. This alerts readers to your whereabouts on social media and can earn you new followers. Retweet or post these shares whenever it feels appropriate (do not share more than one or two at a time, look for shares that add to dialogue, etc.).

WHEN TO POST

These statistics are provided by TrackMaven (2014):

TWITTER

- The most effective day to tweet (to get the most retweets) is Sunday, followed by Thursday.
- The most effective time to tweet is 10:00–11:00 PM EST.

FACEBOOK

- The most effective day to post on Facebook (to receive the most interaction) is Saturday, followed by Sunday.
- The most effective time to post on Facebook is 12:00–1:00 AM EST.

BLOG

- The most effective day to publish a blog post (to receive the most interaction) is Saturday, followed by Sunday.
- The most effective time to publish a blog post is 10:00–11:00 PM EST.

EMAIL

- The most effective day to email (to get the most opens) is Thursday, followed by Wednesday.
- The most effective time to email is 2:00–5:00 PM EST.

Curated Content

Note which of the e-newsletters you read curate content from other publications (usually with a title, brief description, and link to the content's original location online). *Mensa Weekly Brainwave* is one example. Reach out to these publications and suggest your recent write-up be included (make it easy by writing a succinct description they can use). Some publications even provide directions for making such suggestions.

Reposts

Take note of which sites post content that first appeared elsewhere (such as with "Reprinted with permission from . . ." or "Originally published by . . ." displayed at the bottom). Let these sites know when you write something they might want to post on their sites, as well (as long as this does not violate any copyright).

Blog Directories

If you maintain a blog, submit it to blog directories like www.blogscholar.com or www.blogarama.com (you can find hundreds more by searching online). You might look into an RSS feeds generator (like www.rssground.com) for this task. Not only can people find your blog through these directories, but increasing the number of backlinks to your work increases your blog's search engine ranking and thus makes it easier for people to find your blog when searching for related topics.

Images

For any online content, include a related image. "Some bloggers find that a large proportion of their traffic comes from Google Image Search. That means people are searching for images using keywords, finding images on a blog, and then finding their way to the blog" (Psychology Today, 2017).

You can add the image yourself on your own blog or post, or you can suggest an image if someone else is managing the content. Journalists overwhelmingly rate images as their preferred visual media for a piece, followed by infographics, data displays, videos, and then social media posts (Cision, 2019a). See the "Guide to Slide Design" eResource (described in Chapter 7) for image options.

EXPOSURE FOR YOUR SPEAKING ENGAGEMENTS

Most tips for sharing your speaking engagements and broadcasting appearances were already covered in the previous sections. Additional tips are presented here.

Social Media

Announce your appearance beforehand on social media (in an inviting, "Join us!" style) with a link to where guests can register or watch the event. Event organizers are often happy to provide an image you can use to call more attention to these posts.

If a recording of your appearance is housed online after the broadcast, share the link on social media. This gives you another chance to catch viewers who missed the initial airing.

If your speech is online with a designated title, periodically search for its title on Twitter (or whatever automatically populates tweets when readers click the Twitter "share" icon that accompanies your presentation), LinkedIn, and other sites. This will show people who have shared your speech but did not know your handle or account name in order to copy you on the share.

"Like" all of the shares (of your appearance) you find. This alerts audiences to your whereabouts on social media and can earn you new followers. Retweet or post these shares when it feels appropriate and not self-gratuitous.

Local Media

Contact local media about your visit. "Local media are always looking for uplifting stories tied to supporting . . . their communities;" even if a story does not result from this outreach, it can establish you as a resource for reporters, who then ask you to contribute to future stories (Boyle, 2017, p. 1).

HUNTING AND HARVESTING

GUIDE TO HUNTING AND HARVESTING

This book directs you to many opportunities to share your expertise with the world, but you can hunt and harvest to land even *more* great opportunities. This involves finding opportunities through memberships, online communities, events, internet searches, and social media. See the "eResources" section near the start of this book for details on accessing the "Guide to Hunting and Harvesting".

CONCLUSION

I hope over the course of reading this book you have come to view me as a supportive friend. I hope you will remember that, through this book, I am here for you anytime, and you can return to me again and again to add to your repertoire of research-sharing avenues.

If you found this book helpful, please share it with your colleagues to help them expose the world to their research findings, too. Whatever your opinion, I would be grateful if you posted a review for the book on www.Amazon.com, www.BarnesandNoble.com, and www.GoodReads.com so that others can learn from your impressions.

 FINAL SCRAPPY TIP

When you post book reviews, publishers might contact you for permission to include your review in a future edition of a book.

If you have now pursued even 1% of the opportunities presented in this book, you have already shared your discoveries with new audiences who can apply them to helping others. Do not lose steam, and you will continue to expand your studies' impact.

As your influence grows, never forget from where you came. Remember what it was like to yearn and struggle to get your research out into the world, and help those who stand where you once stood (for example, do you have to turn down a radio appearance because it does not fit your schedule? Introduce the interviewer to someone you know who would be great for the opportunity). The more we help our peers to share quality information, the more we help our field and our world.

As you share your research extensively, also remember to learn from your different audiences. "While scientists have a duty to speak about their work, they have an equal duty to listen to the public so as to strengthen the quality of public discourse and increase the perceived and actual relevance of science to society" (National Academies of Sciences, Engineering, and Medicine, 2017, p. 19).

As you close the pages of this book, please pour yourself a glass of something celebratory and pat yourself on the back. You are the kind of researcher not content to limit the reach of your expertise to the usual, comfortable outlets. You know your work will have greater impact if you step onto the world stage, so you have officially launched that endeavor. With your mindset and determination there is no limit to the influence you will have on your field and our world. *Thank you*. Few lives leave behind such a legacy, and you should feel very proud.

REFERENCES

Academia. (2017a). *Academia*. Retrieved from www.academia.edu

Academia. [noreply@academia-mail.com]. (2017b, June 13). *The Academia community just hit a big milestone!* [email].

Associated Press. (2018). *About us*. Retrieved from www.ap.org/about

Berger, J. (2013). *Contagious: Why things catch on*. New York, NY: Simon & Schuster.

Bernazzani, S. (2019). 20 examples of social proof in action in 2019. *HubSpot*. Retrieved from https://blog.hubspot.com/marketing/social-proof-examples

Boyle, D. [acquisitions@ascd.org]. (2017, November 7). *ASCD AuthorPULSE: Building relationships with local media*. [email].

Cacean, V., & Harzing, A. (2019). *How to increase the visibility and academic impact of your research*. Retrieved from https://harzing.com/download/impactguide.pdf

Cision. (2019a). *Cision's 2019 global state of the media report*. Chicago, IL: Cision.

Cision. (2019b). *Media pitching manual for PR and comms professionals*. Chicago, IL: Cision.

Elsevier. (2018). *About SSRN*. Retrieved from www.elsevier.com/solutions/ssrn

Espinoza Vasquez, F. K., & Caicedo Bastidas, C. E. (2015). Academic social networking sites: A comparative analysis of their services and tools. In *iConference 2015 Proceedings*, 1–6.

Grant, A. (2016). *Originals: How non-conformists move the world*. New York, NY: Penguin Books.

Heath, C., & Heath, D. (2008). *Made to stick: Why some ideas survive and others die*. New York, NY: Random House.

IGI Global. (2016, April 11). Maximizing your publication's potential: A how-to guide by Dr. Victor C. X. Wang. *IGI Global*. Retrieved from www.igi-global.com/newsroom/archive/maximizing-your-publication-potential-guide/2502

Jeng, W., DesAutels, S., He, D., & Li, L. (2017). Information exchange on an academic social networking site: A multidiscipline comparison on ResearchGate Q&A. *Journal of the Association for Information Science and Technology*, *68*(3), 638–652. doi:10.1002/asi.23692

Jordan, K. (2014, November 3). Academics and their online networks: Exploring the role of academic social networking sites. *First Monday: Peer Reviewed Journal on the Internet*, *19*(11). http://dx.doi.org/10.5210/fm.v19i11.4937

Mangan, K. (2012, April 29). Social networks for academics proliferate, despite some doubts. *The Chronicle of Higher Education*. Retrieved from www.chronicle.com/article/Social-Networks-for-Academics/131726

National Academies of Sciences, Engineering, and Medicine. (2017). *Communicating science effectively: A research agenda*. Washington, DC: The National Academies Press. doi:10.17226/23674

NBC Learn. [@nbclearn]. (2015, August 26). *If you or another educator want to be involved in our next #NBCLearnChat, let us know!* [Twitter moment]. Retrieved from https://twitter.com/nbclearn

Niyazov, Y., Vogel, C., Price, R., Lund, B., Judd, D., Akil, A., et al. (2016). Open access meets discoverability: Citations to articles posted toAcademia.edu. *PLoS ONE*, *11*(2), e0148257.doi:10.1371/journal.pone.0148257

Psychology Today. (2017). How to promote your blog. *Psychology Today*. Retrieved from www.psychologytoday.com/how-to-promote-your-blog

Reddick, R. J. (2016). Using social media to promote scholarship. In M. Gasman (Ed.), *Academics going public: How to write and speak beyond academe* (pp. 55–70). New York, NY: Routledge, Taylor & Francis.

ResearchGate. (2017). About us. *ResearchGate*. Retrieved from www.researchgate.net/about

Routledge. (2017). *Promoting your book: Metadata surveys*. Retrieved from www.routledge.com/resources/authors/promoting-your-book

Routledge, Taylor & Francis Group. (2017). *Author directions: Navigating your success in social media: 5 key tips for authors using social media.* Boca Raton, FL: CRC Press.

Sandberg, S. (2013). *Lean in: Women, work, and the will to lead.* New York, NY: Alfred A. Knopf.

Stein, K. (2016). How to write an influential press release. In M. Gasman (Ed.), *Academics going public: How to write and speak beyond academe* (pp. 105–117). New York, NY: Routledge, Taylor & Francis.

TrackMaven. (2014). *A complete guide to the best times to post on social media (and more!).* Retrieved from www.slideshare.net/TrackMaven/when-to-postslidesharepdf/ 18-TrackMavenEmailWhen_to

Index

Note: Numbers in **bold** and *italic* indicate tables and figures respectively on the corresponding page.

263

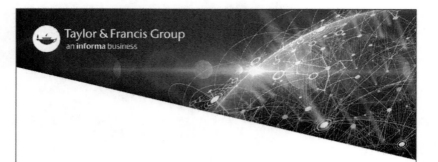